EVERYTHING
HAPPENS
FOR A REASON

EVERYTHING HAPPENS FOR A REASON

My Life in Rugby

DANNY CARE

EBURY
SPOTLIGHT

Ebury Spotlight, an imprint of Ebury Publishing
Penguin Random House UK
One Embassy Gardens, 8 Viaduct Gardens,
Nine Elms, London SW11 7BW

Ebury Spotlight is part of the Penguin Random House group of companies
whose addresses can be found at global.penguinrandomhouse.com

Penguin
Random House
UK

First published by Ebury Spotlight in 2024

www.penguin.co.uk

A CIP catalogue record for this book is available from the British Library

ISBN 9781529946154

Printed and bound in Great Britain by Clays Ltd, Elcograf S.p.A.

The authorised representative in the EEA is Penguin Random House Ireland,
Morrison Chambers, 32 Nassau Street, Dublin D02 YH68.

Penguin Random House is committed to a sustainable future
for our business, our readers and our planet. This book is made
from Forest Stewardship Council® certified paper.

MIX
Paper | Supporting
responsible forestry
FSC
www.fsc.org   FSC® C018179

To Jodie, Blake, Koha & Rocco.
You are my proudest achievement.
Thank you for letting me chase my dreams x

Contents

Prologue

November 2018

We hadn't played great against Japan – the fans had booed us off at half-time, which is never a good sign – but we'd dug deep for the win. Eddie didn't seem too concerned, although he told us to have a couple of days off at home before the game against Australia the following weekend. That wasn't a very Eddie Jones thing to do, so I probably should have known that something strange was afoot.

Having enjoyed a bonus Sunday with the family, I'd just put my son Blake to bed when I saw I had a missed call. I remember the voicemail as clear as day: 'Danny, Eddie here. Didn't think you were sharp enough at the weekend, I don't need you this week. Cheers.' Short and in no way sweet.

I was livid. How had I gone from being one of only two scrum-halves in the squad to being bumped completely? I'd worked insanely hard for four weeks, and been part of a win over South Africa and a narrow defeat by New Zealand. Actually, I'd worked insanely hard for Eddie for three years, and he thought a three-second voicemail was the right way to drop me. I should have been used to Eddie's games by then, but this really didn't sit well with me.

I wanted to have it out with Eddie this time, but I'd seen what had happened to guys who'd challenged him in the past – they invariably got binned, never to be seen again. I asked my

1

wife Jodie what she thought I should do, and she said, 'Go and speak to him. Be honest, say you don't understand his rationale and you feel a bit hurt. Surely he'll hear you out?'

Jodie was right. I'd spent too long not standing up for other people when I'd seen Eddie belittling them, but I should at least stand up for myself. Besides, he couldn't get angry if I just asked why he'd dropped me. Could he?

I had to clear out my hotel room so that one of the other boys could move in. When I bumped into Wiggy in the corridor, he shook my hand and said sorry. I told him it wasn't his fault and we had a bit of a laugh about it.

I called Eddie on the way there and asked if I could see him, and he told me to come and find him in his office. So after I'd said goodbye to Wiggy and the rest of the lads, I girded my loins and made my way to the dragon's lair.

When I walked in and asked if we could discuss what had happened, Eddie said of course and pulled a chair out for me. His desk was covered in computer screens, like a City trader's; there were charts, graphs and lists all over the walls; Post-it notes were stuck to everything. And in the corner was his dog, Annie, a little big-eared thing that yapped at anything that moved.

'Eddie,' I said, 'I just feel that dropping me is a bit harsh. I don't understand how I can go from starting against Japan to not being involved at all. We've done well over the last few weeks. We beat South Africa, we nearly beat New Zealand. The Japan game was always going to be tough because we changed a lot of players. And Japan played well. But we still managed to get back into it and win the game.' I thought I'd made my case quite eloquently, but Eddie just said, 'That's a shit attitude, mate. That's justified my decision.'

I was momentarily dumbstruck. Then I said, 'I don't think I've got a shit attitude. Actually, I've got a good attitude. I've never once complained about not starting. And I've contributed a lot to this team since you came in. I just don't think I played that badly to warrant you dropping me.' Eddie narrowed his eyes and said, 'Nah, shit attitude, mate. You've got to get better.'

Suddenly, I wasn't so punchy. I told Eddie that he was right about me not having my best game and that I could give him more. But I still had bit of fight left in me. 'I just think I deserved more than a three-second voicemail,' I said. 'I thought we had a better relationship than that.' There was a pause, before Eddie said, 'Whatever, mate. Go back and play for your club and we'll see if you can get back in the room.' I thanked him and shook his hand, and I swear to God his dog started growling at me.

I loaded up my car, rang Jodie and said, 'I think I'll be home for a while now. Actually, I don't think I'll be going away again.' She couldn't believe it. Jodie had heard stories about what Eddie was like and had met him a few times – but she didn't know the real man. 'Surely it can't have been that bad,' Jodie said when I got home. 'Only if I'd done a flying headbutt and knocked him out could it have been any worse,' I replied.

How could the kind of conversation that happens all the time in professional sport – a coach drops a player, the player asks why, the coach explains, no hard feelings – have had such disastrous consequences? Well, apparently it could where Eddie was involved. Just a few days earlier, I thought I was a shoo-in for the 2019 World Cup. Now, I appeared to have no chance.

I had a horrible few days, and might even have shed a tear or two. Hurt was the overriding emotion. I'd worked so hard for the previous three years, my body was in pieces, and I was mentally drained. I'd spent so much time away from my wife, who was learning how to be a mum, and a young son who could have done with having his dad around more. So to be ditched in such brutal fashion, as if I meant absolutely nothing, was very difficult to take.

I also regretted not saying what I really thought about Eddie in front of all the players and staff. When he was belittling one of his analysts, I wish I'd stood up and said, 'That's bang out of line, Eddie!' Maybe my departure from camp could have been like that scene in *Dead Poets Society*, when Robin Williams's teacher character gets sacked and all his pupils climb on their desks and say, with quivering lips, 'O Captain! My Captain!'

Who am I kidding. Professional sport is every man for himself, so nobody would have backed me up, just as not a single person phoned me and asked, 'How could Eddie treat you like that?' And I behaved like a coward because I didn't just want to play for England, I desperately needed to.

My fear of Eddie and the power he wielded bordered on paranoia. I worried that if I gave him both barrels in the media, he'd have me barred from Twickenham, which would have put the kybosh on any potential media work. Maybe I'd have needed to hire someone to taste my meals for me. Besides, I didn't want to come across as bitter. So I did as Eddie had told me: went off and played for my beloved Harlequins and tried to get back in the room.

○

I barely heard from Eddie in the three years after that traumatic meeting, save for a few brief chats at games and corporate events. So when I was offered the chance to write my autobiography in the summer of 2021, I accepted.

I'd almost given up hope of playing for England again, and I wanted people to know what had unfolded in my career and how my dreams of playing in the 2019 World Cup had been shattered. But having written the proposal and been offered a deal, I decided to pull the plug.

I'd only *almost* given up hope of playing for my country again, and while saying what I really felt would have given me some short-term satisfaction, it probably would have ended my England career. So I carried on playing as well as I could for Harlequins and did my best to forget I was well into my thirties. It wasn't that I thought my England career *deserved* a good ending, I just believed it would have one. And I never stopped thinking, *Everything happens for a reason.*

Chapter 1

Football Mad

The real world is a very strange place to me because I've never really lived in it.

All my adult life, I've done the same as I was doing when I was a two-year-old in the garden, kicking and throwing a ball about. Lucky so and so.

Dad had an inkling I'd be a decent sportsman: when he rolled a ball towards us, my brother, Simon, would always manoeuvre it onto his right foot before hitting it, but I'd hit the ball with whichever foot it came to. Dad would often say, 'Any player who can't kick with both feet shouldn't be playing professionally.' And from when I was tiny, I desperately wanted to be a professional footballer.

Dad was a football-mad West Bromwich Albion fan and always claims he was a natural goal scorer. He still talks about a cup final he played in as a teenager, when West Brom sent some scouts to watch. He hardly got a kick in the first half but really turned things on after the break, scoring four goals in a man-of-the-match performance. Unfortunately, the scouts left at half-time. So instead of becoming West Brom's new Jeff Astle, he went and worked in a bank instead, which is where he met my mum.

Mum and Dad are both proper Yam Yams from the Black Country, Mum from Wolverhampton, Dad from Smethwick, which is halfway between Birmingham and West Bromwich. The rivalry between their respective football teams is fierce, but they rose above it. And after a short stay down south, they ended up in

Leeds, which is where they had my brother, me and then my sister, Sam, seven years later. Sam was born on Christmas Day 1994 – when Mum went into labour, Si and I were dropped off at family friends', where we had chicken nuggets and chips for dinner (they had already eaten, to be fair!). None of us caught Mum and Dad's Black Country accents – I think we dodged a bullet there!

Home was a lovely little village called Adel, 20 minutes out of Leeds city centre, on the road to Otley. It was paradise for two little boys with a taste for action. If we jumped over a couple of garden fences, we'd gain access to a massive expanse of playing fields, where we'd play football from dawn till dusk. There were only two years between us, so things were quite competitive. Si being older, he never wanted me to beat him at anything, however trivial. As the younger brother, I wanted to be as fast, as strong and as brave as Si. And I often got the snot beaten out of me by him and his mates.

When you're a little kid with an older brother, you assume that nothing is tighter than the bond between you – until his mates enter the picture. But at the risk of sounding like some old bastard writing a letter to the *Telegraph*, all the rough stuff never did me any harm. In fact, constantly competing with an older brother (and his mates) put some steel into me. Si, I never thought I'd say this, but thank you for all those kickings.

Mum and Dad wanted us to be competitive – their attitude was, *If you're going to enter a race, you might as well win it.* And I loved that feeling of winning. On sports days, I'd win everything, and I'd never be embarrassed. Neither would Mum or Dad. One year, one of the other mums complained about me – 'It's not fair your boy winning everything' – and Mum replied, 'He's no different from your boy, he's just faster. You can't have a go at him for that.' It's not as if I was some genetic freak, towering over everyone else; I was the smallest in my class. My legs just turned over quicker than everyone else's.

I was even competitive when it came to schoolwork. I wasn't necessarily the best at everything, but I certainly wanted to be. I'd have to finish a book before anyone else in the class, and usually did, but spelling was my specialist subject. Ask me to spell anything and I could see it straight away in my head.

Despite Dad's love of football, I started playing rugby first. My brother was playing for West Park in Bramhope, and whenever we watched him, I'd nag Mum to let me join in. The club told us I'd have to wait for two years, which was agonising, because I reckoned I was better than most of the players out there. So Mum had a word and they let me start playing for the under-sevens a year early.

I then started playing for the local football club in Adel, which was run by a good mate's dad, Tony Walker. At first it was rugby on Saturday mornings, football on Sunday afternoons, playing up a year in both. But when I was nine, rugby and football started clashing, so Mum and Dad told us that we had to choose one or the other. Si chose rugby, while I chose football.

I enjoyed rugby, especially the social aspect. After football matches, everyone would jump straight in their cars and go home, while rugby would be an all-day affair, with adults sharing a few beers in the clubhouse and all the kids running around with fizzy drink and crisps swilling around their bellies. But we'd started tackling in rugby, and being the littlest by a mile, I was constantly getting pasted by the big kids. Meanwhile in football, I was running rings around people. I was still smaller than everyone else, but I was skilful.

My parents weren't pushy, but they did want me to do as many sports as possible rather than focus on just football. I was actually pretty good at gymnastics, although I came to hate it. I remember a coach trying to push me down into the splits and me telling him I couldn't do it anymore. But it must have helped with my strength, balance and agility, which came in very handy on the football pitch (and later with rugby).

By the time I reached secondary school, football had become an all-consuming passion. I didn't watch rugby at all when I was growing up – I couldn't even have named any teams or England players. Not even Will Carling. And whenever I went to the park with my mates, we never took a rugby ball. We'd boot a football about for hours, using a little cricket pavilion as the goal.

You can blame Santa Claus for my shocking change of allegiance from Leeds to Liverpool, because it was him who gave me a Liverpool annual for Christmas (I'm pretty sure it wasn't on my wish list). I think the red of Liverpool just seemed more exciting than the white of Leeds (it can't have been a glory hunting thing, because Liverpool hadn't won the league for years) and I read that annual over and over again.

It was the time of the so-called Spice Boys – Robbie Fowler, Jamie Redknapp, Steve McManaman, David James and the rest of them – and they were quite an alluring bunch for an impressionable boy, what with their cream FA Cup Final suits, sports cars and pop-star girlfriends. I'm still mad about Liverpool now, although I get plenty of grief for it. People know I'm a proud Yorkshireman, and that I should be a Leeds fan, so they'll often say to me, 'How many games have you watched at Anfield?' And I grit my teeth and reply, 'One.' Horrific really, but football makes a man do strange things.

My dream was to play for Liverpool, and I wanted to be like Michael Owen, because he was small and quick like me. I was actually pretty good with my feet but preferred to use my pace and knock the ball past people, just like Owen. Remember that ridiculous goal he scored against Argentina at the 1998 World Cup? I scored a goal like that once, beating four or five players before smacking it from 20 yards out. I'm still annoyed that Dad didn't record it.

When I was about 11, a local guy called Colin Morris asked my dad if I wanted to start training at his academy, which was like a feeder camp for Yorkshire teams. The first night we turned up, it was immediately apparent that some of the kids were quite a bit older than me. But when Dad asked Colin what group I'd be training in, Colin replied, 'There's only one group. He'll learn a lot faster by playing against these big lads.'

Some of these lads weren't just big, they were also quite hard. Proper kids, in other words; kids who came from towns and cities, not picturesque villages. I was scared at the start, thought I'd get clumped every time I beat someone, or even tried to. But I soon earned their respect. And as time went on, I was holding my own against kids four years older than me.

Colin would take me if Dad was busy elsewhere, and this being the olden days, he'd smoke five or six fags during the half-hour journey. I'd be leaning out of the window coughing and spluttering and by the time we got to training I always felt sick as a dog. But Colin was a good man, and after about six months, he referred me to a guy called Clive Baker, who ran the Sheffield Wednesday academy. And after a couple of trial nights, Sheffield Wednesday signed me.

Wednesday were a big team back then, and I'd see the likes of Paolo Di Canio and Benito Carbone wandering around the place, as well as first-team manager Danny Wilson. Playing for Liverpool remained the ultimate dream, but this seemed like a good enough stepping stone.

I was a bit intimidated when I first turned up because kids were gobbing on the floor and swearing. And while the game was a bit rougher than I was used to, with lots of tough tackling and fouling when necessary, it didn't take me long to adjust. Colin had been right: I had learnt a lot faster by playing with all those big lads.

I was the top goal scorer in my first two seasons, playing in the same team as Jamie Vardy, who would go on to have an incredible career with Leicester and England. Jamie was exactly the same as he is now – spiky, feisty, whatever you want to call it. He was from inner-city Hillsborough, where Wednesday's ground is, and while he was small like me, he could handle himself. He tackled hard and was cocky as hell, the sort of kid who'd say, 'Just give me the ball and I'll do something.' But Jamie and I got on well, especially on the pitch.

We were very similar – nippy, elusive, loved scoring goals – and Clive would either play us both on either wing or one of us on the wing with the other one up top. Clive, a legend of a bloke, loved kids who could pass well and play intricate football. And for the first three years, it was great. But then Clive left, a new guy came in and everything went pear-shaped.

These being less enlightened times, some might say the Dark Ages, there were still lots of youth coaches in England who acted as if Maradona and Pelé had never happened and thought that small kids couldn't make it in men's football. That old chestnut. So despite the fact that I was still carving things up and scoring loads of goals in training, I was suddenly warming a lot of benches at weekends, while bigger kids started ahead of me. Shockingly, Jamie suffered the same fate.

Twice a week, Mum would drop me at Dad's work in Leeds, I'd sit at his desk waiting for him to finish, then he'd drive the hour and a half to Sheffield. Dad would stand in the cold with a cup of tea watching me train, then he'd drive back to Adel. We wouldn't get home until 11 o'clock. Then at the weekend, poor old Dad would have to ferry me to Middlesbrough or Newcastle, where I might get 10 or 15 minutes off the bench. You tend to take your parents for granted when you're a kid, but I do remember thinking, *This must be so crap for Dad.*

The final straw was a game against Manchester United. We lost 2–0, and for the first time the coach didn't put me on at all. The whole game, I was sat on the bench thinking, *I could do something here, maybe win us the thing.* And as Dad and I were trudging off after the final whistle, I said to him, 'I don't want to do this anymore. I'm not enjoying it.'

'I know,' Dad replied, 'I can see that.' At the next training session, Dad asked them if they could release me from my contract so I could go and play for my local club, and they said yes.

Looking back, I'm happy that I wasn't one of those kids who spends all his childhood years in an academy, when he could have been playing with his mates, only to be rejected at the end of it. You don't get to live those years again. My son Blake used to play at one of Chelsea's many academies, and I'd sometimes stand on the touchline, watching hundreds of kids of all different ages. How many would make it? Not just for Chelsea, for anyone? Not many. Maybe none. It's quite sad when you think about it.

At the same time, I do have some lingering regrets about my football career that never was. Towards the end, I played against

Derby County, who had future Spurs and England midfielder Tom Huddlestone in their team. We couldn't get anywhere near him – it was like playing against Patrick Vieira – but I scored two goals and their coach said to my dad, 'If you ever leave Wednesday, give us a call.' Leeds said something similar, but I was so disillusioned by then, we never followed it up. Dad's attitude was, *Whatever makes you happy, that's what you should do.*

I admire him for that, and I loved playing football with my mates in Adel again, but I do sometimes think we should have made contact, at least with Leeds (driving to Derby twice a week probably would have finished Dad off). Was I good enough? I reckon I was as good as Jamie Vardy at the time, and even though he had to go all the way down the leagues he eventually got to the very top of the game (what was that Wednesday academy manager thinking?). And I sometimes watch football now and think, *I could have been better than him.*

The dreamer in me says I could have played at some level if I'd stuck with it, and I probably would have earned more money playing football for Barnsley or Bradford than I have playing rugby for Harlequins and England. Then again, would making a living at Oakwell or Valley Parade have topped regularly playing in front of 80,000 people at Twickenham? I don't think so.

Chapter 2

Blagging It

Mum and Dad sent me to a secondary school whose main sport was rugby, Prince Henry's Grammar in Otley, and while it was a bit of a laugh and useful for attracting girls, I didn't take it seriously – certainly not while I was still at Wednesday.

I was as elusive on a rugby pitch as I was on a football pitch, although when I was 12, my best mate Albear (Alex Bearpark) got counter-rucked, flipped onto his back and landed on my left leg. Ignoring my screams, the captain suggested I run it off, but when I put my left foot down there was nothing there and I promptly collapsed in a heap. I didn't know what pain was until then; it was absolutely excruciating. There was hardly anyone watching, just my mum and another lad's dad standing on the far touchline, so I had to crawl off the pitch. The dad scooped me up, put me in Mum's car and she whisked me off to hospital, where they discovered I'd snapped my tibia. As you can imagine, Wednesday were over the moon about that.

I found rugby quite easy. My school team would win most games, including the under-13 Yorkshire Cup final, and I'd usually bag a couple of tries. The same year I was let go by Wednesday, I was selected to play for Yorkshire Schools Under-15s, but football was still my game. It certainly never crossed my mind that I could play rugby as a job.

The turning point was probably when some of my mates persuaded me and my dad to go on a tour of Dublin with Otley

Rugby Club. Dublin was different from anything I'd experienced in football. Whereas I didn't really know any of the lads at Wednesday (let's face it, they were my competitors rather than my mates), and the little football club in Adel didn't have much of a social scene, that tour was my best mates and me all in it together. There was nothing cynical about it; we were all shapes and sizes – little lads, lanky lads, skinny lads, fat lads – but each of us had a role to play and felt wanted and loved. And while we obviously wanted to win our games, having fun was just as important, which is why we all dyed our hair blond. And just like the Romania team at the 1998 FIFA World Cup, we looked utterly ridiculous.

We'd run Irish teams ragged on the pitch then go out drinking with our dads, and we were only 16. This was a bit of me. And I soon found out that they didn't just drink when they were on tour, they did it quite often. Apart from the night my dad found me spewing in the toilet after one too many WKDs, it was the best craic I'd ever had, and probably the exact moment I fell in love with rugby. Soon afterwards, I became a paid-up member of Otley.

Prince Henry's was nominally a grammar school, but it was actually just a normal comprehensive, albeit with a decent reputation for rugby. I'm sure some of the lads played rugby just so they could beat up posh kids from private schools. They'd always be particularly revved up for those fixtures, and one game against Leeds Grammar (which was a private school, confusingly) had to be abandoned at half-time because our boys kept swinging punches. To add insult to the Leeds boys' injuries, our lads nicked a load of their kit from the changing room.

But despite the occasional thuggery, we were pretty good at rugby, and our coach Pete Latham (who knew nothing about the thieving) has to take a lot of the credit for that. Pete had four daughters, none of whom were into rugby, so I think he saw his students as his projects. He was so passionate about us doing well and had a real knack for taking a talented all-round sportsperson and turning them into a rugby player.

The same year we won the under-16s Yorkshire Cup, I was selected for Yorkshire, North of England and then England Schools, which was almost unheard of. You normally didn't get into the England Schools team unless you attended private school, so everyone at Prince Henry's was going mad about it.

I didn't understand what all the fuss was about until I turned up to camp, where everyone spoke posh, even the kids from up north. They all went to very expensive schools with impeccable rugby pedigrees, places like Millfield and Barnard Castle, and our skipper Sam Stitcher went to Wellington College, alma mater of my future England team-mate James Haskell. But it's not as if I was walking around with a chip on my shoulder – I didn't go to a school that cost ten grand a year, but I wasn't exactly from the mean streets! – and I got on with Sam and most of the rest of the lads just fine.

It was cool wandering around the place in my England kit, but I still thought of myself as a footballer. Funnily enough, I had watched quite a lot of rugby league – my dad would take me and Si to watch Leeds Rhinos on a Friday evening, and we were even mascots once – but I didn't watch union on TV, I'd never been to a game and I'd have struggled to name you more than a few England players until they won the 2003 World Cup. Martin Johnson, Jonny Wilkinson, Jason Robinson maybe. But beyond that, no one.

I didn't really know what I was doing on a rugby pitch, because I wasn't steeped in the game like the other lads. Most of them had dreamt of being rugby players since they were little, just as I'd dreamt of being a footballer, so their game intelligence was on a different level to mine. I could pass and kick off both feet, and I could skin people with my pace, but I was blagging it really.

That was when I first met several of my future senior England team-mates, including Dan Cole and Tom Youngs. I vividly remember Tom saying to me, 'My little brother's a scrum-half and he's going to be quite decent,' and me thinking, *Yeah, we'll see ...*

My first England roommate was the enigma that is Danny Cipriani, and there was no one better to learn from than him. I'd watch him in training and think, *Jesus, that's a proper rugby player.* He was only 15, a year younger than the rest of us, but he passed and kicked just like Jonny Wilkinson and glided around the pitch like Barry John (not that I had a clue who Barry John was back then). Cips had scary confidence – what you might call swagger – a total belief that he was the best player on the pitch, which he was. But I didn't find his approach off-putting; we bonded straight away, maybe because we weren't as posh as the rest.

One night, Cips and I snuck out of our room and tried to listen in on the coaches' selection meeting. We were crouched outside the room with our ears to the door like a couple of spies, but we couldn't make much out. And the following day, I got picked and he didn't. That raised a few eyebrows, the consensus being, 'How on earth is Cips not in the team when he's the best player here by a mile?' Maybe they didn't want him to get too ahead of himself, but it would be a theme of his career.

Before playing for England Under-16s, I'd been invited to a trial for the Leeds Tykes academy. Stuart Lancaster was the academy boss, and he ran a deadly serious ship. It was very technical, all about core skills, and I was still pretty raw – a footballer just trying his hand at rugby. I thought I was good enough to be there, but I didn't want it as much as some of the other lads.

A week or so later, I received a letter from Lanny, explaining that I'd not reached the required standard. (Dad kept that letter, along with everything else from my rugby career – 40 folders' worth! And I showed it to Lanny when he became head coach of the England team.) But after I played for England Schools, Lanny sent me another letter asking if I wanted to join Leeds's academy after all. So I signed up, and suddenly things were beginning to get a bit serious, at least in terms of rugby.

○

Once my sport took off, schoolwork fell down my list of priorities. I wasn't a bad kid; I just wanted to be kicking or chucking a ball about rather than sitting in class learning stuff that didn't seem to have any relevance.

I became known for being that kid who did stuff nobody else had the nerve to do, like the time a school mate and I were daring each other and I called 999 to tell them there was a fire. I didn't give any more details, but ten minutes later, three fire engines were parked outside. This lad's mum came storming up the stairs, asked what was going on, and eventually I owned up. She was, understandably, livid and booted me out of the house. And the poor guy got the mother of all bollockings.

I ran to a payphone and rang home. 'Mum,' I said, 'just to let you know, I'm not feeling well so I'm coming home a bit early.'

'Danny,' Mum replied, 'get yourself home now. I know exactly what you've done …'

My mum's not a scary person – unless you really mess up – but she was certainly the disciplinarian of the household. So when I came jogging down the road, she was standing by the front door, and I could see the fury in her eyes. Mum never hit me, but I wasn't taking any chances. I ran past her, locked myself in the bathroom and prayed that she'd soon calm down.

Readers – she didn't soon calm down. Mum was banging on that door for what seemed like hours. I kept shouting, 'I'm not coming out!' and she kept replying, 'We need to talk about this!' Mum would be handy in sieges, because I eventually opened the door, and she gave me what for, and then some. The bollocking my mate got from his mum paled into insignificance next to the bollocking I got from my mum. It was the mother, the father, the son and the holy ghost of all bollockings. To be fair, Mum had every reason to be angry, because I'd put three fire engines out of commission and people could have died. Once her own fire had subsided, she said to me, 'Why is it always you?' What I thought, but didn't say, was, *Because everyone else always bottles it.*

I enjoyed being good at rugby, which meant that some people wanted to take me down a peg or two. I'd like to think that none of my schoolmates would have described me as arrogant, but you've got to be confident to succeed in any sport. As Morrissey almost said, there are people in this world who hate other people being successful at sport, and they attempt to rationalise their hatred by convincing themselves that those successful people are arrogant, even when they're not. That happened with me, and it pissed me off. No one accused kids of being arrogant because they were good at exams, but because I was doing something a bit sexier, at least on the face of it, I was a problem.

Throw girls into the mix and that hatred can become quite dangerous. I was playing in the school's first team with my brother at the age of 16, so older girls who otherwise wouldn't have looked twice at me suddenly became interested. I wasn't exactly a player, but I did have a couple of girlfriends who were two years above me, which greatly confounded not only my brother but also some of the more thuggish elements of Prince Henry's sixth form.

Armed with fake ID, I frequented a nightclub in Leeds called Heaven and Hell – stone cold dance classics in Heaven on the top floor, heavy house in Hell on the bottom floor, R&B and hip-hop in Purgatory in between. Saturday nights would be like a scene from *The Inbetweeners*, in that almost every person in there was underage, including an arch enemy of my brother who hated me by association and claimed to knock about with the Otley Crew.

The Otley Crew weren't exactly the Crips, but this particular kid was quite big and had it in his head that something was going on between me and his girlfriend (I think I'd spoken to her once on a bus). So there I was, larging it in the VIP section behind the velvet rope, when this kid wandered over. We had a bit of a scuffle, and he said to me, 'I'll get you tonight, Care.'

'We'll see,' I replied.

I'd had a few drinks and didn't think anything would come of it, but after I left the club, I was crossing the road to catch a bus when this kid came out of nowhere and sucker-punched me in the back of my head, before giving me a few more digs while I was down. He was on his toes before my mates could react, and I was left with a mashed-up face all covered in blood. That was an early lesson that while being good at rugby had its upsides, it also put a target on your back.

Some of the Leeds academy lads trained every day, but because I was still at school, I could only do Monday nights. We'd train at Chandos Park, which was basically a battered old shed and a pitch that resembled a potato field.

It was a big step up for me, and felt like proper big boys' rugby. Some of the lads were playing for the under-19s, others were in the second team already. These were people who were nearly making it, like Tom Biggs, Rob Webber and Rob Vickerman, who would go on to have long and successful careers.

In 2003, when I was still 16, I made my first-team debut, coming on as a winger in a pre-season friendly against Exeter. And the following season, the under-19s won the National Colts Cup. With the first team battling against relegation most seasons, naturally the club was getting excited about this new crop of kids that they thought were going to change their fortunes.

For all our successes, there were times when I didn't particularly like Lanny. I was convinced he wasn't keen on me because he was constantly saying I needed to be more like this and more like that, like a very pushy and annoying dad.

At other times, Lanny was more like a strict teacher. As far as he was concerned, you needed to arrive for everything ten minutes early, while arriving a minute late was a heinous crime. One morning, Mum got stuck in traffic and I walked into the gym at nine o'clock. Lanny gave me one of his laser stares and ordered me to do 5km on the bike, 2km on the running machine and a 1km row. And if I didn't complete the set in a certain amount of time, I'd have to do it again. I was terrible at rowing because of my stubby arms, but when I protested that I wouldn't make the time if I attempted it 100 times, Lanny said to me, 'Okay Danny, I understand, you're really terrible at rowing ...' Ouch.

If I had a big game for Leeds on the weekend, Lanny would tell me I couldn't play for my school on a Wednesday. He'd also tell my school coach, a guy called James Tiffany who also worked at the academy. But one week, Lanny's order not to play coincided with a particularly big school game, and there was no way I was missing out on that. I had so much fun playing for my school team; it was rugby at its purest, and I didn't want to let my mates down.

Having been told by Tiff that I wasn't playing, I told him I'd put my kit on, warm up with the boys and support them from the touchline. We usually hammered teams, but this was a bit of a tussle, so when one of our lads started hobbling around with ten minutes to go, I started nagging Tiff to put me on.

When Lanny told you to do something, you knew full well that you were dicing with death if you did the opposite – but I couldn't resist on this occasion. Without telling Tiff, who was probably more scared of Lanny than I was, I subbed myself on and ended up scoring a crucial try at the death.

The following day, I trained with Leeds before heading to the shed. When Lanny, very sternly, read out the team for the weekend, I wasn't in it. At the end of the meeting, he told me to stay behind, like when you've been naughty at school, before giving me the full Alex Ferguson hairdryer treatment. He kicked things off with, 'Who the hell do you think you are?'

It was a proper mum or dad telling-off, as if I'd let Lanny down in some terrible way, and I couldn't get my head around it. I said to him, 'This is bollocks, I only played ten minutes with my mates.' But he kept going on about how this wasn't football and how I had the opportunity to be a professional rugby player, but only if I started taking things more seriously. And now, when

I look back on that moment, I understand where Lanny's fury came from. In truth, it was probably more frustration than real anger. I was this talented kid, and he was worried I didn't want it enough and would blow my opportunity.

Before that dressing down from Lanny, I was just going with the flow. But now I was thinking, *I need to knuckle down if I'm going to have any chance of making it. And I don't want to be shouted at by Lanny again.* What's more, I'd found England's World Cup win in 2003 incredibly inspiring. And while Jonny Wilkinson got most of the plaudits for his match-winning drop goal, I was just as impressed by Matt Dawson's involvement. First, he did a little dummy, so that the Australian defenders had to take a couple of steps back; then he threw a long pass that was bang on the money and gave Jonny all the time he needed to execute his kick. That was incredible skill from Dawson under immense pressure, and he became my first real rugby hero. I was under no illusion that I'd have a long career, let alone win a World Cup like him, but I was going to give it a crack.

Suddenly, I wanted to be the first to arrive for training, the last to leave and the best trainer in between. Having been a reluctant lifter of weights, I now realised I'd never make it without putting on some bulk. And once Lanny realised that I did want it after all, he threw himself behind me 100 per cent. Then one day, he told me he thought I could play for England. I spent hours on the pitch with Lanny, practising my passing. He'd dip balls in a bucket of soapy water and say, 'If you're going to play for Leeds, you'll need to learn how to pass a wet ball.' Lanny even kept on at me about my schoolwork, presumably because he was hearing stories about me messing about all the time instead of studying. No doubt about it: I owe Lanny a lot.

My time in the sixth form at Prince Henry's was a bit of a whirlwind, to put it mildly. I signed a professional contract with Leeds in my final year, and a couple of weeks later I made my competitive debut against Spanish side Valladolid in the third-tier European Shield, starting at fly-half (I had been playing ten at school, to get my hands on the ball a bit more in space and because we had a really talented younger lad who could play nine).

Valladolid weren't great – we beat them 121–0 in the first leg at Headingley – so it was the perfect opportunity for head coach Phil Davies to try out a few youngsters. And it was fun for the first 23 minutes. I scored a length-of-the-field try, set another one up and kicked four conversions. This pro rugby lark seemed like a piece of piss. Then I went for another show and go, got tackled and snapped my ankle. My foot was facing the wrong direction, which is never nice to see, and I was in shock. Then the pain kicked in, which was on a par with when I'd knackered my other leg.

After a trip to the hospital, where I was medicated up to the eyeballs and had my right leg set in a plaster cast, I ended up going to a restaurant where a massive piss-up was taking place, this being the first time Valladolid had hosted a professional team. They put on an incredible spread in a massive cavern, with tapas, beer and wine on tap and a banging live band. Everyone was up on their feet, dancing like idiots, and I was sat in the corner with my leg up.

The lads had slung a few drinks down my neck, which dulled any pain, but when I eventually needed to go to the toilet, I had to wait for my doctor, Terry Crystal, to finish singing. He'd clambered onto the table and asked if he could use one of my crutches as a microphone. My team-mate Rob Rawlinson ended up piggybacking me to the toilet, and I passed Terry on the way. 'Nice one, Terry,' I shouted. 'Top doctoring …' (I should add that Terry is an absolute legend and a fine doctor who also worked for England.)

I rounded off my school rugby career with a try and victory in the *Daily Mail* Vase final at Twickenham. That was an emotional day. Playing with your best mates at Twickenham is the stuff of dreams, and it was largely because of their enthusiasm that I'd started to take rugby seriously, but I knew we wouldn't have many more games together. At the same time, I had an inkling that this could potentially be normal life now, or at least could become so. I was an actual real-life rugby player.

Chapter 3

Right at Home

I was 17, on £12,000 a year, and I felt like a king. A few of the new boys had come from elsewhere in the country and were living in an academy house, which they had to pay rent on. But I was still living at home, with a grand a month in my pocket, nothing to spend it on (apart from the little blue Fiat Punto my parents bought me) and my mum doing all my cooking and washing.

I'd underperformed in my A levels (although I did get a B in PE and was offered a place to study sport and exercise science at Leeds Metropolitan University), so I needed to give rugby my undivided attention. I had vague notions of becoming a PE teacher or a fireman if rugby didn't work out, or maybe even giving football another crack, but I've always been a glass-half-full kind of person, and I thought rugby would probably work out if I kept grafting.

Those first couple of seasons at Leeds were mainly about watching and learning from team-mates, and we had a great squad on paper, including Iain Balshaw and Mark 'Ronnie' Regan, both World Cup winners with England. Balsh was one of the most dangerous backs England has ever had, but he was also one of the greatest moaners in rugby – and he was up against some very stiff opposition – while Ronnie was one of the most unintentionally funny people I'd met. He once showed me a video of him parking his new Bentley. When I asked why he'd carpeted his garage, he replied, 'So that she can sleep nicely ...'

We also had England lock Tom Palmer, former England full-back Tim Stimpson, Scotland fly-half Gordon Ross, Wales back-rows Alix Popham and Richard Parks, some proper club stalwarts like Mike Shelley and Rob Rawlinson, who always kept an eye out for me, and a former All Black in Justin Marshall, one of the greatest scrum-halves of all time.

Being an understudy to a bloke who'd won 81 caps for New Zealand was a bit intimidating for a kid straight out of school. But while Marshy didn't offer me much advice, I'd constantly ask him questions about tactics and technique and he'd always answer.

Besides, watching Marshy train was a daily revelation. In terms of core skills – passing and kicking – he wasn't up there with the very best, but he was big, physical and quick. And when it came to actual games, which he was being paid the big bucks to perform in, he'd really turn on the class.

Marshy had only retired from international rugby in 2005, after the All Blacks' whitewash of the British and Irish Lions, so opposition players were terrified of him. And watching him manipulate defences was mesmerising. He'd glide across the pitch, throw defenders with his eyes and wait for a mistake. Then he'd either go through the gap himself – he scored a lot of tries for a scrum-half – or put a team-mate in, often with a ridiculous offload. I loved that he backed himself, whether it was the right or wrong decision. If a quick tap and go or drop goal didn't come off (he'd try drop goals from anywhere on the pitch), never mind, at least he had the audacity to go for it.

But what I loved most about Marshy was his swagger off the field. If anyone else was late for a meeting, Phil Davies would lock the door so they couldn't get in, then read them the riot act after the meeting was over (if you were running more than five minutes late, it was best not to show up at all and pretend you were ill, preferably dying). But Marshy would regularly stroll in late, safe in the knowledge that Leeds were paying him a load of money and he was the best player in the team by a mile, which made him virtually unbollockable, and certainly undroppable.

One time, he kicked the door open 15 minutes into a meeting, wearing shades as usual, with a sandwich in one hand and a coffee in the other, and casually said, 'Sorry Phil, bit of a queue in the café.' Phil replied, 'No worries, Marshy, take a seat …' Some of my team-mates would get upset that Marshy was able to get away with stuff they couldn't, but I'd be thinking, *That is class. That's how I want to be.* Not that I wanted to be late all the time, but I liked the idea of being so good, and having done such great things in the sport, that I could do whatever I wanted and the coach wouldn't give a toss.

In hindsight, Phil was probably sending out a coded message to the rest of us: 'Marshy has earned the right to be Marshy. If you're ever as good as him, you'll have all the privileges that he has.'

Even our World Cup winners were treated like paupers next to Marshy. If we played badly on a Saturday, Phil would make us do '100s' on the Sunday morning, which meant running 100m over and over again until he stopped blowing his whistle. He'd stand on the sideline shouting, in his thick Welsh accent, 'Fuckin' run, boys!' And I'd be thinking, *I didn't even play at the weekend!*

Not that I said anything, because the best way to earn respect as a young recruit in a sports team is to speak when you're spoken to, make tea and drink beer when you're told to, play well and, most important of all, train hard. However, Iain Balshaw was a ten-year professional veteran, as well as one of the greatest moaners in rugby, and he once shouted at Phil, 'How is this helping us play better rugby?!' Phil shouted back, 'Shut the fuck up, Balsh, and keep fuckin' running …' I thought that was hilarious, a World Cup winner being slapped down like that. Having said that, Balsh was probably right.

For all the talent in our ranks, results were terrible, which meant a lot of '100s' on a Sunday morning. We lost our first seven Premiership games of the 2005–06 season and got battered by Cardiff in the Heineken Cup. Inevitably, players started questioning Phil's methods and his authority began to wane.

I didn't get the bus home after that Cardiff game because I was on duty with England Under-19s, but I heard that it all kind of came to a head on the journey, with comments exchanged between players and the coach. Phil soon stepped aside from hands-on training duties. He gave me my first professional contract and I loved working with him, and just because he couldn't get that team to gel didn't mean he wasn't a great coach.

Daryl Powell, a rugby league man I'd seen play for the Rhinos many times, took over from Phil, with Lanny helping out. And Daryl decided to throw some youngsters in, academy lads like Rob Webber and Jordan Crane, both future England players, sevens star Rob Vickerman, winger Tom Biggs and a lad called David Doherty, who made his debut not long after turning 17, making him the youngest player in Premiership history (when I saw David in-and-out London Irish full-back Michael Horak, which not many people did, I thought he was destined for greatness, but unfortunately he never quite hit the heights we all thought he would and he was playing for Jersey in the Championship a few years later).

I spent quite a lot of that season either playing for England Under-19s and Under-21s in world championships or for England Sevens. Nowadays, the sevens circuit is sealed off from 15s, but back then it was like a finishing school for club prospects. I was part of an awesome squad that finished second at the 2004 Commonwealth Youth Games in Australia (along with Cips and future England centre Anthony Allen) before graduating to the senior England Sevens team and playing tournaments in Wellington and Los Angeles and at the 2006 Commonwealth Games in Melbourne. Our squad for Melbourne included a load of top Premiership talent, including past and future England 15s players Henry Paul, Magnus Lund, Tom Varndell and Mat Tait, and we finished runners-up to New Zealand. We had a lot of fun on those trips, but we also gained a lot of experience of major games, on the biggest stages, and returned to our clubs as better players.

When Leeds' second-choice scrum-half Mark McMillan got injured, I became a fixture on the bench, the hope being that I'd replace Marshy with 10–15 minutes left on the clock and use my pace to run teams ragged. I did get on a handful of times and I absolutely loved it, but we kept giving up leads and losing at the death. I'd look around the changing room afterwards, at all those great players we had, and think, *How the hell have we lost again?* But I was far too young to put in my two penn'orth, and I can't say it knocked my confidence particularly because I was still just happy to be there.

My highlight of that season – and one of the highlights of my entire career – was the four minutes I played against Cardiff at Headingley. Not because we won 48–3, gaining revenge for our defeat at Cardiff a few months earlier, but because they had Jonah Lomu playing on the wing. Like everyone else, I'd watched open-mouthed when Lomu destroyed England at the 1995 World Cup. I'd also spent hundreds of hours playing *Jonah Lomu Rugby*, the best computer game ever made. He was the most famous rugby player who had ever lived, a man who had changed the game forever – before Lomu, backs weren't supposed to be as big as him – and a global superstar who had appeared in adverts for Adidas and McDonald's (they even named a burger after him in New Zealand), so the prospect of spending even a minute on the same pitch as him was surreal.

Lomu's best days were behind him by the time he pitched up at Cardiff – he'd had a kidney transplant in 2004, so it was remarkable he was playing at all – but he was still a colossus who ate scrawny little kids like me for breakfast. I'd only been on the field for a minute or so when he broke through the line and ran straight at me. I thought, *This is going to hurt*, and I fully expected him to run straight over the top of me. In truth, he had several options – step left, step right, a stiff arm right on the end of the nose – but just as I was about to dip into the tackle, I saw what I thought was a kindness in his eyes. Presumably he was thinking, *I could probably kill this boy, but I'd rather not.* It was a textbook tackle, my right shoulder into his thigh, which felt like a large oak tree, but it didn't put him down. I slid down to his knees, then his ankles, and eventually he crumpled to the floor next to me, although he'd long since offloaded the ball. I remember thinking, *This is insane, I've just tackled Jonah Lomu.* Then he jumped up, ruffled my hair, pulled me to my feet and said, 'Well done, kid,' before trotting off. I felt almost grateful to him for giving me that moment, and I'll never stop telling my grandchildren about the time I tackled the greatest player ever.

With Leeds teetering on the brink, Marshy said in a newspaper interview that he intended to stay even if the club went down. But when Leeds's relegation was sealed a couple of weeks later, he changed his mind and signed for Welsh side Ospreys. I didn't know what to make of that: I was now probably Leeds's number-one nine, but I couldn't imagine life at the club without Marshy.

Marshy's departure triggered a mass exodus, but I didn't know what to do. Leeds was my boyhood club; it's where I'd been given me my chance, and I had it pretty cosy, what with living at my parents' house and trousering a kingly grand a month. To be honest, I really didn't want to leave, and I didn't think I'd be allowed to anyway. Then, one day, a team-mate sidled up to me and said, 'Mate, have you checked your contract?'

It turned out that somebody in the HR department had accidentally left a release clause in a lot of our contracts, not just mine, so suddenly leaving was a possibility. My agent advised me to at least think about it, on the grounds that playing Championship rugby wouldn't be great for my England prospects.

When I told the owner Gary Hetherington that I was thinking about leaving, he was livid. I wasn't surprised because I wasn't the only academy graduate to jump ship. The club felt betrayed, but we had to think of ourselves.

○

My agent at the time was a very lively guy who had lots of bright young things on his books, including Jordan Turner-Hall and Dom Waldouck. He was super confident and very proactive, and he soon lined me up with three Premiership teams. He drove up from Surrey to Leeds and we went on a little tour, starting with Northampton, followed by Saracens and finishing with Harlequins.

Northampton's pitch wasn't the most inspiring, but they did offer me £35,000, which was three times what I was earning at

Leeds. I obviously thought that was great, but my agent was angling for quite a bit more. And as much as I kept telling myself it wasn't about the money, I also knew it kind of was.

In contrast to Northampton, Sarries rolled out the red carpet. Their new director of rugby, Alan Gaffney, and Eddie Jones, who was there in a consultancy role, took us out for a slap-up meal and said all the right things. They talked me up as a player, explained why I was a perfect fit for the team and how playing for the club would be great for my England prospects. And halfway through the main course they announced they'd pay me a hundred grand a year for the first three seasons. I tried to play it cool but almost choked on my ravioli. My agent was a bit more composed – 'Let us have a chat and see if we can make that work,' he told them – but when I shook Alan's and Eddie's hands to say goodbye, I couldn't stop myself from saying, 'I'll probably see you soon.'

A hundred grand a year was serious money for a rugby player in 2006. Not only was it an £88,000 pay rise, it also would have made me the best-paid teenager in Premiership history – by miles. When we got back in the car, I half expected my agent to start screaming, 'Show me the money!' à la Jerry Maguire. I couldn't comprehend it; it was like something from a very surreal dream.

I'd played with quite a few Quins lads for England youth teams – the likes of Mike Brown and Jordan Turner-Hall – and they'd been nagging me to join for ages. I was also still close with Cips, who was in London with Wasps. But it was going to take one hell of a pitch to stop me joining Saracens. I'd already pictured myself running out at Vicarage Road in Sarries' black and red kit.

However, within ten minutes of meeting Quins' director of rugby, Dean Richards, and coaches Andy Friend and John

Kingston, I was sold. They told me they'd been fans of mine for a couple of years, reeled off loads of stats about how many games I'd played and tries I'd scored, and said they wanted to play an exciting brand of attacking rugby, with the team built around me. But the line that really got me was, 'We know you're going to be a long way from home, but we'll do everything to make Harlequins feel like your home.' I was sat there thinking, *Crap, I'm gonna have to tell Eddie I'm not signing for Sarries after all*, and they hadn't even mentioned money. As it was, Quins offered me a better deal overall, and I got my poor agent to call Eddie.

I was absolutely buzzing when I got home. As for Mum and Dad, they couldn't get their heads around the salary. I remember Dad saying to me, 'You're earning more money than me and your mum combined,' and me thinking, *How lucky am I? They're going to pay me all that money to play a sport I love playing for nothing. Wow.*

I wasn't bothered that Quins had only just been promoted from the Championship; it just felt right. And it was only really when I joined Quins that I started to think of myself as a proper rugby player. Before then, I still wondered if I was a lad who hadn't made it as a footballer and was just about getting away with it in rugby. But if someone was willing to pay me that much money to play for them, I must have been decent. At least I'd better be.

A year earlier, Anthony Allen had joined Gloucester straight from school for something like £35,000 and people thought that was crazy. And when the press found out about my salary, there were stories about how rugby was getting out of control and going the way of football. That was a gross exaggeration – footballers were earning my annual salary in a week even back then – but I did feel the pressure. Being ordinary at Quins wasn't going to cut it, I'd need to be a superstar in every training session to justify the money.

Mum and Dad sat me down and gave me a talk before I headed to London. They weren't controlling, but because they both worked in banks, they wanted me to invest at least some of my money wisely. So I ignored my agent's flippant suggestion to buy a Ferrari (that would have gone down well with the old soaks at Quins) and pootled down to London in my Fiat Punto.

I was a proper mummy's boy, a bit wet behind the ears, so those first few weeks in London were tough. Luckily, David Strettle, who I'd played with for England Sevens, had found a flat in Isleworth for the two of us. Stretts was a fellow northerner but was a few years older than me and had been to university. So he took me under his wing, and was almost like a big brother.

I remember Stretts watching me unpack with utter contempt, because I'd turned up with a PlayStation and a load of board games. I was virtually unbeatable at Pictionary in those days. He said to me, 'Mate, you've got no idea what's about to hit you. You won't need those games where we're going ...' An hour later, we were supping pints in a pub in Richmond.

I didn't drink a lot before moving to London, other than a few with the Leeds boys after a game. I was very committed to my rugby and getting pissed didn't seem like something I needed in my life, so mostly I was hanging out with my then girlfriend or at home with Mum and Dad. But when Stretts introduced me to the London lights, things changed.

I got a bit of ribbing from some of the older lads who played in the amateur days or signed for peanuts – if we went out for coffee, they'd make me foot the bill for all the first-team players – but there weren't that many of them at the club. Quins had a young squad, including something like a dozen new signings, so nobody was made to feel like the odd man out.

But while I was made to feel right at home at Quins, just as they'd promised, I spent a lot of the 2006–07 season twiddling my thumbs.

After the first game, against London Irish at Twickenham, I asked Dean Richards why I wasn't in the squad, and he told me that I wasn't quite ready and that Simon Keogh, who could cover scrum-half and wing, was his preferred option. That was a bit of a shock, because he'd previously told me I'd be vying for a spot in the first team with Steve So'oialo and at least starting on the bench every week. Plus, I thought I'd performed well in pre-season.

It was incredibly frustrating, especially as a load of the other young lads were playing. Deano didn't see me as an option even after we lost our first few games of the season. After missing out on yet another squad, I knocked on his door, asked why he wasn't playing me, and he said, 'Actually, Danny, on that subject, we're going to sign Andy Gomarsall. We think he's the club's missing ingredient and he's gonna be great for you. You'll learn a lot from him.'

I couldn't believe it. Gomars had been part of the 2003 World Cup-winning squad, but he wasn't exactly the future. He was 32, had had a lot of injuries and had recently been released by Worcester one year into a three-year deal. I walked out of Deano's office thinking, *What the hell is going on here?* I'd left my home-town club, I'd turned down a great deal with Saracens, and now it looked like the boss didn't fancy me. Had I made a terrible decision after all?

One day, I really trained the house down and thought I must have caught Deano's eye. After scoring a particularly good try,

I looked over at Deano and shrugged my shoulders, as if to say, 'Come on mate, put me in, you know it makes sense.' He just laughed and said, 'Soon, mate, soon ...'

While the likes of Mike Brown, Jordan Turner-Hall and Chris 'Robbo' Robshaw were playing most weekends, plus my house-mate Stretts, I was back to hanging around with Mum and Dad and my sister, Sam, in Leeds. I said to them once, 'Have I had a shocker here? Should I have stayed at Leeds? At least I'd be playing.'

I did have the consolation of captaining England in the Under-20s Six Nations Championship and playing in the Hong Kong Sevens, which makes me sound like a bit of an ungrateful brat in hindsight. But I was only available for selection because I wasn't being picked for Harlequins.

Another silver lining was getting to play quite a few games with another All Blacks legend in Andrew Mehrtens. Quins signed Andrew from Super Rugby's Crusaders after being relegated to the Championship, but while he was still an unbelievable player, he was in and out of the first team a fair bit when I joined. However, he loved living in London and was quite happy to muck in for the seconds, when he quite easily could have had his feet up.

Before a game against London Irish, he said to me, 'Dude, let's go and have some fun.' And that's exactly what we did. His body was creaking, and he wasn't really trying, but it still looked so easy. He was kicking beautiful spirals off both feet, and no one could get anywhere near him. I'd never seen anyone take the piss more in a game. And afterwards, he was first up to the bar.

Andrew's final first-team outing for Quins was the last Premiership game of that season, against Sale on his 34th birthday. He contributed a try, five conversions, two long-range penalties and a drop goal in a 49–0 victory. Remarkably, he managed to play several more seasons in France, winning second division titles with Toulon and Racing, helping Racing reach the Heineken Cup, and leading Béziers to promotion from division three. He retired at 40, having squeezed every last drop from the sport. What a guy.

Looking back, that first season at Quins was a blessing in disguise. I thought I was ready, but I definitely wasn't. Maybe if Deano had thrown caution to the wind and put me in, I'd have been chewed up and spat out, as happens quite often in pro sport. Instead, I learnt an awful lot from watching and speaking to Gomars and Steve So'oialo, just as Deano had predicted.

Established players are sometimes guarded with anyone they perceive as a rival for their place in the team, but Steve was always generous with his advice and genuinely wanted me to do well. He was also hard as nails, like most Samoans, and toughness was something I needed to add to my game (Steve was also very handy at computer games – he once suffered a bad neck injury that required him to lie on his back for weeks, so he stuck a TV on his ceiling and played *Call of Duty* non-stop, eventually becoming the best in the world at one of the disciplines!).

As for Gomars, he couldn't have been kinder. I assume Deano had explained to him that I wasn't quite ready and needed some mentoring, because Gomars would grab me before every training session and make me pass 100 balls. Sometimes I'd think, *Jesus, not again*, but I soon worked out that while Marshy had been mainly about instinct, Gomars was mainly about hard graft and getting the basics right.

Gomars would say to me, 'I'm not the fastest, I'm not the strongest, and I'm not the most gifted, but I'm one of the best at passing, kicking and organising. And that's because I practise.' He'd also tell me I had a great chance of playing for England, but only if I worked hard on my core skills like him, nailed my kicks and passes and made as few mistakes as possible.

For many years, Gomars's rivals for the England number nine shirt had been Matt Dawson and Kyran Bracken, and he used to talk about how Dawson was the flair player who could run at defences, Bracken was the technical one and he was the reliable one who didn't make many mistakes. As such, he was always in and around the England set-up, even if he wasn't starting.

Because I'd only started taking rugby seriously relatively recently, I hadn't honed those core scrum-half skills. I was essentially a winger playing at scrum-half, someone who just loved scoring tries. In contrast, Gomars was a controlling nine, a good box-kicker who also loved little dinks to the corner. And while I hated box-kicking, and did so for years, I added parts of Gomars's game to the more attacking stuff I'd learnt from Marshy – a bit of swagger, some of that trickery and manipulation of defences – and tried to blend it all in with my natural approach, which was to have a go and see what happened.

Having been in the international wilderness for three years, Gomars was selected for the 2007 World Cup and ended up starting in the final. That's what being Mr Reliable does for you. And with Steve also in France with Samoa, Deano didn't have a choice but to throw me into the mix.

Before the first game of the season, against London Irish at Twickenham, Deano said to me, 'Right, this is your time, go and show what you can do.' He'd decided he wanted to play a more up-tempo game, which suited me down to the ground. Whereas Gomars was all about putting the team in the right areas, I was more about quick taps and getting the team playing from anywhere, and we were brilliant that day, winning 35–27.

Unfortunately, I got injured in that game, and by the time I returned to action five weeks later, Gomars and Steve were back from France.

That meant I was relegated to EDF Energy and European Challenge Cup duty. But when Steve got injured and Gomars's form dipped (he was dropped after two games of the Six Nations), I was promoted to the first team ahead of him for a Premiership game against Sale and never looked back.

The game when everything clicked into place, in terms of the style Deano wanted us to play, was against Saracens away at Vicarage Road. I set up a couple of tries and won man of the match in a 15–6 win, and afterwards Deano put his arm around me and said, 'Now you're ready.'

'Thank you,' I replied, before giving him a hug. He'd been right all along.

Chapter 4

Trauma Down Under

England's summer tour of New Zealand had been in the back of my mind for most of that season. It wouldn't have been much of a surprise had I not been picked, because I was still very green, but I thought I offered something a bit different from Sale's Richard Wigglesworth, who had nicked Gomars's starting spot during the 2008 Six Nations.

I'd also worked with head coach Brian Ashton when he was in charge of the national academy and I loved his way of thinking, all about playing what you see and attacking space. But having led England to a World Cup final the previous autumn, Brian was out on his ear as soon as the Six Nations was over.

I'd heard whispers about what had gone on during the World Cup – the lads had apparently decided they needed more structure and pretty much taken over the running of the team, and I wasn't really big on structure. Then when Martin Johnson was appointed England's new head coach, I thought that was my chance of an international call-up gone, at least in the short term.

No one knew what Johnno's coaching philosophy was because he'd never coached before, but him being a brute of a second-row, all about toughness and doing the basics well, I don't think many people expected him to pick a 21-year-old running nine against New Zealand in their own backyard. As it was, Johnno's first touring squad was quite bold, with six uncapped players involved. And one of those six uncapped players was little old me.

I was obviously excited, but I couldn't help thinking, *How on earth am I going to play against that lot?* How the All Blacks hadn't won the 2007 World Cup I do not know, because they were probably the greatest team I'd ever seen. They were missing a few key players through injury in 2008, but still had Dan Carter, Ma'a Nonu, Conrad Smith and Mils Muliaina in the backs and Richie McCaw, Jerome Kaino, Brad Thorn, Ali Williams and Keven Mealamu in the forwards. These weren't just good international players, they were some of the finest All Blacks in history.

Johnno couldn't travel to New Zealand, so Rob Andrew, who had a top job with the RFU, filled in as tour manager. And it was Rob who told me I was on the bench for the first Test at Eden Park in Auckland, where the All Blacks hadn't lost a Test since 1995 (a streak that continues to this day). The next thing I remember, I was standing on the pitch watching the All Blacks do the haka – Nonu, Carter, McCaw and the rest of them screaming at me with their eyeballs on stalks.

Whenever I'd seen the All Blacks doing the haka on TV, I'd thought it was cool: just a dash of culture. But now I was experiencing it from a few yards away, I thought, *Why are they allowed to do this? It's literally a war dance. They look like they want to rip our heads off and we haven't done anything wrong. We only came here to play a game of rugby against them. It's ridiculous. What am I doing here? Why didn't I join Leeds United?* Players usually claim that the haka doesn't bother them, but they would say that, wouldn't they? I don't mind admitting that it put the fear of God into me.

It was a horrible evening, cold and wet, as it always seems to be down there. But when the whistle went, I couldn't believe the speed at which the All Blacks played – apart from Dan Carter, who looked like he had all the time in the world. He set up one try for Conrad Smith and scored one himself as New Zealand rattled up 20 points in 11 first-half minutes, and by the time I was thrown on with half an hour to go, the game was over as a contest.

I was picked to start the second Test in Christchurch, and Matt Dawson, who had been a bit of a mentor to me and was in New Zealand doing some media work, came to my room the night before to see how I was. I told him I was crapping myself and couldn't get my head around the fact I was starting against the All Blacks. To be honest, I still had imposter syndrome. I wanted to play in these kinds of games, but I wasn't sure if I really belonged in that kind of company. Players like Carter, Nonu and McCaw were icons of the game, while I was just some kid who had become a rugby player by accident.

Matt said to me, 'Mate, you're never gonna be prepared for what's coming, but you're here because you're good enough. It will be a learning experience, but this is just the start of a long international career. It will be over in a flash but do what you've been doing for your club and try to enjoy it.' And while he was trying to help, the line that struck the loudest chord was about me not being prepared. *Jesus*, I thought, *is it gonna be that bad?*

Matt was right, I wasn't really prepared. And while I did manage to enjoy the occasion, it was rugby like I'd never experienced before. While standing under the sticks after New Zealand had run in their second try, Mike Tindall looked at me as if to say, 'How good are these boys?' And for probably the first time in my career, I was thinking, *There's absolutely nothing we can do to stop this lot.* They were too fast, too physical and too skilful.

I did manage a couple of half-breaks, one or two offloads and a tackle on Nonu in the first half (I remember thinking, *Jesus, I've just tackled Ma'a Nonu, how cool is that?*). But nothing I did put much of a dent in the All Blacks.

Carter was even better than he had been in Auckland, scoring a try, setting up two more, kicking seven goals and missing none. Without any shadow of a doubt, he was the best player I'd played against by a distance.

We thought that if we put pressure on him, his team wouldn't function properly. But we couldn't put pressure on him because he saw things seconds before anybody else did. However, what surprised me more than his silky handling skills was how physical he was. He was probably their smallest player, and I'd assumed he didn't enjoy too much contact, but when I tried to tackle him, I really felt his power. Even our big lads were bouncing off him.

We were already doomed by half-time, but I still thought I could do something for the team. Eight minutes into the second half, we had a penalty 5 metres from their try line, so I decided to take a quick tap and see what happened. A few seconds later, I was scurrying over for my first England try.

I couldn't celebrate because we were so many points down, but that was a huge moment for me. I'd wanted to make quick taps my own, a point of difference between me and the other English scrum-halves. And I thought, *If I've scored a try against New Zealand, maybe I do belong at this level.*

There was, as usual, a lot of negativity in the English press, but I'm not sure it was entirely warranted. We had some good up-and-coming players – Tom Rees, James Haskell, Mike Brown, Dave Strettle, Tom Varndell – but not a lot of experience (prop Andrew Sheridan was the only survivor from the World Cup final just eight months earlier). Meanwhile, New Zealand's team was packed with seasoned superstars, who each had a point to prove after their quarter-final exit in France, so it was always going to be tough for us to compete with them.

For me and many other England players, that tour was a crash course in what it took to compete at the highest level. In short, when we made mistakes, the All Blacks almost always punished us. But when they made mistakes, we didn't punish them enough. However, as chastening as those two Test matches were, we now knew that if we were going to thrive in that kind of company, we'd have to raise our skill levels, our speed, our physicality and our ferocity.

But the most traumatic lesson on that tour wasn't delivered by Carter and co., it was handed out by the media, and it had nothing to do with what happened on the pitch.

After our defeat in Auckland, I received my cap at the post-match dinner before being plied with drink on the bus and made to sing a song ('Lean on Me' by Bill Withers), along with the other debutants. Win, lose or draw, we always respected those traditions. We then hit the town, drank even more, and I ended up going home with a girl, quite a lot earlier than most of my team-mates because I had consumed a few beers.

The following morning, Stretts knocked on my door and reminded me that we needed to check in with the physios and go for a swim to flush the legs out. So I said goodbye to the girl, who was really nice, before going into the adjoining room, where I expected to find Mike Brown snoring his head off. However, Browny was nowhere to be seen. Instead, Topsy and a female were in there. So I apologised for the intrusion, reminded Topsy about physio and swimming, made a hasty exit and headed downstairs.

I was waiting in the lobby when the lift doors opened and the girl I'd seen in Browny's room appeared, along with a few of the other lads. She'd been laughing on the way down and then said goodbye to our team liaison guy.

A few of the lads had been out until 5am, so I spent most of the recovery session finding out what they'd been up to. It sounded like a good time had been had by all – lots of drink, lots of fun, nothing illegal – and I didn't think anything more of it until I got off the plane in Christchurch and clocked a gang of police officers.

As the team filed past, wondering what the hell was going on, Topsy, Browny, Dom Waldouck and I were taken aside, pulled into a room and informed that someone had made a very serious allegation of sexual assault. All the blood seemed to drain from my body, even though I knew I'd done nothing wrong. I'd been on such a high after making my England debut and now this was happening. Talk about crashing back down to earth with a thud. God knows how Dom must have felt – he hadn't even gone out and they'd only collared him because his room was next to ours.

When the police spoke to me on my own, they told me that the girl had accused two boys of sexually assaulting her while two other lads watched. I told them that the only times I'd seen this girl were when I went into Browny's room that morning and when she appeared in the lobby, and I left that meeting thinking it was all nonsense. I thought, *None of us has done anything wrong, so everything will be okay*, which was exactly what a naive 21-year-old would think.

Still, having that hanging over me while I was preparing to make my first start for England was far from ideal. It was decided that the best course of action was for nobody to say anything until things were sorted. And while it had quickly been established that the girl's story was a pack of lies and the RFU was confident no charges would be brought against us, our names were inevitably leaked following the second Test. The *Sun* ran a story calling us 'The Auckland Four' (Dom had by now been absolved of any blame), along with a picture of us all singing the national anthem. I wished I could just speak to the media and explain what had and hadn't happened. It was a horrific situation.

Before the *Sun* ran their story, the management team told me I was going to be named, having previously told me I wouldn't. So I had to make a heartbreaking phone call to my mum and explain that I was about to be accused of sexual assault in a national newspaper. She believed me when I told her I hadn't done anything wrong, but her life was turned upside down and she was worried sick. Hearing her so upset was probably the worst part about the whole episode. I'd been quite naive before then, but I now understood the malevolent power of the press. They didn't just mangle the lives of the people they wrote about, they also mangled the lives of their nearest and dearest. It certainly took the gloss off my try in the second Test.

The British tabloids have no morals, but the biggest problem is that their readers assume that whatever their journalists write must be at least partly true. In other words, they believe that there's no smoke without fire. It didn't help that the New Zealand police carried on investigating the case after we'd returned home, so stories were popping up in the papers for weeks.

Once we were back on English soil, the RFU handed our case over to our clubs, because we were no longer on England duty. Luckily, Stretts, Browny and I had a great lawyer at Quins and eventually the case against all four of us was dropped. What did the tabloids have to say about that? Not nearly as much as they had to say about us being accused of sexual assault in the first place.

Browny and Topsy were found guilty of misconduct and fined (although only for staying out late and missing physio and recovery, not for any illegal activity). They were also relegated to the second-string Saxons squad, as was Stretts (Topsy never played for England again, while Stretts and Browny didn't earn a recall until after Johnno was gone). Johnno's first elite squad was missing 13 players who toured New Zealand, but thankfully I was included. It had been a traumatic tour, but compared to the rest of the Auckland Four, I'd come through it relatively unscathed.

I'll never forget the first time I met Johnno – when we shook hands, mine disappeared inside his. It was like he was wearing a baseball glove. But while he was an absolutely enormous bloke, and had a real aura around him, he wasn't as intimidating as you might expect.

Johnno would ask me about my family, and he was a big Liverpool fan like me, so we chatted about them a lot. When he spoke about rugby, players just stared at him like little puppy dogs. But he was surprisingly attack minded. He'd say to me, 'Enjoy yourself. If you young lads bring the energy and get stuck in, the rest of the boys will follow, and this team will do good things.'

People had their doubts about Johnno because despite leading England to their only World Cup triumph in 2003, he'd never coached before. In hindsight, the decision to appoint him was a bit mad. Can you imagine an NFL franchise appointing a head coach who had never been in charge of an American football team? No. But at the time, I couldn't think of anyone I'd rather play for. *Of course he's going to be a success*, I thought, *he's Martin Johnson. The guy's a bloody hero, he can do anything ...*

Johnno was a proper tracksuit coach who got involved in training, whether it was putting on a tackle suit and wrestling with the lads or flying into rucks. I loved it; it was like having an extra player on the pitch. One day, we were doing a restart session and Leicester second-row Tom Croft wasn't quite getting it right. So Johnno took up Crofty's position, asked Jonny Wilkinson to put a kick up, caught the ball one-handed on the run and went on a 30-metre gallop. Then he said, 'There you go, Crofty, that's how you should do it,' before tossing him the ball. I thought that was class, this legend of English rugby taking the piss out of lads who were 15 years younger than him.

Unfortunately for Johnno, he didn't have much of a honeymoon period. Those autumn internationals are never easy, but they were particularly challenging early on in my England career. In 2008, we kicked off with a game against the Pacific Islanders, which was meant to be the easy one, before games against Australia, who had some great players back then; world champions South Africa; and New Zealand – on consecutive weekends.

Johnno only had us for three training sessions before the first game, which isn't much time to mould a bunch of lads from lots of different teams – each of which have a different style of playing – into a cohesive unit. And while we beat the Pacific Islanders quite handily, we were well beaten in the other three games, which included a 42–6 hammering at the hands of South Africa.

As strange as it might sound coming from an England international, I felt like a little boy in that South Africa game, as well as a fraud and an imposter. I was looking around at all these superstars, like their second-row pairing of Victor Matfield and Bakkies Botha, Schalk Burger and Bryan Habana, and thinking, *These are proper men, and this is proper rugby.*

Bakkies Botha hit me late in that game, about three seconds after I'd passed the ball, and I'd never felt anything like it. While I was attempting to catch my breath, looking like a man who had just crawled out of a serious car crash, Botha pushed my head into the ground, like someone grinding out a cigarette. I heard him laughing as he was running off. He reminded me of some fairytale ogre who ate scrum-halves for breakfast.

This was only five years after England had won the World Cup, which isn't that long in the grand scheme of things, so I couldn't help thinking, *Is this team a bit crap now because of me?* Along with quite a few of our young lads, I just couldn't see how we'd ever be able to compete with a team like that. I certainly realised I needed to toughen up and become more streetwise.

Before that series, people were writing articles about me and Danny Cipriani forming a half-back partnership that might last for ten years. But after that defeat by the Springboks, Cips was dropped to the bench for the All Blacks match before spending the next six years in the international wilderness.

I knew what a brilliant player Cips was, but it was always going to be a big ask for him to run that team against the three best sides in the world, especially as he'd only just returned from a career-threatening injury. The media was desperate for him to be the new Jonny Wilkinson, and that was a big burden for a lad of only 21. Cips was also a more instinctive player than Jonny and took more risks, which didn't always come off. Those kinds of fly-halves become vulnerable when results aren't going a team's way.

Cips and I had shared so many good times down the years. When we roomed with each other at age-group level, we'd have what were essentially sleepovers, with ham and cheese sandwiches and pints of milk. We both rated ourselves quite highly and loved playing with each other, because we saw the game in a similar way. But while neither of us wanted to be a robot, I was always a team man, whereas Cips wanted to do things his own way.

I've sat in a lot of meetings with many England coaches and it's not often that players have questioned anything. There are a lot of yes men in professional rugby, because they feel they have to be: if you're agreeable, you've got far less chance of being dropped from the team. But Cips didn't have that filter. He was a non-conformist to his core, and if he didn't agree with something, he'd say it. That's why he was never around an England set-up for very long.

Other coaches would have recalled Cips somewhere down the line, but that was never going to happen with Johnno, because they were polar opposites in terms of personality. I'm sure if Johnno was being completely honest, he'd say he simply didn't like Cips as a person, which is why he probably didn't have any qualms about never picking him again.

○

Harlequins had only just missed out on the Premiership play-offs in 2008 (in the final game of the season, Leicester wing Tom Varndell scored a ridiculous late try to clinch the final spot ahead of us), but we did manage to scrape into the Heineken Cup. And we started the following season like a runaway train, playing some scintillating attacking rugby and scoring a stack of tries.

Sometimes I'd think how weird it was that I was starting every week while Gomars was on the bench. He'd taught me so much and almost won the World Cup with England a year earlier. But instead of being angry with me for taking his place, he was like a proud big brother, delighted by my progress.

Not much had changed personnel wise – we still had Browny, Stretts, Ugo Monye and Jordan Turner-Hall in the backline, and the likes of Nick Easter, Robbo and our skipper Will Skinner up front – but sometimes you only need to add one extra ingredient to elevate things to the next level, and that one extra ingredient for us was New Zealand fly-half Nick Evans.

Nick decided to join Quins after Dan Carter usurped him as the All Blacks' first-choice ten, but he was still only 28 and arguably at his peak. He was one hell of a scoop for the club, and we were all excited to see him in action, although I don't think anyone realised exactly how influential he'd be.

We knew Quins were paying him bags of money, and that combined with the terrible swag he wore made him an instant target. In the early days, he'd wear three-quarter-length cargo shorts, like he was off to fit a kitchen, and because some of the lads were quite fashion conscious, what with living the London life, they'd really get stuck into him. I'll never forget the bemused look on Nick's face when the flak started flying – it was actually quite uncomfortable.

But he soon put us in our place. One of his first nights out with the boys was at Chinawhite, a celebrity haunt in Soho. We reserved our own table, ordered a load of beer and vodka and got stuck in. But after half an hour, Nick disappeared. I thought he'd decided it wasn't really his scene and headed back to his hotel. Fair enough: Chinawhite wasn't to everyone's taste, especially blokes who wore cargo shorts. But about two hours later, I peered into the VIP suite and saw Nick lounging on a sofa next to the owner, who turned out to be a massive All Blacks fan, surrounded by girls and champagne.

From thinking that we were doing Nick a favour by showing him the most exclusive joints in London, we suddenly realised we might spend the next few years hanging on his coattails (I should add that Nick never made it to his hotel that night – instead he woke up on mine and Jordan Turner-Hall's sofa, which was nothing like as comfortable as the VIP ones in Chinawhite).

Nick – or 'Snapper' as we called him, because of his love of fishing – soon got used to all the abuse about his swag and started to show us what he could do on a rugby field. He was quick, skilful and a superb kicker out of hand and off the tee. He was also brilliant at making the best of bad situations. If I threw him a bad ball, he'd usually be able to readjust and find the right pass or even step a couple of defenders.

I always felt that Snapper played with a chip on his shoulder, having been displaced in the All Blacks team by Dan Carter. But while Carter was obviously an unbelievable player, Snapper wasn't too far behind him and made the game look every bit as simple. And every time he did something great, I imagined him thinking, *That's what New Zealand are missing out on …* Had Snapper stayed down under, he probably would have played many more times for the All Blacks, and maybe even starred in a World Cup final in 2011, when Carter got injured and New Zealand were scrabbling around for a replacement. But New Zealand's loss was very much the Quins' gain.

Weirdly, if you rolled Snapper a football, he was utterly clueless. He'd mince around it for a few seconds before toe-punting it like a toddler. The first time I saw him do it, I said to him, 'What the hell is wrong with you?' I couldn't get my head around the fact that a sportsman as talented as Snapper, especially someone who kicked goals for a living, had no concept of how to kick a football. But as Snapper explained, he'd never played football, so it was completely alien to him. However, like lots and lots of other Kiwis, he did grow up with a rugby ball in his hands, so he knew exactly what to do with one of them.

We'd shown flashes of what we were capable of in the previous couple of seasons, but Snapper had a way of making things work on a weekly basis. Like all great players, he made everyone around him better and gave us the belief that we could compete with the best teams out there. I have no doubt whatsoever that Snapper is the best overseas signing in Premiership history.

Chapter 5

Crazy Gang

Of course, even the great players require a good environment to thrive in, and there was no better environment than the one Deano created at Quins.

The more time I spent with Deano, the more I loved him. He was such a warm, caring person – and one of the most unique people I've ever met. He was professional when he needed to be, but he still had those amateur vibes about him, as you'd expect of a man who combined a rugby career playing for Leicester, England and the Lions with a day job as a copper.

When I first arrived at Quins, the lads would tell me that Deano went on every major piss-up, wherever it happened to be. I only knew Deano as this bloke who always looked quite grumpy in post-match interviews, so thought they must have been exaggerating. But sure enough, he was front and centre at the first couple of socials I attended, along with the rest of the coaches. He'd still be standing and making sense when some of the lads were under tables.

End-of-season socials were a massive deal for Quins, and I learnt very early on that if Nick 'Minty' Easter, our very keen social secretary, demanded everyone wear fancy dress, you didn't just turn up on theme, you splurged a lot of money and went a big as possible (we called Nick 'Minty' because he sounded and looked like the *EastEnders* character of the same name, despite attending the exclusive Dulwich College). One year, Deano came as Friar Tuck, while head coach John Kingston came as Mrs Doubtfire, and it was the best Mrs Doubtfire costume I'd ever seen: he was the spitting image of Robin Williams (although I have absolutely no clue what the theme was that year!).

Deano loved playing the one-inch punch game. We'd all sit in a circle and he'd always sit in between some props, usually young ones he wanted to toughen up a bit. He'd shape as if he was going to jab them with a couple of fingers before making a fist, pulling his arm back and banging them as hard as he could. Then he'd demand they did it to him. The one-inch punch game often ended up in a brawl, which Deano absolutely loved. He was in his mid-40s by this stage but probably still the hardest bloke at the club, even while dressed as Friar Tuck and with 15 pints of bitter swilling around in his belly.

Every now and again, those fancy dress socials would get a bit out of hand. One year, we started out in Putney and by the time we reached Parsons Green, everyone was steaming. And who should we bump into? The entire Bath squad, who were also on an end-of-season jolly. What's the worst that could happen?

Will Skinner had spent months making a Transformers costume, which was a marvel of engineering – when he sat down, he was a car, but when he stood up, he was a full-on Transformer (Skins was in his mid-20s at the time, in case you were wondering). But while he was standing at the bar, Bath's Aussie lock Justin Harrison, who had a tendency to make a nuisance of himself, grabbed Skins's costume and ripped it off his back. Skins had come from Leicester, where fighting was encouraged. But while I'd never seen a man angrier, he just gave Harrison a long, cold stare before walking out of the door. I remember thinking, *That's odd, I thought he would have whacked him.*

Skins was away for a while, and we all assumed he'd gone home and wasn't coming back. But as we were gathering outside this pub, getting ready to hit another one, Skins reappeared. He should have been wearing a ten-gallon hat and spurs on his boots, because it was like something out of a cowboy movie. He marched straight towards Harrison – quite briskly, but almost in slow motion, if you know what I mean – and threw the biggest right hand I'd ever seen. For a little lad, Skins could punch, because Harrison was laid out cold on the concrete. I thought he was dead. Luckily, he wasn't.

I'm not a fighting man, and people getting punched makes me feel quite queasy. But as punches go, it was a beauty. And while the Bath boys went home, the Quins boys carried on drinking. Good old Skins had won the day.

Then there was the Infernos fish tank story, which is luckily only famous among Harlequins players of a certain vintage. At least until now.

That year's fancy dress theme was the Olympics, so one group of lads went as judo players and the other group went as Mexican boxers, wearing boxing gloves, ponchos, sombreros and handlebar moustaches. We arrived at Infernos, a nightclub in Clapham, at about ten o'clock, already three sheets to the wind. And completely inevitably – in hindsight, of course – scraps kept breaking out between judokas and boxers.

At one point, Stretts wrestled me to the ground and kicked me in the face (accidentally, probably). I wasn't having that, so I whacked him. I was wearing big, padded boxing gloves, but there was still enough power in the punch to knock him over. Stretts bounced back up, we locked eyes, and it was going to go one of two ways: either we were going to have a proper fight, or we were going to hug it out. Luckily, Stretts was in a hugging mood.

Unluckily, one of the bouncers wasn't. In a story as old as time, he thought Stretts and I were having a proper fight, and it didn't matter how many times we told him we were only messing about, he wanted us out.

If I was ever in trouble, Jordan Turner-Hall acted as my personal bodyguard. I'd call his name – 'Jordy!' – and he'd appear by my side from nowhere, like the Bat-Signal had gone up. So while this bouncer was dragging me up this steep staircase towards the exit, Jordy was hanging on to him – until the bouncer got irate and tried to chuck me back down again. I grabbed hold of the bouncer, in order to stay upright, and started doing that thing where you speed up running downhill to keep your balance. The bouncer then grabbed hold of Jordy, for the same reason I'd grabbed hold of him, and we all crashed into a huge fish tank at the bottom of the stairs.

It was a terrible scene. There was water everywhere, crashing over us in waves. And, of course, lots of fish – tropical ones, all the colours of the rainbow, thrashing around for dear life. And amid the carnage, kickin' and a-gougin' in the mud and the blood and the beer, were Jordy, me and this bouncer, while team-mates and random punters watched on, open-mouthed.

Jordy and I eventually managed to escape the bouncer's clutches, get past his colleagues on the front door and hotfoot it down Clapham High Street. I was shedding my outfit as I ran, so that by the time I reached Clapham Common Station, I was no longer a Mexican boxer, but a relatively normal bloke in shorts and a poncho. It was like a cheap version of the final scene from *The Usual Suspects*, when Kevin Spacey morphs into Keyser Söze.

How that incident never ended up in the papers will always be a mystery to me. It was far worse than some of the things I got nicked for down the line. I'm told that people were wandering around Infernos with fish in their drinks. I didn't even get barred, because they didn't recognise me. To the staff of Infernos, I will always be that mysterious Mexican boxer, there one minute, gone the next. I'd turn up with the lads looking sheepish, and a bouncer would say, 'Did you hear about those dickheads who crashed into the fish tank?'

○

Deano flogged us in training, don't worry about that, but he understood that there was more to team bonding than dying for and fighting with each other on the pitch – what you might call the Leicester way (which was slightly ironic, because there were few bigger Leicester legends than Deano).

He believed that you learnt more about each other on the beers than you did on the training ground, which is why he'd sometimes send us down the pub with the order to just sit around drinking and chatting nonsense. Because of Deano, playing for Quins was like being back at school with your best mates.

At clubs like Bath or Gloucester, most of the lads lived quite close to each other, but because Quins were based in London, we were spread all over the place. So after every home game, Minty would say, 'Right, everyone down the St Margaret's Tavern. You can do whatever you want afterwards, but you're having a couple of pints at least.' Had Minty not done that, some players might have drifted off every week and never got to know their team-mates properly. But it never felt like we were forced into being mates, and some of the older lads loved getting on the beers more than us young, free and single kids. We'd say to Minty, 'Mate, you're almost 30, why are you even coming out?' But he was mad for it: first in the pub and last out.

You didn't earn Minty's affection easily – he was quite grumpy and very old-school, almost like a throwback to rugby's amateur days – but once you were in with him, he was one of the funniest blokes you could possibly meet. He'd spend weeks putting together his end-of-season video, in which he and a few others reenacted all the daft stuff the lads had done during the year. You knew you'd made it if you appeared in one of Minty's videos, and his impressions of the boys were off-the-scale funny.

Minty somehow combined his love of a night out with never in my mind offering to buy a round (which is probably why he's got so much money now), but there was a group of us young-sters – me, my old housemate Stretts, my new housemate Jordan Turner-Hall, Ugo Monye – who had a bit of cash and didn't mind spending it. Don't get me wrong, we weren't as rich as footballers – those boys earned more in a week than we did in a year – but we would do silly things like playing credit card roulette for the bill (everyone would put their card in a hat and whichever card got pulled out first – or last, for dramatic effect – would foot the bill). That would usually mean some poor bastard leaving a nightclub or restaurant £1,000 lighter.

Looking back, I can't help thinking I could do with some of that money now that I've got a wife and three kids. But at the time, we were just living for the moment and having fun. And it was largely down to all that extra-curricular daftness that we were so close, and had so much fun, on the pitch.

Deano would ask the lads to send him photos and videos of ridiculous things they'd got up to on Saturday night. All day Sunday, he'd be texting people, 'Come on, lads, some-one must have something for me!' And on the Monday, he'd hold his 'dick of the week' meeting, which involved presenting a giant dildo to whoever had done the stupidest thing over the weekend.

Before Deano's arrival, we'd balance a bucket of water on top of the meeting room door, so that when he walked in, the bucket would tip and he'd get soaked. It was such a basic, schoolboy gag, and we'd all be screaming with laughter. If we'd played badly, Deano would kick off the meeting by saying, 'Bad game, lads, got to be better than that. Right, on to dick of the week …' Then he'd smile, rub his hands together, lower the lighting and show all these photos and videos.

A winning video was of one of the lads sleeping naked in a dog bed, which meant he had to carry the dildo with him at all times until the following week (unless he did something else just as stupid, in which case he'd have to hand the dildo back to Deano, and Deano would present it to him again).

We trained at Roehampton, the old stomping ground of Wimbledon FC's Crazy Gang, and I like to think we kept their spirit alive. Quins had a reputation as city slickers and champagne Charlies, but the training facilities at Roehampton were appalling. It was essentially a public field off the A3, where lonely horses grazed. There would be muck all over the pitch, and sometimes one of the horses would break free and go on an alarming gallop, causing the lads to scatter in different directions.

The changing rooms, in which the likes of Vinnie Jones and John Fashanu caused mayhem back in the day, were tiny. Our meetings took place right next to the kitchen, and lads would nick meat for dinner, much to Joe the chef's chagrin. We'd have to drive to the gym to do weights and to the track to do shuttles. But the facilities being so bad only brought us closer together.

We embraced how awful it was, and recognised that it made us different from other clubs.

Just like the Crazy Gang, it was us against the world – and the abuse was relentless. The physio room was banter central, but players would get abuse everywhere they went – it was impossible to escape it. You were willing team-mates to do something stupid so that everyone could take the piss out of them, because you knew that all that piss-taking acted as a social glue.

Deano was a big watcher. For example, he was known to call lads in for a meeting and pretend to be on the phone for five minutes. When I asked him why he did that, he said he liked seeing how people reacted, whether they just sat there calmly or started looking awkward as the minutes ticked by. He also didn't do any hands-on coaching – while we were warming up, he'd be indoors watching horse racing, then he'd wander out and observe from the touchline.

He wanted us to be tough and scrappy (you can take the man out of Leicester, but you'll never take the Leicester out of Deano), but he surrounded himself with coaches who had a sophisticated understanding of attacking rugby.

Andy Friend left for the Brumbies in his native Australia in 2008, but not before he'd instilled an expressive style of playing at Quins. John Kingston was a magician when it came to design-ing trick plays at line-outs, while Collin Osborne was a brilliant skills coach who had been working with a lot of the lads since they joined the Quins academy. Add in Tony Diprose, who was in charge of defence but had been a talented footballing number eight for Quins, and a bunch of young lads who wanted to play the game fast, chuck the ball around and entertain the crowd, and you had a nice blend of grit and flair.

We thought that if we were going to be the best team in the Premiership, we needed to play the game faster than anyone else. And to play the game faster than anyone else, we needed to be the fittest. As such, we ran a lot in training, but it wasn't mindless running, like other clubs did, it was running as you'd expect to do in a game, almost non-stop, with the ball in hand the whole time. And we did that every Monday, Tuesday and Thursday.

We became so tight, on and off the field, that we thought we could beat anyone, and we developed something of a swagger. Our mindset could be summed up as, 'Play what you see, and let's have fun doing it.'

We weren't too worried about tactical kicking; it was attack, attack, attack, score as many tries as possible and get the fans on their feet. But it wasn't completely reckless, because we had older heads like Minty, Snapper, second-row Olly Kohn, Irish prop Mike Ross, Welsh prop Ceri Jones, Samoan hooker Tani Fuga and South African hooker Gary Botha to keep us from disappearing up our own backsides. Not that those older lads were averse to some ridiculous behaviour off the field. After one big night out, I wrestled Olly for an hour in a hotel corridor – he was about 22 stone, I was about half that – and our epic clash was only brought to an end by the club doctor, whose sleep had been rudely interrupted by all the banging and growling.

It was also those boys who insisted that however heavy the weekend's drinking had been – Saturday nights often carried over into an all-day session on Sundays – we made it in for training on the Monday. As I say to our young lads now, 'However many drinks you had last night, and however bad your hangover, you pitch up and you work hard. You can go home and sleep later.'

Chapter 6

Bloodgate

While we were flying in the Premiership, the best evidence of how far we'd come was our Heineken Cup form. Prior to that season, we hadn't reached the quarter-finals since 1998, and we weren't expected to advance from a pool that included French giants Stade Français, who had only ever lost once at home in Europe. But we fully deserved our win at the Stade de France, managing to block out the pre-match can-can girls (difficult) and the jousting tournament (only in Paris!) and outscoring them two tries to one; and the following week, Snapper kicked a last-gasp drop goal as we beat them 19–17 at the Stoop.

That wasn't the first time Snapper had pulled out a moment of magic to win us a game. It was becoming clear that that's just what he did. He was a go-to clutch guy, who would get us out of a sticky situation with a wonder try or a goal from nowhere. And not many teams had one of those blokes in their ranks.

We drew Leinster at home in the quarter-finals, and with Snapper back after a four-week injury lay-off, we thought we had a good chance of winning. We weren't just entertainers; we also had a pack of forwards who were rock solid at the set-piece and fearsome at the breakdown. The back row of Minty, Robbo and Skinner were very physical; some argued they were cynical, in that they played right on the edge and were brilliant at slowing down opposition ball.

Then again, Leinster were a giant of a team, and we knew we'd have to play well to beat them. Leinster also had Brian O'Driscoll back for the first time since the Six Nations, and he was never not the best player on the pitch. Like Dan Carter, he seemed to have more time on the ball than everyone else and made everything look easy, as if he was born with a rugby ball in his hands. He glided around the pitch, but he also had a physical presence, despite being quite a small centre. And while he was mostly about doing the basics extremely well – running the right lines, pinpoint passing, solid tackling – he also had the ability to make opponents look very silly. He was one of the few players I watched and thought, *Wow, that's cool. I might try that.*

O'Driscoll had Ireland team-mate Gordon D'Arcy alongside him in the centres, Argentina's Felipe Contepomi at fly-half and a pack full of Irish internationals, supplemented by Wallabies flanker Rocky Elsom, who might be the most appropriately named rugby player in history. There was one thing I was absolutely certain of – this team wasn't going to be a pushover.

A lot of people expected a classic: two teams full of attacking flair going end to end for 80 minutes. It was actually more like an old-fashioned international, very physical, tight and intense, with no quarter given. But it would turn out to be one of the most notorious rugby matches in history.

The first half was brutal – one for the purists, as they say. Snapper was still able to conjure a bit of magic despite his heavily strapped leg (one journalist said he was swathed in more bandages than Tutankhamun), but we were unable to get over the try line and two Contepomi penalties made it 6–0 to Leinster at the break. Then, shortly after the restart, Leinster number eight Jamie Heaslip hit Snapper with a thumping tackle, which left Snapper hobbling and proved to be the trigger for all the madness that followed.

We spent the majority of the second half camped deep in Leinster territory, mostly to no avail. I had what I thought was a legitimate try disallowed, Gary Botha was held up over the line, and Minty and Robbo fell just short. We did finally break Leinster's resolve with 15 minutes remaining, Browny going over in the corner, but Snapper's replacement Chris Malone missed the extras, leaving us trailing by a point.

A few minutes later, Chris tore his hamstring off the bone and was replaced by Tom Williams, who usually played on the wing. That meant Browny was our only recognised place kicker, although he didn't actually kick that often. And with eight minutes left, Browny pushed a penalty attempt wide of the posts.

When you're a scrum-half, you spend so much time in the middle of the pitch with your head in a ruck that you normally don't have a clue what's going on in terms of who's coming on and who's going off. But on this occasion, I do remember seeing Snapper hobbling back on and thinking, *How is that happening?* What I didn't see, however, was Tommy Williams being helped off the pitch with blood all over his mouth, or Leinster head coach Michael Cheika remonstrating with officials. I was just trying to find a way to win the game.

Hindsight is a wonderful thing, and now I wonder why Deano didn't just put Gomars on at ten or put him at nine and move me to fly-half. Either one of us had it in us to knock over a goal. Instead, Snapper, who could barely stand, had a late crack from 35 yards out and the ball drifted left of the upright.

After the final whistle, the Leinster coaching and medical staff were going bonkers, but because I was so gutted to have lost the game, I didn't pay much attention to it. It was only when I got back to our changing room and Leinster coaches were trying to force their way in that I realised something controversial had gone on. Then one of our older lads who hadn't played arrived with an ashen look on his face. He sat down and said, 'Lads, we have fucked this. It's very bad.' We asked what he was going on about, and he told us it was something to do with Tommy going off with a fake injury.

At first, all the newspaper reports focused on Deano's games-manship. Because Snapper had apparently been substituted for tactical rather than injury reasons (which would have been big news to Jamie Heaslip), he was able to return to the field if anyone suffered a blood injury. Hence why Deano said after the game, 'You have to know the rules.' There was no mention of fake-blood capsules or anything like that, although it was widely noted that Snapper had spent most of his time on the sidelines riding an exercise bike and Tommy had winked at a team-mate while being helped from the pitch.

The media scrutiny died down after a week or so, and the management told us the tournament organisers were investigating and that we had nothing to worry about. But rugby teams are worse than sewing circles when it comes to gossip, and as soon as we were back in training, the rumour mill went into overdrive.

It soon became clear that shortly after Browny had pushed that penalty wide, Tommy had pulled a fake-blood capsule out of his sock and popped it in his mouth before hitting the deck and pretending to be injured, thus allowing Snapper to re-enter the fray. And having had the attitude that it was nothing to do with me, I suddenly realised that the club had really messed up and was in a lot of trouble. This wasn't rule-bending, this was outright cheating.

I can understand why people would say, 'Come on mate, you must have known what was going on.' But hand on heart, I never knew clubs, let alone mine, used fake blood to get players off the field. I was only 22 and still quite naive. And I wasn't the only one who was in the dark. Quite a few of us were saying to each other, 'Fake-blood capsules? How is this even a thing?'

It was only when I started asking some of the older lads questions that I discovered that club physios all over the world had been slicing players' lips open for years, and that things had recently gone to the next level, with clubs buying fake-blood capsules. And where did these fake-blood capsules come from? In our case, apparently, a joke shop on Clapham High Street! You couldn't make it up.

Despite the gravity of the situation, the lads obviously found elements of it hilarious. After watching the game back, we realised just how badly executed the cheat had been. We had coaches and medical staff pushing and shoving on the touchline, trying to make it look like Tommy was badly injured, but only making it look more fake with their overacting. There was the 'blood' gushing from Tommy's mouth – it looked more like he'd been eating a jam doughnut. There was co-commentator Stuart Barnes asking, 'Who's punched Tom Williams in the mouth – Tom Williams?' There was Tommy staggering from the pitch as if he'd been whacked by Tyson Fury. And, of course, there was Tommy's wink, in response to our lock Jim Evans telling him to tough it out. Let's just say Tommy hasn't got a future on the stage. It was a farce from start to finish.

I just kept thinking, *If Deano had just brought on Gomars, none of this would have happened* … Try as I might, I couldn't make sense of it.

Then we started hearing about all the murky details, although how many of those details were true or not was difficult to work out. How when Tommy had taken to the field, he'd told our physio Steph Brennan that he'd be coming off at some point with a blood injury. How Steph had handed Tommy the capsule the next time he was on to treat a player. How Tommy had fallen to one knee after his first major contact, fished out the capsule and bitten into it at the second attempt. How Leinster wing Shane Horgan had shouted from the bench, 'It's not real blood!' And, murkiest of all, the scene that played out in our physio room: Leinster medics and tournament officials banging on the door because they wanted to see the 'injury' (they smelt a rat as soon as they saw Snapper warming up on the exercise bike); Tommy pleading with our doctor Wendy Chapman to cut his lip, to prove the injury was genuine; Wendy refusing and Tommy threatening to do it himself; Wendy finally agreeing, but only because she feared Tommy doing himself some proper damage.

I was mates with Tommy but there were a few competing stories, so I didn't know who to believe. Our poor captain, Will Skinner, was in and out of meetings with our board and lawyers and independent investigators, although I'm certain he knew nothing about the use of fake-blood capsules either. He'd just been playing a game of rugby and now he'd been sucked into one of the greatest scandals in rugby history.

The lads were split between thinking, on the one hand, that Tommy should stay quiet, go along with whatever the club asked him to do and take the punishment – more recently, Tommy said there was a bit of borderline bullying going on, with team-mates saying stuff along the lines of, 'Loose lips sink ships' – and on the other hand, that Tommy had every right to stick up for himself. After all, Tommy hadn't bought that capsule from a joke shop in Clapham and it hadn't been his idea to fake an injury.

Tommy disappeared from the club for a while, presumably because things were getting a bit tense between the club's lawyers and his. And all the while, that footage of him winking seemed to be playing on a loop on Sky Sports News. Then in July, three months after the game, the independent disciplinary panel announced its punishments: a £215,000 fine for the club and a 12-month ban for Tommy. Misconduct complaints against Deano, Steph and Wendy were dismissed, which raised a few eyebrows in the camp. But members of the media did more than raise a few eyebrows: their reactions ranged from bemused to apoplectic.

Deano's old England team-mate Brian Moore, a trained solicitor, wrote: 'It is curious that the club have been fined when their two medical staff and coach were cleared of wrongdoing.' A Scottish journalist wrote that the investigation's findings 'were rank with the aroma of fudge and contradiction'. Meanwhile, Damian Hopley, chief executive of the Professional Rugby Players' Association (RPA), called the decision to ban Tommy for a year 'extraordinary' and 'entirely disproportionate'. Plenty pointed out the apparent madness of banning Tommy for a year while other players had only received eight-week bans for poking a finger in an opponent's eye. 'Bloodgate', as the media were now calling it, wasn't going away any time soon.

The club had originally offered Tommy compensation if he swallowed the one-year ban, but after a meeting with some of our senior players, during which he said he was going to take the money and the hit, he changed his mind, deciding instead to tell all for a reduced ban. That annoyed some of the team, because it seemed like Tommy wanted things both ways: to take the money (he'd already accepted the club's offer) and to tell all.

A couple of weeks later, Deano resigned. And following a 14-hour European Rugby Cup hearing, during which Tommy spilled all of Bloodgate's ugly details and it was revealed that the club had faked a blood injury on four previous occasions, Deano was handed a three-year ban from rugby. Steph was banned for two years and later struck off by his regulatory body (although he overturned that on appeal); Wendy escaped punishment again but was later suspended by the General Medical Council, having admitted that she deliberately cut Tommy's lip (her suspension was later reduced to a reprimand); Charles Jillings, the club's co-owner and chairman, also resigned; and the club's fine was increased to £260,000. Talk about a bomb going off. Imagine if Snapper's kick had gone over and we'd won, before going on to win the whole tournament? They'd still be sifting through the carnage now.

Quins escaped a ban from European rugby and Tommy had his suspension reduced to four months, but trying to put a positive spin on the situation was like trying to find a silver lining in a mushroom cloud.

It's difficult to sum up the emotions that were swirling around the club in the aftermath of Deano's departure, but for me it was a mixture of bemusement, embarrassment and sadness. Bemusement that a moment of madness in a game of rugby had led to such devastation; embarrassment that my once proud old club was now both a laughing stock and a pariah; and sadness that a man I adored – an icon of the game, the person responsible for Quins' rebirth, the reason I'd joined the club in the first place – was no longer around.

I know what Deano did was wrong, but I still felt so sorry for him. It was impossible not to because he was just such a great person who always looked out for me, and rugby had been his life for so many years. He didn't even get to say goodbye to the players: he was there one day, gone the next.

I reckon everyone in that squad would have gone along with Deano's ruse. I certainly would have done, because when Deano asked you to do something, you did it. Deano always stuck up for his players, and a few would have said they owed their England careers to Deano's influence – Minty and I certainly did. All of which probably explains why a few of the players closest to Deano didn't like how Tommy had gone about things.

Maybe some of the lads thought, *Other clubs are at it, so why not us?* – the old Lance Armstrong defence – but we deserved everything we got. We were the ones who got caught cheating, so we just had to wear it – the reams of criticism in the media (every second newspaper story about us included a blood-based pun as a headline), opposing fans booing and chucking blood capsules at us, which went on for years, and not to mention the oppro-brium from our own supporters. I'd been so proud of being a Harlequin, and we'd developed such a swagger, but now people thought we'd been cheating the whole time. Even today, 15 years later, people give me grief about it. Even though I wasn't directly involved, in some people's eyes I'll always be guilty by association.

As you can imagine, the grief us Quins lads got the next time we were in the England camp was off the scale. Haskell proba-bly spent all week beforehand writing jokes about it, and I was surprised he didn't turn up dressed as Dracula. But mostly the lads from other clubs laughed at us. They weren't angry that we'd cheated, they just couldn't believe that we'd cheated so badly.

Bloodgate was probably the worst thing that had happened in the club's history, but instead of feeling sorry for ourselves, we used it as a motivator.

A lot of people hated us anyway, because of our reputation as underachieving champagne Charlies, but now we were the scum of the earth as well; it was as if Spurs had merged with Millwall. It felt like us against the world, which can bring a team closer together and make them more dangerous. We also felt we had a responsibility to win back the trust of our fans, which meant trying to entertain even more than we did before.

Chapter 7

Moments of Madness

While the Bloodgate saga was in full swing, we still had a season to finish. And it didn't finish well. Having come second in the regular season table behind Leicester, we were well beaten by London Irish in the play-off semi-finals.

We went into that game confident of winning, but Irish came up with a great game plan that messed with our rhythm. We didn't help ourselves by missing four first-half kicks at goal (Snapper still wasn't quite right) and they nabbed a couple of second-half tries to win 17–0.

But the thing I remember most about that game was being hit high by Mike Catt. And while I was flat on my back and seeing stars, I thought I felt a cheap shot. From that day on, I didn't particularly like Catty (although when he became England backs coach a few years later, I had to pretend I did).

That game probably put paid to any chance I'd had of being picked for the Lions, despite appearing to have a good chance of being selected just a few months earlier. And the story of my slide down the ranks is almost as tragicomic as Bloodgate.

When Johnno named his squad for the 2009 Six Nations, Northampton's Ben Foden and I were the only two scrum-halves in it, and Ben wasn't even a full-time nine. There was a Lions tour to South Africa that summer, so when Johnno confirmed I was his number one, I was buzzing, because first-choice England scrum-halves almost always go on Lions tours.

I was picked to start the first game against Italy and life seemed rosy. Italy weren't much cop at the time – there were even rumours doing the rounds that they were going to start flanker Mauro Bergamasco at scrum-half – so I thought it was a chance to run them ragged and really catch the eye.

It snowed heavily a few days before the game, meaning training got curtailed. And while most of the lads took the chance to put their feet up, Ben Foden, Shane Geraghty and I grabbed some tackle pads and went sledging.

We'd run down the hill, dive on the tackle pad and slide for miles. It was so much fun – like being a little boy again. But the problem with little boys is they always want to go faster and make things more dangerous. So after a while, we switched from sledging on the tackle pads to snowboarding on them. It was a time in my life when I didn't think anything could go wrong. I was in the zone, life was beautiful. Then I hit a tree stump, went flying, tried to brake using my foot and rolled my ankle. As mothers of little boys all over the world know all too well, it's all fun and games until somebody gets hurt.

I was writhing around in the snow, clutching my ankle, and the other lads thought I was winding them up. A minute later, we were spitballing ideas, trying to think of a convincing excuse. I could see Johnno's giant angry face, those glowering eyes, that furrowed brow. How the hell was I going to explain this to him? How the hell was I going to explain this to the physios? The best we could come up with was that I'd slipped on the road leading up to the hotel. You know what they say: keep your lies as simple as possible. 'Right, lads,' I said, 'you take this to your deathbeds. If Johnno finds out the truth, I'm dead.'

By the time I got to the physio's room, my ankle was up like a balloon. And a few minutes later, Johnno burst in, asking what had happened. When I told him I'd slipped on some ice, he went off like a volcano. 'Idiots! I told them to salt that road!' I hadn't seen him that angry since he punched Robbie Russell in the face playing for Leicester against Saracens.

I was told that after storming out of the physio's room, Johnno went straight to reception and started ranting and raving about the road not being salted. 'One of my players has just slipped over and injured himself!'

It was at that point I started panicking, thinking that the hotel manager might put him right and cause Johnno to start questioning my story. I could picture him demanding to see the CCTV footage, before leaping over the desk and ripping the tape from the machine, as the receptionists cowered in fear.

I had a scan and they told me it wasn't that bad, so I thought Ben Foden would replace me at nine for a couple of games and then I'd come back in. Instead, Johnno called up Leicester's Harry Ellis and started Ben on the bench against Italy. Harry had fallen out of favour with England, but I thought he was a great player, and I did think to myself, *Crap, this isn't good for me.* And watching the game, I was in that terrible position of wanting England to win but not wanting Harry to play that well. That's a horrible thing to admit, but I reckon anyone who's played professional team sport would say the same.

As it turned out, Harry played a blinder and scored two tries in a scrappy win over Italy (they really did start Bergamasco at scrum-half and he was absolutely awful) and kept his place for the rest of the tournament.

I was back on the bench for the third game against Ireland at Croke Park, and on the morning of the game I met my mum and dad to give them their tickets. I'll never forget Mum saying to me, 'Whatever you do when you get on the pitch, don't do anything stupid.' What did she think I was going to do, launch myself at someone, barge them off the ball and get a yellow card?

We were 11–6 down when I was introduced in the 58th minute, desperate to be England's hero. But I was in the sin-bin ten minutes later, having launched myself at Ireland prop Marcus Horan and barged him off the ball. It was just about the most stupid thing I'd ever done on a rugby field.

Horan was just standing there at the back of a ruck, doing nothing in particular. As one journalist wrote afterwards, I should have been sent to the loony bin instead of the sin-bin. I've watched that moment back a few times on YouTube and it still makes me cringe. Despite Horan going down like a sack of spuds, I somehow manage to look really weedy. Then there was the remonstrating with the referee, and the spread arms as I leave the field, as if to say, 'I've no idea what I did wrong.'

As ridiculous as it sounds, in that moment I couldn't actually remember what I'd done. I think my mind must have been clouded by a combination of desperation to make my mark on the game and frustration at not getting enough of the ball.

As I was trudging off, I looked up at the big screen and saw a repeat of Johnno smashing his gigantic ogre's fists on the table. I'd really messed up this time. It had been my big chance to grab that starting jersey back from Harry and instead I'd probably ruined the game for the lads and made Johnno England's maddest man. Sure enough, Ronan O'Gara popped over the three points and we ended up losing by a point, despite a late try by Delon Armitage. Then I remembered what Mum had said. Never mind Johnno, she was going to kill me.

It's hard the describe the feeling of being responsible for your team losing a major rugby international, except to say that

I didn't want to feel it again. My only saving grace was that our veteran prop Phil Vickery had also been sin-binned, so at least I wasn't the only one who felt like a complete dickhead. But when Johnno walked into the changing room, he didn't look angry like I expected; he looked crushed with disappointment instead.

I thought it best to look him straight in the eyes, tell him I was sorry and that I wouldn't do it again. 'Fuckin' right you'll never do it again,' he replied. Then he put his arm around me, like a dad with a son who had let him down.

Other coaches would have dealt with that situation very differently, screamed and shouted and thrown things around. But Johnno saw things from the players' perspective and understood that big games make people do things they wouldn't normally do (he'd done a few daft things in his career, except in his heyday you'd just get a ticking off from the referee for almost taking someone's head off with a punch). He saw how regretful I was, he saw how low the team were feeling, and he recognised that giving me a bollocking wasn't what the situation required. And because I now knew he had my back, I never wanted to let him down again.

As for my mum, she did a Johnno in reverse, hugging me first before asking me what the hell I'd been thinking. 'Mum,' I said, 'I have no explanation for this one.' At least she didn't bollock me this time.

My moment of madness in Dublin put paid to any hopes I'd had of nicking my starting spot back from Harry: a month after our final game against Scotland, the Lions squad was picked and I wasn't in it. Harry had been selected, along with Wales's Mike Phillips and Ireland's Tomás O'Leary.

But a few days after the squad was announced, O'Leary was ruled out with an injury, and there followed an agonising few weeks for the rest of Britain and Ireland's top scrum-halves, all waiting to hear who would be chosen to replace him. I thought I offered something a bit different from the other guys in contention, but I knew I was up against some stiff competition, including Wales's Dwayne Peel and Scottish pair Mike Blair and Chris Cusiter.

Lions head coach Ian McGeechan was watching from the stands when Quins were comprehensively beaten by London Irish in that play-off semi-final, presumably to see if I fitted the bill. Clearly, I didn't, because a few days later, Geech announced the selection of the very experienced Mike Blair.

Gutted doesn't even begin to describe how I felt, and that decision to go sledging haunts me to this day. I've got 'Everything happens for a reason' tattooed on my arm. Even so, I'll be sitting on the sofa and suddenly think, *If I hadn't gone sledging, would I have gone on that Lions tour? Or maybe I'd have started against Italy and been comprehensively outplayed by Mauro Bergamasco? Or gone on the Lions tour, been badly injured and never played again?* Then I look at my kids and think, *It was only a few games of rugby …*

○

Quins made a terrible start to the 2009–10 season, which was hardly surprising. The squad was almost unchanged from the season before, but from being relative unknowns in the grand scheme of things, we were now this very famous, scandalous, cheating team. That's going to scar players mentally.

Attendances at the Stoop were down (why would people want to be associated with the biggest cheats in the country?) and many of the fans who did turn up were angry and upset with us, so the atmosphere at home games was hardly conducive to celebratory rugby. What's more, the abuse our fans got from other teams' supporters was brutal. People were turning up to matches with fake blood all over their mouths and chucking capsules, and while it was all fair game, it must have been wearing. Suddenly, shopping for a few bits and pieces at B&Q must have been a tempting Saturday afternoon alternative.

John Kingston was in charge for most of that season, but only on an interim basis. That meant a few of the lads were on edge because their contracts were up soon and they didn't know if the permanent appointment would be their kind of coach. But when Conor O'Shea took the reins with a handful of games to go, I immediately knew he was the perfect coach for me.

Conor hadn't been involved in club rugby since leaving London Irish in 2005, but I'd heard great things about him as a coach and a person, and his philosophy seemed to fit Quins like a glove. (Mark Mapletoft, another big fan of attacking rugby, was also brought in as attack and backs coach.)

He made it clear that we still had a lot of work to do in terms of restoring our reputation, and the best way of doing that was to play expressive rugby. One of Conor's favourite phrases was 'Live by the sword, die by the sword.' This meant playing what we saw, throwing the ball around and having fun. He saw that my game was all about tempo and unpredictability, and he wanted that to be the template for the whole team. As such, I was given licence to do pretty much whatever I wanted, within reason. And if playing that kind of expressive rugby didn't come off, Conor would take the flak.

Not many Premiership scrum-halves were quick-tapping back then, but having already been an advocate, I started doing quick taps all over the pitch. Along with quick line-outs, they were a very effective way of catching defences off-guard, and Conor would be disappointed if I didn't do three or four a game. He'd say to me sometimes, 'Why didn't you quick tap there? You would have caught them unawares.' For the first time in my career, I had a coach who wanted me to be even looser than I was naturally, which was very exciting.

Conor believed we'd win more than we lost by playing expressive rugby. And if we did lose by playing that way, he didn't seem to care, as long as we'd also had fun. His first season in charge was a rocky one – we finished eighth in the Premiership table and lost all six of our Heineken Cup games – but he retained the confidence of a man who knew his methods would bear fruit eventually. However, playing an even looser brand of rugby week in, week out for Quins made the switch to international rugby more difficult for me.

I believed the way I played for Quins suited me best, and that if I tried to play any other way, I wouldn't be doing my best by the team. As such, I couldn't understand why England wanted me to play in a more conservative manner, especially as Johnno had said when he first took over that he wanted me to play with the same energy and enthusiasm for England as I did for Quins.

Rather than a running threat and a risk-taker, England wanted me to be a distributor, an organiser, someone who box-kicked the ball until it was bent out of shape, none of which made much sense to me. Only later did I realise that Johnno had come up with a game plan that suited what he thought were the best players available. And while those players came from lots of different clubs, only a few of them came from Quins. The fact that it meant little Danny couldn't be his authentic self wasn't a major consideration for him.

Plus, while Quins would usually get away with playing from anywhere on the park in the Premiership, international games are decided by smaller margins, which makes mistakes more costly and difficult to rectify. I'm sure Johnno had been genuine when he told me he wanted me to bring my Quins energy and enthusiasm to England, but when he started losing a few games, expediency kicked in.

Maybe England played like the Harlem Globetrotters in Johnno's wildest dreams, but his game plan couldn't be too complicated or loose in real life because he'd only get a week with the players before a Six Nations started.

Lads who had been kicking the hell out of each other in the Premiership for months would suddenly find themselves standing side by side on the training field and be expected to know each other's games inside out – but elite rugby doesn't work like that. There are new calls and plays to learn, and different people play the game in subtly different ways. I was used to playing with Nick Evans at fly-half, and however good Jonny Wilkinson or Toby Flood were, I had to adjust my own game to dovetail with theirs.

Meanwhile, players from New Zealand and Ireland, countries with central contracts, were playing with each other all the time (sometimes, Ireland's starting XV would be Leinster and a couple of others). They'd also be fresher than us, because their unions would restrict how many minutes they played for their clubs.

I was picked to start alongside Jonny Wilkinson against Australia in autumn 2009, which was up there with the most surreal experiences of my life. Jonny was this almost mythical legend of English rugby, the man who had won England the World Cup, and suddenly I was passing him hundreds of balls in training every day. I even roomed with him. I remember thinking, *How weird is this? Jonny Wilkinson is asleep in that bed next to me.* My mates would bombard me with texts, asking me what Jonny was like. They even asked me to nick some of his kit.

Jonny was everything you'd hope he would be: a wonderful bloke with an unassuming but arresting presence. When he walked into a room, I shut up. When he spoke, I listened. And I believed every word he said. But he wasn't at all arrogant. In fact, I've never met anyone who's said a bad word about him. That's rare in any walk of life, but especially in professional sport.

As for watching him train, I couldn't buy that kind of education. He'd fizz passes off both hands with unerring accuracy, he'd go flying into tackles, and he almost never missed a kick. If I had to choose someone to kick a touchline conversion to save my kids' lives, I'd choose Jonny in a heartbeat.

Jonny and I shared a villa in Portugal once. One morning, I got up at about nine o'clock and wandered down to the restaurant for a bacon sandwich and a cup of tea, and when I got back to the villa, I noticed that Jonny wasn't in his room. When I asked the other lads if they'd seen him, they told me he'd been kicking balls on the training pitch since 6am.

It's because of those lonely sessions, when his team-mates were still tucked up in bed, that he almost never missed a kick; it's why he was able to drop the goal that won England the World Cup. That wasn't luck, that was thousands of hours of practice bearing fruit. But at no point while I was eating my bacon sandwich and slurping my tea did I think, *I really should have been practising with Jonny since 6am,* because that just wasn't how I operated.

Yes, I found Jonny inspiring, and just being in his presence felt like a privilege. But while I sometimes stayed longer than normal after training because that's what Jonny was doing, his approach would never have worked for me long-term. Don't get me wrong, I did work bloody hard, and I knew what I needed to get better at, but I'm not an obsessive or compulsive person. And if I'd been forced to work the hours Jonny did, I'd have burnt out in no time. Even Jonny admits that his quest for perfection wasn't always healthy.

Sadly, my half-back partnership with Jonny only lasted one game that autumn, because after losing to the Wallabies, London Irish's Paul 'Dodge' Hodgson replaced me in the starting line-up for the games against Argentina and New Zealand. That was annoying because Quins and London Irish didn't really like each other – they thought we loved ourselves a bit too much and we thought they were a poor imitation of us. At the same time, I rated Dodge very highly – he was very nippy and feisty, with incredible skills – and if I hated everyone who'd nicked my place over the years, I'd have a lot of enemies.

So I had a little sulk, came to terms with the fact that Dodge probably deserved his place ahead of me, and worked hard on the things they wanted me to get better at. I needed to release the ball quicker and my box-kicking needed to improve. I also needed to be more of a leader. The best nines run the team, however young they are. It didn't matter that I had a legend in Jonny Wilkinson outside me, or veteran forwards like Simon Shaw and Lewis Moody in front of me, I needed to boss them around a bit more, be more of a pain in the arse. I also needed to show more restraint and cut down on the mistakes. I'd always had a gung-ho attitude to rugby – attack, attack, attack – but I needed to show that I could be one of the team's go-to guys, a key decision-maker, even though I was still only 23. Having said all that, I also needed to make sure I didn't stop being me, because that was what made me different.

Si and me at our grandparents' house in Smethwick, 1988. Simon's smile suggests he's just beaten me at something.

A couple of cool customers rocking their Sweater Shop turtlenecks – the height of youth fashion in early '90s Yorkshire (or so we were told).

Us two brothers playing for Adel FC, 1993. All I wanted to be at that age was a footballer.

Dad, rocking the same haircut he's had for 50 years, showing off his skills. As a boy, he'd dreamed of playing for his beloved West Brom.

With Grandad Geoff at West Park Bramhope RUFC. I was a decent little player, but rugby didn't grab me like football back then.

West Park Bramhope Under-7s – we were all small at that age, obviously, but I was smaller than most.

Corridor cricket in Dad's pads. Si probably spent that whole day bowling bouncers at my head.

My family will kill me for including this photo! I'm wearing my most prized possession, a Chicago Bulls leather jacket bartered from a Turkish market (although I somewhat spoil the look with the King Charles hand-in-pocket pose). What I'd give for a head of a hair like Mum's here ...

Sam and me at Anfield for a stadium tour. Despite being a proud Yorkshireman I've been a mad Liverpool fan since I was small.

With Jamie Redknapp, one of my favourite Liverpool players – I still wonder what I could have achieved in football!

Sheffield Wednesday's training ground, Under-14s. Still dreaming of playing for England at Wembley, about to be written off as too small.

Lads and Dads tour to Dublin with my best mate Albear – when I finally fell in love with rugby.

I loved playing a few games alongside my big brother for Prince Henry's Grammar School.

At the Yorkshire Cup final in 2004. Look closely and you'll see I'm wearing Sheffield Wednesday socks.

Our little school from Otley made it to Twickenham for the Daily Mail Vase Final in 2004. The legendary coach that is Pete Latham is on the right.

My first try at Twickenham – the old place would one day feel like a second home.

Stuart Lancaster came to the house so I could sign my first professional rugby contract with Leeds Tykes. Hidden under the table, my leg is in a cast – I'd broken it during my debut.

Leeds Tykes, National Colts Cup winners 2004. That very handy team would soon be scattered to the winds.

Winning a silver medal at the 2006 Commonwealth Games in Melbourne. Our team included quite a few future England XVs players.

A dream come true! I'll be telling my grandchildren about my 'massive' hit on the great Jonah Lomu until the day I die.

Diving over for a try for England at the Hong Kong Sevens – I thought the sweatband on the forearm look was cool back then!

Chapter 8

Sh*t Happens

I was playing some of the best rugby of my career by the time of the 2010 Six Nations, which led to Johnno recalling me to the starting line-up. You never really think you've got a starting place nailed down in international rugby, but I felt like Johnno trusted me. I wasn't walking on eggshells, worrying that something I did or said might get me dropped. I felt quite at home, like I had my feet under the table. I was already excited about playing in my first World Cup the following year, in New Zealand of all places. Then along came Ben Youngs and everything became a bit more complicated.

You might recall that Ben's older brother, Tom, had tipped me off about him when we played together for England Under-16s. Back then, Tom was a centre rather than a hooker, a massive kid with farmer strength who would run through opposition teams like a bowling ball through skittles. As such, I knew he probably wasn't exaggerating when he told me how good his younger brother was. And he never tired of telling me, to the extent that it became a running joke. All the way through from Under-16s to Under-20s, Tom would be saying, 'My brother's going nowhere, and he keeps getting better ...'

When Ben was only 17, he played for Leicester in the 2007 Premiership final. I remember watching that game and thinking, *Damn, he's even better than Tom was making out.* We played against each other a fair bit over the next few years and there was always a

89

bit of added pressure in those games. There was lots of talk about Youngsy being England's next big thing, so I always wanted to perform against him, as well as wanting him to play badly.

Youngsy made his England debut in the 2010 Six Nations, coming on as a replacement against Scotland. I said to him when he ran on, 'Where you going, mate?', and he replied, 'I'm on the wing for Ugo.' Ugo Monye had been knocked out and stretchered off, and I remember being quite relieved that Youngsy wasn't replacing me. I'd love to be able to tell you I thought he was a bit of a twat, but he was actually a top lad, and I was delighted for him. All the same, I didn't want Johnno to give him too many opportunities at nine.

I started the first Test against Australia that summer, with Richard Wigglesworth on the bench. We butchered the Wallabies up front that day in Perth, but they still beat us 27–17. Our lack of attacking threat was probably down to our preparation, but guess who was the only player to get dropped for the second Test? That's right, me. Youngsy was down to start in Sydney and Wiggy was out of the squad altogether.

Wiggy and I were both northerners and he was a bit like an older brother to me. And while we didn't want Youngsy to have a shocker, it's probably fair to say that we didn't want him to play a blinder either. Just before kick-off, Wiggy and I had a quick conversation along the lines of 'Right, let's see how good this kid really is.' And it didn't take us long to find out.

I can still see it now: Tom Croft rising high at a line-out and tapping the ball down to Youngsy; Youngsy throwing an extravagant dummy before carving through the Wallabies' defence; Youngsy curving outside Drew Mitchell, one of the fastest wingers in the world, and diving over the line. I jumped off my seat and cheered like everyone else, but I also turned to Wiggy to see what he made of it. The look we gave each other said: 'We're screwed.'

Anyone who has played professional sport will tell you that they go through a rollercoaster of emotions when someone nicks their place and performs well. So while I was genuinely happy that Youngsy had scored (we went on to win the game 21–20, the first time we'd beaten the Wallabies in Australia since the 2003 World Cup final), after I'd stopped applauding and plonked myself back down on the bench, I thought, *I'm going to be fighting tooth and nail for caps from now on, and I'd better get used to sitting here.*

After a while, I grew more sanguine about losing my starting spot to Youngsy. He was a lovely lad, and I had to concede that he was perhaps a better all-round rugby player than I was, maybe because he'd taken it seriously from an earlier age than me. His dad, Nick, played scrum-half for Leicester and England, while I'd only started thinking about a career in rugby after my footballing dream had died. I did things on a rugby pitch that Youngsy wouldn't even consider trying, but he was more polished and had more feel for the game. I'd look at Youngsy and Wiggy and think, *These lads know exactly what they're meant to be doing, they're in control, while I'm still blagging it a little bit.*

But it's not as if I thought, *Oh well, I'll let Youngsy be number one from now on and concentrate on being number two.* Instead, I decided to get my head down and get better. I had to, not just because of Youngsy, but also because of the other great scrum-halves who were breathing down my neck, like Wiggy, Dodge and Northampton's Lee Dickson. But more than just getting better, I needed to show Johnno that I offered something different than Youngsy and the rest, so that if plan A wasn't working, I could be a key part of plan B.

Social media was well established by 2010, which meant the criticism didn't just come from grumpy journalists, it came in torrents from every Tom, Dick or Harry with a computer. Suddenly, I was only one click away from thousands of random punters telling me how badly I'd played, or that I was a wanker or a prick or any number of other terrible names, and that I should be dropped from the team and never picked for England again.

People would tell me not to look, but it was just so tempting. If I thought I'd played okay, I'd go on my phone straight after the game to see if people were saying nice things about me. And even when I tried to avoid it, such as when I knew I'd made a bad mistake, like an awful pass or a missed tackle, people would clip it up and tag me on Twitter. Or they'd send me a newspaper article written by Stephen Jones or Stuart Barnes, neither of whom were my biggest fans, maybe accompanied with the words, 'They think you're shit.' I wish I could say it didn't get to me, but of course it did. Imagine how you'd feel if thousands of people slagged off your performances at work every week.

One of the main criticisms of me was that I'd take a step before or while releasing the ball. That was fair, because while I usually got away with it in the Premiership, I sometimes didn't get away with it in the international arena.

Wales's Mike Phillips had a similar issue, but he defied the scrum-half rulebook. While most nines were well under six foot, Mike was 6'3" and strong as anything. Sometimes when I played against him, I'd look up at him and think, *Mate, this isn't fair. You're massive and you've chosen to play in the easiest position. You should be playing in the back row or the centres.* But his size and strength meant it didn't matter as much that he took a step when he passed, because he was so good at breaking the line and offloading.

For me, that one step meant defenders were that bit closer to my forwards or my fly-half, who wanted the ball on a plate. As such, one step could be the difference between scoring a try and not scoring a try, or winning and losing a Test match. I was still learning how to be a scrum-half and my first instinct was to run with the ball. On top of that, I probably thought that by taking a step, I kept all my options open – running, kicking or passing. But mostly my team needed me to get that ball away from the breakdown as quickly as possible, so I really needed to erase that pesky step from my game.

○

Talking of steps, it felt like England were taking one forward and one back during the first couple of years of Johnno's reign. But this was the bloke who had captained England to World Cup glory, and he was such an inspiring human being, so I was never going to complain.

Johnno was a lovely man, and I hung on his every word. I certainly believed him when he said we were going to turn things around eventually. We had a bunch of good players and we had good coaches, we just needed to work out how to put it all together.

I could usually work out what Johnno was trying to achieve, although our attack coach, Brian Smith, was a little bit eccentric. He spent a lot of time tinkering with our attack structure and at one point wanted us to play the Australian way, with 9/10/12 on a pendulum the whole time. That meant 12 would some-times end up playing the ball from a ruck and 9 would end up playing 12. I'd be thinking, *I ain't an international 12, how on earth is this going to work against anyone, let alone teams like New Zealand and South Africa?* Lo and behold, it didn't.

Some days, we'd walk into a room and there'd be desks lined up with exam papers on them. The exam would be on where everyone needed to be during our moves, not just our own position, but our team-mates' positions as well. If you didn't get a certain percentage, you were on the bench, and you weren't going to play until you got it all right. I look back now and think, *Why were we wasting our time with that stuff? Why did I need to know where the hooker was going to be on the third phase of a four-phase move?* I didn't. If everyone knew their job and did it properly, we'd be all right. But I think certain coaches just wanted to stamp their authority on the set-up.

Then someone had the bright idea of making us wrestle. We'd be pitched against anyone, with no consideration for height and weight, which was obviously a nightmare for me. I remember going up against giant Bath wing Matt Banahan, him tossing me out of the ring with one hand and everyone doubled over laughing. The coaches would say to me, 'Dan, you need to do better than that,' and I'd be thinking, *How the hell do you expect me to beat Matt Banahan in a wrestle? And what's wrestling got to do with rugby anyway?* Only after Youngsy and Jonny Wilkinson got injured did they decide that wrestling wasn't the wisest way to prepare for a rugby international.

But while the lads would laugh about some of the quirky stuff that went on, nobody said anything. I've always tried to be fairly open and honest in my career, and I'd hate to think that anyone saw me as a yes man. I played with quite a few lads who won more caps than perhaps they should have, simply because they kept their heads down and stayed schtum, but I'd be lying if I said I didn't employ the same tactics at times, biting my tongue instead of saying what I really thought. Saying what I really thought would have put my England career at risk. And once you're out of the England set-up, for whatever reason, it's not easy to get back in. Just ask Danny Cipriani.

We managed only two wins in the 2010 Six Nations and lost to New Zealand and South Africa – again – in that year's autumn internationals, having looked sensational in beating Australia 35–15. We looked to have turned a corner in the 2011 Six Nations, only to get well beaten by Ireland in Dublin with the Grand Slam on the line. But we still won the Championship for the first time since 2003, which was a weird situation to be in.

Some of the older lads were a bit down because we'd missed out on the Grand Slam, but Minty and I kept saying, 'Sod it, we still won the Six Nations!' My old England team-mate Phil Vickery accused us of not caring, based on the fact that we were smiling with the trophy. Of course we cared – Phil didn't see the desolation in the changing room – but most of that squad had never won a tournament with England, and we were in Dublin, so we were going to grin and bear it before getting stuck into the Guinness.

That criticism from Phil touched a nerve because he'd only just retired from England duty. I was thinking, *We're already dealing with journalists slagging us off all the time, we could do without our old team-mates joining in.* One of the things I admired about Irish rugby was the togetherness. I always got the sense that the fans and the media were right behind their team, while it felt like many of our sports reporters actually wanted us to play poorly just so they could tell us how bad we were. Journalism isn't my trade, but maybe it's easier to be negative than positive on the page.

○

Johnno told me I was going to the 2011 World Cup right before the warm-up game against Wales at Twickenham. I was buzzing, naturally. Not only was it a dream come true to play in a World Cup in New Zealand, but I also thought we had a chance of winning it. Yes, we'd lost that game against Ireland in Dublin, but we'd won the other five games, and there seemed to be something building. We were more cohesive, playing better rugby, and we were a tight-knit unit off the pitch as well. Imagine playing in a World Cup on the other side of the planet with a bunch of your best mates. It doesn't get any better.

Youngsy was recovering from knee surgery, so I started at Twickenham, with Wiggy on the bench. England won, I had a decent game, and pundits were suggesting that I might have done enough to be our starting nine at the World Cup. Wiggy started the return fixture in Cardiff the following week, which was a bit of a relief. I really didn't want to play in that game at all, but I thought I couldn't come to much harm if I came on for the last 20 minutes. Don't do anything unnecessary, just pass the ball, stay out of trouble, job done.

Thirty minutes into the game, Wiggy stayed down after a tackle, clutching his head. My first thought was, *That doesn't look good for Wiggy*, followed by, *And it's not good for me, either, because I might have to play for 50 minutes. Come on, Wiggy, it can't be that bad. Please get up, mate* … Wiggy did get up eventually, but only to walk off the field.

When Wiggy failed his concussion test, I had to go on, and I soon found my rhythm and started playing quite well. But a few minutes before half-time, I got the ball off a line-out, passed it, and it was already in the fly-half's hands when some knob-head hit me from behind. Because I wasn't braced, my foot got caught in the turf and my big toe went over. I knew something must have happened, because I felt a snap, although I couldn't feel any pain.

Adrenaline must have got me through to half-time, because when I went to stand up after the team-talk, I could hardly put any pressure on my foot. I told our doc, Mike Bundy, that I thought I'd done something but that I wasn't in pain, and he told me to crack on and see how it was at the end of the game. We didn't have another scrum-half anyway, so I guzzled some pain-killers and went back out. And while I spent some of the second half hobbling around, it really didn't seem that serious. I thought I might have just stubbed it.

After the game, which we lost, Mike examined my foot and booked me in to see a specialist in a couple of days, but said that I'd probably be okay. But because I knew Ugo had injured his toe before, I gave him a call on my way home. After describing how I'd done it and what it felt like, there was a silence. But eventually Uges said, 'DC, do you really want my honest opinion?'

'Yeah, of course,' I lied.

Uges sighed and said, 'Mate, it sounds exactly like mine. I think you've snapped your plantar plate, the ligament that keeps your toe attached to your foot. If you have, it's surgery and a four-month recovery.'

Ben Foden was in the car with me, and I said to him, 'It can't be that bad, I played fifty minutes on it, and it didn't really hurt.'

Plus, how could it be serious if I'd never even heard of a plantar plate? Uges must have got things muddled up.

A couple of days later, Mike – who's the nicest man in the world and a brilliant doctor – took me to see a specialist called James Calder, who was the go-to man for foot and ankle injuries and had even fixed up Dave Grohl from the Foo Fighters. James explained that even if I wasn't in any pain, a snapped plantar plate would mean I'd lost most of my power and spring. Then he told me he was going to inject some dye into my foot and stick it under an MRI scanner. If the dye leaked through to my big toe, that meant the plantar plate was snapped, I'd need surgery and miss the World Cup.

James injected the dye and stuck my foot in the MRI scanner, and then the three of us sat glued to this little screen, waiting to see what the dye would do. And when the dye started seeping through to my big toe, Mike started blubbing. I had to turn away. James may as well have put some sad music on. It was like watching the most depressing film ever made, or a pet dog being put to sleep.

Eventually, James said, 'I'm really sorry, Danny, but we're going to have to repair that, otherwise you might not be able to play rugby again.' I was still in shock. An injured toe felt like such a small thing, how could it have destroyed everything? I said to James, 'If it's that bad, how was it possible to play for fifty minutes on it? Surely I can just crack on if you stick an injection in it? I feel like I could play now if you told me to.' James was unmoved. He told me I wouldn't be able to do what England needed me to do. He explained that I could do some serious damage just by walking on it for a couple of days, let alone playing rugby. Then he passed me a tissue and gave me a big cuddle.

James rang Johnno, who was devastated for me. He told me I was going into the World Cup as his number-one scrum-half, but that shit happens, and I'd come back stronger and play in World Cups down the line. I told him I appreciated everything he'd done for me and that I'd be the biggest fan of the team. Then I wished him luck, put the phone down and shed a few tears.

The floodgates opened back at my flat. I'd been thinking about that World Cup for three or four years. I'd have given up all my Six Nations caps to play in it. I thought England had a great chance of winning it. And now it was over for me. So while Johnno was right when he said shit happens, it didn't really help that much.

I phoned Uges and he came over with a crate of beers. Uges had become one of my very best mates (he'd later be godfather to my first son and I'd be godfather to his first daughter), and while he couldn't make me feel much better about things, he tried to help me put things into perspective. The fact was, we played a ridiculous sport and I just so happened to get really, really unlucky. Similar incidents had happened a thousand times during my career and I'd got away with them, just not on this occasion. That's sport, and at least I lived to fight another day. Still, I couldn't help asking Uges, 'Who was that knobhead who hit me?' Uges didn't have a clue, or at least he said he didn't. I'm still none the wiser. If anyone does know, get in touch.

Minty was the only Quins player picked by Johnno – Uges, Browny and Robbo were all left at home – so at least I had plenty of company while the World Cup was going on. And it wouldn't have been good form to keep banging on about my misfortune when they were all hurting as well. I also had the opportunity to do some punditry for ITV, which I absolutely loved.

People assume it must be agony for an injured player to watch his pals play in a major tournament, but I got a similar buzz from doing live TV in front of millions to the one I got from being out there on the pitch. I wanted to sound like I knew what I was talking about, and I must have done, because I'd been with them every step of the way until the eve of the tournament. I was able to give viewers little nuggets of information about players that nobody else could, and eventually I found myself in the novel situation of being an England fan.

Saying that, I had to watch a lot of England's progress through my fingers. We didn't look too clever during the pool stage, winning all our games but only just seeing off Argentina and Scotland. But off the pitch, it was one of the most spectacular car crashes in sporting history.

It started with the infamous 'Mad Midget Weekender' in Queenstown, when the lads were accused of throwing dwarves in a nightclub (apparently they were just spectating); and it ended with Manu Tuilagi jumping off a ferry in Auckland. In between, there was a bungee jumping outing that didn't go down well with the English media, an accusation of sexual assault (which turned out to be false, again), a suspension for two coaches for switching balls during a game and a fine for Manu for wearing the wrong kind of gumshield. Oh, and a disheartening defeat by France in the quarter-finals.

Watching all this unfold, I found myself thinking, *Bloody hell, that looks like a lot of fun. I wish I was there.* Then again, maybe it was for the best that I didn't go. It sounded like a massive stag do – before Manu's ferry jump, I wondered how the lads could push things any further, and when I read about that, I thought, *Yep, that's how you do it* … And knowing me, I would have been right in the mixer. Mum said to me, 'You couldn't have picked a better time to get injured.' And as Mike Tindall still says to me, 'If you'd been at the Mad Midget Weekender, we would have been throwing you.'

It came out after the tournament that the Irish and Welsh lads had been having even more off-field fun than ours, but none of that was reported. That was partly down to the fact that the Irish and Welsh media weren't in the business of undermining their teams' chances like the English media was. But you also have to take into account the performances of the England team. If they'd been going on the piss and playing well, the media might have gone easy on them. But because they were going on the piss and performing badly, they may as well have played with targets on their backs instead of numbers.

People wonder how a team led by Martin Johnson could ever get so out of control. But it's no real mystery to me. Yes, Johnno could be intimidating, but he'd also been a rugby player, so he knew exactly what rugby lads were like. He probably thought that a bit of off-field looseness was the best way for the players to bond, but if you give a bunch of rugby lads enough rope, some people will take things too far, especially when you've got a blend of older guys playing in their last World Cup and younger guys who enjoy pushing the boundaries. And once that loose mindset has set in, it can be difficult for a coach to rein things back in. Suddenly, the rugby is getting in the way of a great lads' holiday.

I really enjoyed working with Johnno and it was clear how much the England rugby team meant to him. But while I don't blame him for England's 2011 World Cup debacle – he was ultimately let down by his players – and I felt awful that such a great man had been humbled in that way, you have to question the

RFU's wisdom in offering a bloke who had never coached before the job in the first place. Having said that, at the time it never crossed my mind that Johnno wasn't the right man for the job. It was Martin Johnson, one of the greatest rugby players of all time – of course everything would be fine. Except it wasn't.

Chapter 9

Road to Ruin

Quins experienced a couple of average seasons following Bloodgate and that was probably down to the fact that the scars still hadn't fully healed. Plus, everyone was desperate to beat those cheating bastards from London. But we were still able to pull the occasional rabbit out of the hat, including winning the European Challenge Cup in 2010–11, my first piece of silverware.

During the build-up to the semi-final against Munster, I kept hearing the phrase, 'Nobody beats Munster at home.' That was almost accurate, because only one visiting team had won at Thomond Park in 16 years of European competition. But at Quins we'd developed this view of ourselves as a cup team, the kind of side that can be stumbling along in the league but still slay the odd giant when the mood takes us.

Munster had one hell of a side, including a half-back pairing of Conor Murray and Ronan O'Gara, Doug Howlett and Keith Earls on the wings and Paul O'Connell, David Wallace, Denis Leamy and Donncha O'Callaghan, all vastly experienced and tough-as-teak Ireland internationals. They were only in the Challenge Cup because they'd been pipped by Toulon in the pool stages of the Heineken Cup (despite hammering Toulon 45–18 at Thomond Park), so most people expected us to get taken to the cleaners.

Munster came at us with all guns blazing but they weren't able to cope with our pace and physicality. One of my abiding memories of that day is our Samoan blind-side flanker Maurie Fa'asavalu, who struck fear into almost everyone he played against, repeatedly running straight over the top of O'Gara. Tries from me and George Robson gave us a 14–0 lead, and we led 20–7 when Minty got sent off with 12 minutes left. Howlett scored another try for Munster with a couple of minutes to go but we hung on for a rare victory.

The Munster fans had given us a typically rough welcome that day but gave us a standing ovation after the game, which says everything about our performance. We'd stood toe to toe with a European powerhouse and won comfortably on points.

Awaiting us in the final in Cardiff were Stade Français, whose team included the great Sergio Parisse at number eight, formidable French lock Pascal Papé – and James Haskell. They also had the freakish Mathieu Bastareaud in the centres, who I'd had the misfortune of playing against since my England Under-19s days. The first time I laid eyes on him I thought, *How the hell is this guy the same age as me? How is he a back? And how the hell am I going to tackle him?* He was like a grown man playing against kids, just so much bigger and stronger than everyone else. He also happened to be a lovely bloke who was always generous with a cuddle once battle had ceased.

We were bloody awful for most of that final, sloppy in attack and leaky in defence, but somehow we were only six points down with four minutes to play. That's when Haskell came up too quick in defence, Joe Marler made a half-break, offloaded to me, and I put a grubber kick through off the left foot. Gonzalo Camacho, our little Argentinian winger, ran onto the ball, stepped past a defender and went over in the corner, and I thought, *Wow, we might actually win a trophy.*

Snapper still had to nail a conversion from the touchline to clinch it, but nail it he did, which is exactly why the club paid him the big bucks. As soon as he struck that ball, I knew it was going over.

Stade probably should have got a penalty in the dying seconds, because our scrum was going backwards at a rate of knots, but let's not worry about that. Little old Quins had rumbled another European giant and I finally got to do all the things I'd seen other people do on TV: lift the trophy, spray my mates with champagne, do a lap of honour, applaud the fans – all the stuff sportspeople dream about doing at least once in their career.

Another vintage cup display was away against Toulouse in the Heineken Cup in December 2011. Toulouse were the reigning French champions and had beaten us up at the Stoop only nine days earlier. Their pack was massive, as most French packs are, but they were physically superior to us all over the pitch that day. And they probably thought they were going to stick 50-odd points on us at their place.

But having nothing to lose, we threw caution to the wind, trumping their size and power advantage with pace and movement. Browny bagged an early try before our hooker, Joe Gray, scored one of the tries of the season. To clarify, what actually happened was Snapper kicked over the top, Matt Hopper ran onto it and threw an outrageous back-of-the-hand pass to Chris Robshaw, Robbo offloaded to me and I shovelled it inside to Joe, who went over from about 3 yards out. Joe, being one of rugby's great idiots, is always going on about this unbelievable try he scored, and someone always points out that while everything that happened in the lead-up to his try was unbelievable, he just fell over the line.

We were trailing after an hour, which was when Conor sent Tommy Williams on with the simple instruction 'Kick chase.' A minute later, Snapper put up a kick; Tommy chased it, whacked the catcher and forced the turnover. Minty went on a charge and slipped the ball inside to Browny, an unbelievable offload even for Minty, who went over for his second try.

After that game, which we won 31–24, Conor told the media, 'It was the size of the heart against the size of the wallet, and the heart won.' That summed things up perfectly, and if we could beat a star-studded team like Toulouse in their own backyard – Thierry Dusautoir, Yoann Maestri, Louis Picamoles, Maxime Médard, Vincent Clerc, Yannick Jauzion – surely we could beat anyone? We held on to that winning mentality until a month later when we lost 9–8 to Connacht, who hadn't won a game since September. The weather was horrific (as it always is on the west coast of Ireland), the rugby was awful and the result meant Toulouse advanced to the knockout stages instead of us. At least Galway is a good place for a few drinks.

○

Quins' social scene had always been quite loose, and it would be easy to say that the disappointment of missing out on the World Cup – *Why always me?* – made me even looser. But looking back, I'm not sure that was the case.

We were going great guns at the start of the 2011–12 season, winning 11 of our 12 Premiership games before Christmas, while still going out on the beers three days a week. The team was playing well, I was playing well and my attitude was, *We can't stop drinking, or we might start playing badly.* I was going with the flow. I felt untouchable, and maybe a bit of arrogance had seeped in, without me noticing. But while there was some craziness, mostly we were just a normal bunch of lads who went to the pub, got drunk and kept drinking, almost always without incident.

Having said that, there was a short period, before and after Christmas 2011, when I kept making mistakes and the media made out like I was the second coming of Oliver Reed.

The first incident took place after a defeat by Toulouse in the Heineken Cup (and a week before we gained revenge in France). For reasons I can't remember, some of us ended up in a night-club in Weybridge, and it just so happened that some London Irish lads were there as well. Despite the rivalry between us, we saw them out and about quite a lot, and mostly got on well with them. But one of their players had brought along a mate, who was staggeringly drunk and abusive. A loose cannon, in other words.

Us Quins boys were sat around a table laden with a big bottle of vodka and buckets of beers, and this rogue mate wandered over and said a couple of things he shouldn't have. No one reacted, we were just a bit nonplussed. But then he walked over to one of our youngsters, a lad called Sam Smith, who wouldn't say boo to a goose, and shoulder-barged him. Sam fronted up to him, and this bloke grabbed Sam and threw him through our table. There was beer, vodka and glass everywhere, and poor Sam, who was the nicest kid you could possibly meet, was sprawled on his back, a look of shock on his face.

I always made sure I had a good rapport with security (apart from that time I crashed into a fish tank in Infernos), and the bouncer at this place had promised me that if any trouble broke out, he'd be in like a flash. Unfortunately, a flash wasn't quick enough. And before I knew it, I was in the middle of one of the most ridiculous brawls I've ever seen. It was seven Quins against seven London Irish, plus the dickhead who started it all. I'd call it full-on Wild West, minus the chairs being broken over people's heads. People were rolling around on the floor and being thrown through tables and doors (sadly not the saloon type). And because I was the smallest bloke there, and I've never been much of a fighter, I spent most of my time shuttling between combatants, trying to drag them apart.

After a minute or so of chaos, the bouncer came flying in, the lights went up and the music was cut. The bouncer asked me what was going on, I told him we didn't start it, and he told me the police were on their way. It was time to follow Clive Woodward's T-CUP mantra and start Thinking Clearly Under Pressure. I managed to extricate the lads from the nightclub and commandeer a seven-seater taxi, then proceeded to count the lads in, military style. But just as I was about to jump in, the driver told me he didn't have room for me. I didn't have time to argue, so I sent the boys on their way and waited for another taxi, feeling like the hero of the hour – and badly needing the toilet.

I've always had a really small bladder, and if I don't go straight away, I'll probably wet myself. I couldn't go back inside, for obvious reasons, and I couldn't see any alleyways. Then I spotted a mini roundabout covered in grass and trees. So I headed over to it, undid my fly and started having a wee. After a blissful few seconds, I heard someone say, 'Put it away.' When I turned around, there were two coppers right behind me. I said to them, 'I'm dying for a wee, I can't stop once I've started, I've got to finish.' Before I knew it, an officer had tackled me to the ground, while I was still weeing. I just about managed to pull my jeans up before the copper pulled my hands behind my back, snapped some cuffs on me, threw me into a police car and whisked me to the local nick.

They logged my offence as drunk and disorderly and I spent my first ever night in a cell. The following morning, I was released without charge, paid a fine, and got straight on the phone to my team-mates: 'Cheers boys,' I texted, 'I ended up spending the night in a police cell.' They were all very apologetic and seemed genuinely thankful for my T-CUP tactics, and as I made my way home, I didn't think anything more would come of it.

However, my arrest was all over the papers the following morning and every headline referred to my drunkenness and disorderliness, when the truth was slightly more innocent than that. I understand that urinating in the street isn't very pleasant, but 'drunk and disorderly' made it sound like I was some kind of street-fighting lunatic.

The following day, Conor O'Shea marched into the team meeting and said, 'Put your hand up if you were in this nightclub in Weybridge on Saturday night.' It was like being in class back at school. Seven hands went up, rather sheepishly, and Conor told us to stand up. 'Right,' he barked, 'what the fuck were you boys doing? It's a disgrace. You've dragged the club's name through the mud, you've dragged your own names through the mud. We're trying to build something here and you lads are out on the piss fighting with another club. Ugo, Jordan, you should know better at your age. Danny Care, ending up in the nick for pissing in the street? Pathetic. You're lucky this isn't going any further.' There was a short pause, before Conor turned to a terrified-looking Sam Smith and said, 'Sam – never let yourself be thrown through a table again!' The room erupted. That was Conor all over: he had authority, but a smile was never far from his face.

Everyone involved with the Weybridge affair was fined by the club and had to apologise to the group. But Conor also told us that he was glad we'd stood up for each other. In fact, the thing he seemed most annoyed about was the lads driving off in that taxi and leaving me in a vulnerable situation.

I was living with Jordan Turner-Hall at the time, and a few weeks after my arrest for weeing, the two of us planned to attend a New Year's Eve Party at a warehouse in Cobham, not far from our house. However, Jordy went far too hard on the pre-drinks at a nearby hotel and the evening spun off in a different direction.

I accompanied Jordy home in a taxi, put him to bed and then found myself sat in my front room twiddling my thumbs while listening to Jordy snore the house down. Then another mate texted, inviting me to a party down in Southampton. In fact, he'd been texting me about this party all day. I thought to myself, *I'm sat here on my own on New Year's Eve, Jordy's not getting up any time soon, maybe I should go.* I'd had four or five drinks but felt stone-cold sober, and Southampton was only an hour away. It didn't enter my head that I might be over the limit. So I jumped in the car and headed south on the M3.

I was about 15 minutes from the intended destination when I saw a police car up ahead, pootling along in the slow lane. I always panic a bit when I see a police car, so instead of passing, I tucked in behind (I was driving a ridiculous white Range Rover and the road was empty, which made me an easy target). The police car then slowed to about 40mph, and after tailing it for a minute or so, I indicated and went round it. That's when the police car's lights came on – BOOM! – and I thought, *Oh no, I had a few drinks earlier …*

We pulled into Winchester services and this copper, who was actually really nice, said to me, 'I thought it was a bit strange that you pulled in behind me and then decided to go round me. Have you had anything to drink?' I told him I'd had a few earlier in the evening and he said he'd have to breathalyse me. I still thought I'd be okay, but I blew double the limit. Let that be a lesson to anyone reading this: just because you feel sober doesn't mean you are.

The officer said he was going to drive me to a police station that wasn't the closest, so that maybe when I got there my levels would have gone down. But when we arrived, I blew exactly the same number. The copper was almost apologetic. 'Mate,' he said to me, 'I know you're not steaming but you were still drink-driving. I'm gonna have to nick you.' Then he put me in a cell and slammed the door behind me.

Driving a white Range Rover down a deserted motorway on New Year's Eve after a few drinks is the height of stupidity. I might as well have had a massive sign on the side that read PLEASE ARREST ME. I'd never driven drunk before then, and to this day I cannot understand why I got in my car that night. But I'd done it, and now I had to face the consequences.

My mum and dad couldn't believe it when they got my call. They must have thought they had rugby's answer to Paul Gascoigne on their hands. As soon as they got off the phone, they jumped in their car and began the 235-mile journey down from Leeds, no doubt cursing me to high heaven all the way.

The following morning, two coppers drove me back to my car, and then I headed straight home to Cobham. Jordy had only just woken up when I walked through the door. 'Mate,' he croaked, 'what happened last night?' I explained everything and he replied, 'Why did you do that?' It was a very good question, but not one I was able to answer.

I clearly wasn't thinking straight around that time. More accurately, I wasn't thinking at all. And this was a whole different level of seriousness. When I got arrested for weeing in the street, I could claim to be unlucky. But whenever you read a story about someone drink-driving, you automatically think they're a bad person, regardless of whether they've caused an injury or seriously harmed someone by doing so. I still didn't think I was a bad person, but I also thought, *I've given everyone a reason to think I am. They don't know me, so why would they think otherwise?*

My birthday is 2 January, which is the worst day for a birthday in the entire calendar even when you haven't been nicked for drink-driving. All your mates are in bits after Christmas and New Year, everybody's skint, nobody wants to go out, so you normally end up doing nothing. I didn't go out on this birthday either; instead I was subjected to a very long interrogation by my mum and dad. And neither of them was playing good cop.

They thought I was on the road to ruin, and seeing them so upset and bewildered was incredibly sobering. It really hit home that I was letting people down, not least myself. The following day, my old Leeds academy boss, Stuart Lancaster, who had just landed the England head coach job, came to see me in training. First and foremost, he wanted to know if I was all right and hadn't gone full Gazza, but he was also livid, almost like a second dad I'd managed to let down.

Lanny explained that he'd wanted to pick me for the Six Nations but might not be able to. And when I told him about a loophole lawyer I knew who reckoned he could get me off (something about police radios interfering with breathalysers), he got really angry and said he'd never pick me again if I went down that road. Everyone else I'd told thought it was a great idea, but Lanny's view was that if I'd done the crime, I had to admit to it and accept the punishment. If I did that, he said I might be in his first squad after all.

Lanny was right, of course. I knew what I'd done was wrong, so trying to evade punishment on a technicality would have been morally questionable, to say the least. So I told this very creative lawyer that I was going to plead guilty, accept anything they threw at me and try to move on.

Lanny still didn't pick me for the whole of the Six Nations, which I was furious about at the time. But looking back, I'd put him in a sticky spot, while also doing him a favour. After the 2011 World Cup debacle, Lanny had been hired in part to restore discipline to the team, so if he'd let me off the hook it wouldn't have been a great look; not picking me made him look like a steely man of authority (the *Telegraph* headline read, 'LANCASTER REVEALS HIS IRON FIST'). I was more furious with myself than I was with Lanny. Every England cap is a precious thing, and I'd just chucked five of them away.

Conor wasn't exactly over the moon either, so I had three disappointed dads on my case. But once he'd got his harsh words out of the way, he put an arm around me and asked if there was anything he could do to help. And when someone asks you that, you know you're in a bit of trouble.

Drink and I just weren't working well together. It was messing up my rugby career and causing my loved ones a lot of anguish. Not that it was the most important consideration, but it was also costing me a lot of money. Quins slapped me with a £10,000 fine, on top of the fine they gave me for weeing in the street, and the courts fined me £3,000, as well as banning me from driving for 16 months. A three-year deal I'd signed with Nike a few months earlier also went up in smoke, and I missed out on England match fees.

Having promised Conor that there'd be no more trouble from me, I went into hiding. For the next month or so, I only really emerged from my house to shop, train and play games. But when we played Newcastle on a Friday at the beginning of March, I suggested to a few of the lads that we stop off for a night out in Leeds and stay at my mum and dad's before heading south on the Sunday. The last thing Mum said to me before I went out on the Saturday night was, 'Do not get into any trouble.' She even said to my mates, 'Make sure he comes home unscathed.' You probably know what's coming next.

$$\bigcirc$$

We were having a great night out in Leeds, my home patch, when our number two fly-half, Rory Clegg, who lived with me and Jordy, went missing. I was trying to call him for ages, leaving voicemail after voicemail, but he wouldn't pick up. Eventually, Cleggy phoned back and told us he was in a bar near the city centre, so I jumped in a taxi, found him in this bar and said we needed to go home. But as he was getting into the taxi, it suddenly hit me that I was dying for a wee. In case any readers were wondering, you haven't lost your place and you're not reading the same section twice.

Because I was worried the taxi driver wouldn't hang around for too long, I decided to wee next to some steps near the station, rather than find a bar and go there, which might have taken ages. And as soon as I started weeing, the same thing happened as before, except this time there were about ten coppers behind me rather than just two. Transport police, apparently, doing their rounds. I said to one of them, 'Mate, I'm so sorry, I'm just desperate for a wee. Can you just let me finish off and go home?' This bloke gave me a bit of a telling-off and told me to hurry up and be on my way. But as I was zipping myself up, another copper, who had been staring at me intently, said, 'What's your name, mate?'

'Erm ... Gary,' I replied.

'Nah,' he said, looking me up and down. 'You ain't Gary. You're that rugby player who keeps getting in trouble.'

'Okay, that is me. I could really do with not getting in trouble again, if at all possible. Can I just go home?'

'Nah, mate, you're in trouble again now ...'

With that, he pulled my arms behind my back and cuffed me. As the police van pulled away, I could see my mates through the window. The looks on their faces said, 'We are gonna get such a bollocking from Mrs Care ...'

When I woke up the following morning, I was absolutely freezing, because they'd confiscated my socks and hadn't given me a blanket. I suppose that's their way of persuading people not to do something stupid again. But when they brought me a cup of tea and told me my dad was waiting for me, I thought, *Oh God, I'd rather stay in here.* It's difficult to forget the look on my dad's face when I saw him staring at me through the door. I suppose it was a look of disappointment, but that doesn't do it justice.

When we got back to the house, my mates were still asleep in my old bedroom. They asked me where I'd been and I told them I'd been in the nick again. Mum and Dad were as understanding as they could be, gave me a cuddle and told me I needed to get a grip on things, while I just kept saying sorry. And then I jumped in the car and drove back to London. There wasn't much laughter on that trip. It was the darkest journey I'd ever taken.

○

That was a bleak period of my life, maybe even the bleakest, but I wouldn't change any of it. I entered it as a young man who thought he was indestructible and emerged from it emotionally scarred yet far wiser.

While I knew I'd done wrong, and was remorseful, I also kept telling myself I'd been unlucky to get caught. And maybe if I'd evaded arrest on those three occasions, I'd have thought I was untouchable, kept pushing things and got sucked in to an unstoppable downward spiral. So I'm so grateful to those coppers who nicked me, especially the one who pulled me over on the M3. I'd go as far as to say that they made me a better person.

Chapter 10

Redemption

I don't think I had an alcohol problem, as in an addiction, but I was drinking too much, and it certainly made me do stupid things. Whatever the reasons (World Cup woe? Becoming too comfortable? Just a complete idiot?), I couldn't trust myself when things were getting a bit loose, so I made the decision to put myself in fewer of those situations.

My team-mates were on board with that because I was letting them down as much as anyone else. Every time I appeared in the papers for the wrong reasons, Harlequins were dragged through the mud, as were their names by association. Some of the older lads, like Minty and Snapper, would say to me, 'Jesus, Danny, what on earth are you doing?' And the younger lads were probably thinking, *Is this what could happen to me?*

I realised that the quickest way to repair my tattered reputation was to train the house down and play out of my skin at the weekend. Some people would still think I was a dickhead but at least they'd have to concede I was a decent rugby player, which would be a crumb of comfort.

That shock Heineken Cup defeat by Connacht might have been a blessing in disguise, because it meant we could focus fully on the Premiership. And while I wouldn't call getting axed by England for drink-driving a blessing in disguise, it had the same effect.

Finishing top of the table meant we hosted fourth-placed Northampton in the play-off semi-finals, although I missed that game with an injury. Our number-two scrum-half was Karl Dickson, whose younger brother Lee played nine for Saints. Karl was a great player but never seemed that bothered about whether he started a game or was left on the bench, maybe because he had a clause in his contract that said he should get a win bonus whether he played or not. Karl would sometimes sidle up to me before a game and say, 'I need eighty minutes from you today, Danny. I was reffing a game yesterday and I don't really feel up to it.' But to be fair to Karl, he never let the side down when he was called upon, and I think he was desperate to get one over on his brother, who had recently made his debut for England. What's more, all that reffing paid off because he's now one of the top refs in the world.

The brothers Dickson had a bit of a scuffle early on, which led to a Snapper three-pointer, but when Lee went over with ten minutes to go, Saints led by eight. It felt horrible sitting helplessly in the stands, and I thought we might be toast with only a few minutes remaining on the clock. But Joe Marler scored after a driving maul, Snapper kicked the extras and we were on our way to Twickenham.

We were sponsored by Etihad Airways, so the morning after our victory over Northampton, we all flew to Abu Dhabi for five or six days of warm weather training. That was Conor's reward for all the hard work we'd put in that season, and it did a very good job of taking our minds off the big game. It certainly wasn't how most teams prepared for a cup final, but Quins never followed convention.

The accommodation, facilities and food were very nice, but I wouldn't describe it as a holiday. It was pushing 40°C most days, and Olly Kohn got himself into that much of a hole during one fitness session that he pissed himself. But we'd lounge around by the pool after training, play a bit of golf or take a boat trip, and I'd never seen the lads so happy. By the time we returned to England, we were convinced that we'd beat Leicester in the final.

Leicester had beaten us by ten points at the Stoop a few weeks earlier, but while the players were obviously disappointed to have lost, Conor was all smiles in the changing room. When Minty asked him why he was so happy, Conor replied, ''Cos I know exactly where we went wrong and what we need to do to put things right. Our A game is gonna cause them so many problems.'

The media had a lot of narratives to work with before that game. A few of our lads had been overlooked for the Six Nations, and therefore had points to prove, while there was a lot of talk about Quins seeking redemption for Bloodgate. On a personal level, a good performance and a win would maybe stop people talking about those dark few months either side of Christmas. Plus, I was up against Ben Youngs, now England's undisputed number nine.

On the morning of the final, I climbed out of bed, threw open the curtains and saw a beautiful blue sky and a sun already blazing. And I thought to myself, *These are perfect Quins conditions, this is gonna be our day.*

Our squad included some of the best players and biggest characters English rugby has ever produced – including Minty, the finest I've ever played with. He never had a bad game and never got injured. He was terrible in the gym but one of the most powerful blokes I've ever met, the epitome of strength.

I always felt inferior in Minty's company, like a little boy next to someone who represents everything I felt a *man* is meant to be, but I loved that opposing players must have felt the same. He was like rugby's version of Vinnie Jones – I can't imagine Dulwich College has produced many people like him (weirdly, Minty's brother is quite posh).

Our skipper, Chris Robshaw, was just the most hardworking, selfless bloke you could imagine. He never stopped running and always reminded me of a dog with a stick: as long as you kept throwing it, he'd keep fetching it. Robbo knew that other players were bigger and more powerful than him, quicker than him, more skilful than him, so his job was to be the team's engine, whether he had the number six or seven on the back of his shirt.

He wasn't even a great motivational speaker. Instead he was one of those captains who led by example. He was the first on the training pitch, last one off, always working on extras, and would never ask you to do something he wasn't prepared to do himself. And on game day, he'd make 20 tackles, hit 30 rucks and only touch the ball three times in 80 minutes. That meant he didn't get many plaudits, but the team just wouldn't have worked without him.

People sometimes ask me why Minty wasn't captain, given how inspirational he was and how long he'd been at the club. But Minty was almost the captain without actually being the captain, in that Robbo was always asking him for advice. Snapper also had a bit of sway, while I'd take the lead every now and again (by which I mean I'd tap and go when no one had given me permission to).

Joe Marler appeared one day in training and has been in the first team ever since. Sometimes you just know when a young lad has what it takes, and that was certainly the case with Joe. He was a big, tough, ludicrously strong teenager who had no qualms about whacking established names in training. As such, he commanded respect from everyone, even when he started turning up to training with some of the worst haircuts known to man.

Joe has never given a toss what anybody thinks of him, not even Martin Johnson when he was England head coach. The first time Johnno clapped eyes on Joe, he was sporting a mohican and had 'Jolly Hog Sausages' written on either side of his head (he was a walking billboard for Olly Kohn's pork-based business venture, which is still going strong).

Johnno said to him, 'Nice hair.' Joe replied, 'Thanks.'

'Are you gonna shave that all off?'

'No.'

That was the end of it, nothing more was said.

How many youngsters would dare to turn up to an England camp with hair like that? And how many players would stand up to Martin Johnson like that? But Joe's attitude was 'If you wanna pick me, pick me. If you don't, don't. But I'm not changing for anyone.'

Joe didn't come out drinking much – he was more likely to be found at home having a few beers with a barbecue – but he absolutely loved anything to do with fancy dress. One year, he spent £700 on a Bane costume (Batman's enemy) and spent the evening terrifying people. Minty had set a very high bar when it came to fancy dress, but Marler came along and blew everyone out of the water. I reckon he must have shelled out £10,000 on outfits over the years, but he's always best dressed at the party.

Of the backs, Ugo Monye was the most charismatic, effervescent bloke you could hope to meet. Any bar or club we went to in London, we'd send Uges down the front and he'd get us all in, usually with our own table in the VIP area. He'd scored God knows how many tries since joining Quins in 2002 and was still a major threat on the wing.

Then there was Jordan Turner-Hall in the centres, who provided so much energy and ran his body into the ground for the team. He was already creaking badly, and he was only in his mid-twenties.

I should also mention Kyle Sinckler, who wasn't in the squad for the final but had played for us that season. Sincks was so raw and really wanted to hurt people, which is actually quite rare for a rugby player. Like Joe, he was no respecter of reputations and wasn't averse to the odd cheap shot in training. But I enjoyed his spirit and I loved that he'd found something to channel all that youthful aggression into. Not many lads play rugby in Tooting, and if someone hadn't told his mum about the existence of Battersea Ironsides, Sincks might not have either.

Sincks would make me laugh so much in training. He'd go haring across the field, past seven or eight team-mates, to get the ball. The coaches would constantly be saying to him, 'Kyle, that's not how it works, you have to stay in position and wait for the ball to come to you.' Other times, I'd have the ball and hear Sincks shouting, 'Danny! Danny!' from about 30 yards away. I had to admire his ambition, but even I didn't have that kind of pass in my locker.

It took him a while to get the hang of rugby's intricacies, but when he did, what a player. He was a very modern prop – quick, good hands, more than just a scrummager and tackler. He'd hit incredible lines and go on rampaging runs. And he was quite loose on nights out as well. We did take him under our wing and try to look after him, but we weren't always in control of ourselves.

And overseeing the team was the brilliant Conor O'Shea, who just wanted us to express ourselves and whose constant mantra was 'I don't care if you win or lose this game, as long as you play the Harlequins way.'

It sounds like the sort of thing a coach would say to a school team, but it was just so invigorating. We discussed structures, because you have to at that level, but we didn't play in a prescriptive way. Training was full of flair, creativity and fun, which meant it never felt like work. We worked bloody hard, and were extremely fit, which is why we came from behind to win so often. When we did win, Conor would heap praise on his players. But when we lost, he'd say it was all his fault. He was just an incredible boss to have.

○

Whenever Quins play at Twickenham, the players, coaches and staff just wander over from the Stoop, which makes us unique among rugby clubs. And that day, our fans lined the route in force. But while it felt like a home game, most people had Leicester down as favourites. While we'd never won a league title, they'd won nine, including three in the previous four years. But that just made us more determined, not just to win the thing, but also to win it the Quins way: swashbuckling, thrilling, getting people off their seats. In other words, how rugby should be played.

We started so fast they couldn't get a handle on us. Snapper popped over an early penalty before Tommy Williams, one of Bloodgate's central figures, strode over in the corner. He'd obviously read the script. We only led by a point at half-time but Leicester hadn't really been in it. Two Snapper penalties early in the second-half, followed by a Chris Robshaw try, put us in complete control.

An Anthony Allen try and a George Ford penalty got Leicester to within seven points with 11 minutes left, and maybe we'd have blown it 12 months earlier. But when my old mate Billy Twelvetrees opted to run straight at me rather than chucking it wide with nothing left on the clock, I stood firm, Robbo won the penalty and that was that. Quins had won their first Premiership

EVERYTHING HAPPENS FOR A REASON

title, I'd atoned for my mid-season knobheadishness, and I reacted to the final whistle by bursting into tears. It's impossible to describe those kinds of moments, except to say you'd probably break the bank to experience them.

I was so glad my mum, dad, brother and sister were in the stands because I'd put them all through the ringer that year. After months of reading all those lurid stories about me, I'd finally given them something to be proud of.

They joined in the celebrations back over at the Stoop, where Minty serenaded our fans with some of the worst singing in human history. And having told myself I wasn't going to have a drink until the team had done something special, I allowed myself a few. But it really was just a few. I wanted to savour the moment, and be able to remember it, rather than getting myself into a pickle. That night still cost me a fair few quid because I bought 20 bottles of champagne for my team-mates, as an apology for all my off-field misdemeanours. When I saw the bill, I felt like necking a bottle of brandy.

Chapter 11

Bad Timing

It wasn't possible to stay entirely on the straight and narrow with the England lads, especially when Ben Foden and Chris Ashton were involved. Whenever they were in the team, a lot of the madness seemed to revolve around them.

Fodes, a northern lad like me, didn't take life too seriously. In fact, it might have been his idea to sledge down a hill on a tackle pad. He had some terrible habits and the diet of a seven-year-old – sweets, chocolates, biscuits and fizzy drinks – but somehow managed to be absolutely shredded. He was similar to me in that regard, and people would often say to us, 'How the hell are you two not fat bastards?'

Fodes's 2012 wedding to pop star Una Healy was more like a stag weekend. First up was dog racing with all the boys in Tipperary, which quickly descended into complete and utter carnage; and on day two I was introduced to the Manchester City and England footballer Wayne Bridge, who was going out with Una's Saturdays bandmate Frankie Sandford. Being a football nause, I was excited to meet him, and he turned out to be a bona fide legend.

Modern footballers aren't known for their drinking, but Wayne made all us rugby lads look like lightweights. Whenever someone asked him how he was putting so much away, he'd reply, 'It's experience, boys, lots of experience …' It was all fun and games until some party promoter Ben and Una knew got a bit too pissed and started doing a chant about Wayne's former Chelsea team-mate John Terry. Terry had allegedly had an affair with Wayne's ex-partner, which Wayne's ex denied, so Wayne was understandably irritated. He said to this drunk idiot, calm as you like, 'Say that again, mate, and we'll see what happens.' The drunk idiot said it again, Wayne lamped him with a quick right hook, knocked him out cold and everyone started cheering.

The actual wedding day was amazing and full of action. Chris Ashton decided it would be a good idea to see how many cocktail sticks he could embed in his head, which will sound ridiculous to most people reading this but was pretty much par for the course for Ashy. He managed 65 in total, and he thought it was absolutely hilarious. But not so much the following morning, when his head looked like a giant, over-ripe tomato.

At some point in the evening, I ran into a wall and knocked myself out cold. I don't remember it at all, but I'm told I didn't move for about 30 seconds. I'm not sure why there was an ambulance on site, but the next thing I remember I was looking up at two paramedics and suddenly realising I'd done something stupid. Again. I stayed down a while longer, because I was too embarrassed to face anyone, before popping back up and running into the woods. I hid for an hour or so, hoping people would forget about it, and by the time I'd slunk back in, Fodes's dad, who is basically him but 30 years older, and a load of his pals were naked on the dancefloor. That probably didn't go down too well with some of Una's family, but at least it took the focus off me.

We were staying in chalets dotted around the grounds, and when Jordan Turner-Hall and I finally retired for the night, we came across some of Ben's cousins (I think!) wrestling, which included diving off the balcony onto the sofa. This balcony must have been 12 feet up, and Jordy and I found it quite alarming, even in our drunken state. When one of the lads launched into a backflip, Jordy, who thought he was going to kill himself, grabbed him and they both fell through the bannister and landed in a heap on the sofa. It was like a scene from *The Hangover* and just one incident in the loosest weekend I'd ever experienced – and, lest we forget, it was Ben Foden's wedding.

Fodes had terrible teeth, which isn't ideal when you're mixing in celebrity circles, so he decided to get veneers. Me and a few of the lads were sat having a coffee in Pennyhill Park's café when Fodes walked in, asked if we were alright and smiled. We couldn't believe our eyes. These new teeth made him look like a donkey, and not only were they too big for his mouth, so that he couldn't speak properly, they were also white as snow. But Fodes was so laid-back that he didn't really care.

Fodes, Ashy and I were quite into our gambling, and if we weren't betting on horses in the Ladbrokes in Bagshot, we were betting on an online roulette wheel in one of our rooms. One day, Joe Marler popped his head in and we convinced him to stick a grand on a spin. 'Mate, you're gonna win,' we said. 'It's almost impossible not to.' Joe went all in on red, spun the wheel, and it came up black. 'Nah, sorry mate,' said Fodes. 'You've lost.' Joe was utterly aghast – I don't think I've ever seen a man look so bewildered.

Whenever we went on a summer tour with England back then, we'd change our flights so that we had a few days in Las Vegas on the way home. So it was that, the weekend before Fodes's wedding, me, Jordy, Uges and Paul Doran-Jones found ourselves at a pool party, drunk, discussing tattoos. I wasn't much of a tattoo man, apart from the 'Everything happens for a reason' on my arm, so when Uges said we should all get matching tattoos to commemorate a cracking few days, I never thought it would actually happen. But on my way from the pool to the taxi rank, what should we come across? 'VEGAS'S BEST TATTOO PARLOUR'. And who was already in there designing our team tattoo? That's right, Uges.

Twitter was still a bit of a novelty, and hashtags were suddenly a thing, so Uges's bright idea was for us all to get '#ELITE' branded on our arses. A few of us went and had a drink while Uges was getting his done, and half an hour later he came running in, pulled the back of his shorts down to reveal this terrible tattoo and said, 'Lads, now it's your turn.'

I woke up the following morning and immediately thought, *Christ, my arse is sore. What the hell happened last night?* Then I looked at it in the mirror and saw '#ELITE' staring back at me in gigantic letters. It covered most of the cheek. The moral of the story? Don't get drunk with Uges in Vegas, or you might end up looking like an idiot for the rest of your life. (Uges, I actually love the tattoo. It reminds me of some very good times!)

○

The media consensus was that I'd got the better of Youngsy in the Premiership final (although he'd very nearly dragged them to victory at the death), so I was confident of being picked for England's summer tour of South Africa. I was, along with eight fellow Harlequins, but it didn't take me and Lanny long to fall out.

The squad was 42 players strong, meaning quite a few lads weren't going to get within a sniff of the Test team. And before the first session, Lanny told us that 25 lads were going to train on one pitch and the rest were going to train on a pitch next door. It was like being back at school, with Lanny reading the names from a list, and as soon as we heard Lanny call skipper Chris Robshaw and Owen Farrell's names, we knew that whomever they were training with were the players for the first Test. Youngsy soon joined Robbo and Faz, which I'd expected. Lee Dickson's name was also called. When I heard my name being read out to train away from the Test squad, I caught eyes with Lanny and shrugged my shoulders as if to say, *What's happening here?*

Having taken my place on the other field, alongside boys who had never played for England and were unlikely to appear in any of the Tests against South Africa, I spent most of the next couple of hours trying to score as many tries as possible. I couldn't even look at Lanny, let alone speak to him.

As soon as the session was over, Lanny said to me, 'You and me in the meeting room, now.' And once we were in there, he growled, 'Right, let's have it. What are you thinking?'

'Do I have permission to speak openly and honestly?' I said.

'Yes.'

'Okay, perfect. This is bollocks. What's going on?'

'What do you mean?'

'Stuart, I really respect you, and I respect what the team did in the Six Nations [England finished second behind Wales]. But you cannot tell me that Youngsy or Dicko have played better than me this year. I'm just not having it. I've done everything you said you needed to see me do to get back in.'

'But they played in the Six Nations and you didn't. We feel they deserve to retain their place.'

'I disagree. Me and Youngsy are your two best nines.'

'Well, we'll have to agree to disagree.'

'Fine, but I think you need more attacking threats against SA. I'll be trying my hardest to get back into the team.'

I was watching from the stands when we lost the first Test 22–17 in Durban, and it was the same again the following week, when we lost 36–27 in Johannesburg. In between, I was part of our dirt-trackers team that comfortably beat the Southern Barbarians, whoever they are, in Kimberley. But whichever team you're playing in South Africa, the locals will make things as uncomfortable for you as they possibly can. Sitting in the stands for those first two Tests, I could feel the hatred. In fact, I'm not sure it was particularly wise putting us up there, a load of blokes dressed in bright white tracksuits with 'ENGLAND' emblazoned across the back. It was like being stuck in the middle of a load of Millwall fans at The Den while wearing West Ham shirts. I thought, *We are going to get filled in here ...*

Even some of the Southern Barbarian lads were more physical than I could ever dream of being. For South Africans, rugby is war in miniature, and the fans don't just want to see visiting teams get beaten, they want to see them get beaten up. It's a very different rugby culture from New Zealand, where fans prefer to see visiting teams get carved up by athleticism and exquisite skill.

When Lee was picked for the midweek game against the Northern Barbarians, I knew I'd won a place in the squad for the dead rubber in Port Elizabeth. And when Youngsy injured his shoulder, I suddenly found myself in the starting XV.

That third Test wasn't exactly a thriller – we drew 14–14 – but I scored our only try, from a tap-and-go after ten minutes. And afterwards, Lanny told me he thought he should have played me in the first two Tests, which I didn't really know how to respond to. But my England career was apparently back on the rails.

○

If anyone thought Quins would rein things in after winning the Premiership title, our first game of the following season would have made them think again.

After 56 minutes at Twickenham, we were 40–13 behind against Wasps. Their wingers Christian Wade and Tom Varndell, who both made shit off a shovel look sluggish, had run riot in the first half, and when Wasps added two more tries shortly after the break, it was looking like a rank humiliation.

But one of Conor's catchphrases was, 'You're never out of it, just keep throwing the ball about and see what happens.' And just after I was replaced by Karl Dickson, Tom Guest's charge-down try gave us a glimmer of hope, before Snapper, playing his 100th game for the club, took over. First, Browny latched on to his perfectly judged cross-field kick to score his second try, then Snapper scored one himself. And with two minutes on the clock, Snapper kicked a penalty to make it 42–40 to us. It was the biggest comeback in Premiership history, although we've done similar quite a few times since.

My fun with Quins was interrupted by that year's autumn internationals, and I started the first two games against Fiji (which we won handily) and Australia (which we lost by a narrow margin). I was back on the bench for our one-point defeat by South Africa, but the game everyone remembers from that series was our thumping of New Zealand, when Manu Tuilagi looked like he was on a one-man mission to belatedly gain revenge for Jonah Lomu's treatment of the England team at the 1995 World Cup.

I've always said that if I could swap bodies with someone for just one game, I'd swap mine with Manu's. He's such a happy, smiley bloke, and so gentle as well. He was very aware of his own power, so would never hit anyone properly in training, in case he hurt them. But put him in a game and he turned into a monster. There haven't been many better players than peak Manu Tuilagi; he was just the most potent combination of strength, explosiveness and aggression, and he also had a better rugby brain than people gave him credit for. The All Blacks certainly couldn't live with him that day. Just like Lomu in his pomp, he knew that every time he got the ball, he was going to run either through or over someone. And remember, this was basically the All Blacks side that had won the World Cup 12 months earlier, with Richie McCaw, Dan Carter, Ma'a Nonu, Kieran Read and the rest.

That was just one of those rare days when everything clicked, and I don't think I've ever had so much fun sitting on the bench. We did hear afterwards that the All Blacks had been hit by some sickness bug, but never mind that. If we could beat the world champions playing like that, we could beat anyone, especially in our own backyard.

It's amazing what a win like that can do for a team's confidence, and we hit the ground running in the 2013 Six Nations. First up were Scotland at Twickenham, and we blew them away, which was satisfying.

People sometimes say to me, 'It must be amazing playing at Murrayfield.' To which I always reply, 'Not really.' There's a fierce rivalry between the two teams so it's often a bit of a grudge match when England and Scotland play. We'd get off the team bus and people would throw pints at us and swear in our faces. It was always freezing cold and usually pissing down. They'd sing that anthem of theirs, about beating the English in battle 700 years ago. I just never understood their fixation with beating England – I honestly believe that some Scotland fans would be happy to lose every game they played in return for beating us once a season – so I didn't just want to beat Scotland every time, I wanted to beat them at a canter.

The game against Ireland was the first time in my England career that I stayed on the bench for 80 minutes (I've no idea why – maybe I looked at Lanny the wrong way at breakfast) but we edged a low-scoring game for our first win in Dublin since the last time England had won a Grand Slam in 2003.

We also beat France at Twickenham and Italy in Rome (although that was tighter than we would have liked), meaning a Grand Slam was on when we travelled to Cardiff. Unfortunately, they tonked us 30–3, their biggest ever win against England, and retained their Six Nations title into the bargain.

I can't explain what went wrong that day. Training had gone well, our confidence was sky high and we really thought we could beat them. But unlike Scotland, Wales were a very good team, especially if they had the chance to scupper an England Grand Slam and win a Six Nations title in the process.

Sometimes when you're sat on the bench, you sense whether it's going to be a good day or not in the first few minutes. That was one of those days. It was abundantly clear that the Welsh lads were massively up for it, and while they didn't score a try in the first half, they kept forcing us into mistakes and Leigh Halfpenny kept pumping over penalties.

When Wales get on a roll, their fans just get louder and louder, which gets the players even more amped up. It's like a feedback loop, and not something that happens very often at Twickenham. And by the time I was introduced with 15 minutes to go, Wales were over the hill and far away, their winger Alex Cuthbert having just scored their first try. He quickly added a second, and I proceeded to have a nightmare. I just couldn't get into the game, missed a tackle on Sam Warburton that led to a try and tried a cross-field kick to Manu that went straight into touch. And after the final whistle, the rest of the lads and I had to stand there and watch 70,000 Welsh fans celebrating wildly while their team paraded the trophy.

I have fond memories of playing at the Millennium Stadium, especially when the roof is closed, as it was that day. But that game was like torture from start to finish. Having said that, sometimes you've just got to take your hat off to your opponents and admit they were brilliant. Through gritted teeth, of course. When Wales centre Jamie Roberts joined Quins a couple of years later, he told me that had been one of the best nights of his life. 'That's nice to hear,' I replied, 'because it was one of the worst nights of mine.'

That was a season of near misses for me. Quins finished third in the table that season, which meant an away play-off semi-final against Leicester. We had the better of the first half, and if Tom Croft hadn't held me up over the line, we would probably have been ten ahead at the break. Instead, we opted to keep the ball in hand rather than boot it into touch to end the half and got turned over at a ruck. A few seconds later, Leicester wing Vereniki Goneva was touching down under our posts.

That was a big momentum swing – they went in on a high and we went in on a low, when it should have been the other way around – and we couldn't wrest it back. They crossed three more times in the second half and a late try from Ross Chisholm was nothing more than a consolation. That was Leicester's ninth consecutive Premiership final, which tells you what a tough, gritty outfit they were.

We were great in the pool stage of the Heineken Cup, winning all six of our games, but came up against a Munster side bent on revenge in the quarter-finals.

I'd already received a letter telling me I was on the shortlist for the Lions tour to Australia, just as in 2009, and that game doubled as a virtual trial for a place in the squad, at least as far as Conor Murray and I were concerned.

I was a bit more experienced than Conor, which I hoped would count for something, but that was overtaken by events on the field. And with Lions head coach Warren Gatland and a few of his team up on the stands, it was a bad day to have a bad day.

We were excited to be back in the big time, playing a Heineken Cup knockout game at the Stoop, and given Munster's patchy league form, we really fancied ourselves to do a number on them. But when I came out for the warm-up and looked around the ground, it was a sea of red. It transpired that loads of Quins fans had sold their tickets to travelling Munster supporters, so it felt like we were playing away at Thomond Park instead.

That Munster side were very good spoilers. They'd trick you into thinking there was space where there wasn't space; they were quite happy to let their opponents play an expansive game, or at least try to, because they had excellent anticipation, knew players would get isolated and turn them over or win a penalty. And when Ronan O'Gara is your kicker, you'll settle for penalties over tries all day long.

We did create opportunities but couldn't take them. Meanwhile, Conor Murray box-kicked superbly, as he almost always did. No doubt about it, he got the better of me that day, and Munster ended up winning 18–12, O'Gara kicking six penalties to Snapper's four.

I'd had two big games to prove that I was worthy of a Lions spot and blown both. True, I only played 15 minutes against Wales in Cardiff, but that was still enough time to make a few mistakes. And now I'd been eclipsed by Conor Murray in a home game that felt far more like an away game. That's the thing with Lions tours: you can play great for three and a half years, have a couple of shaky high-profile games just before the squad gets picked and suddenly you're right down the pecking order. It's all about timing your run.

When the Lions squad was announced a few weeks later, I wasn't in it, and neither were any other Quins players. Gatland and his team opted for Youngsy, Wales's Mike Phillips and Conor as his nines instead, which I couldn't complain about. Youngsy was starting ahead of me for England, Mike was a great running nine, and while I thought I could offer something a bit different to Conor, he'd been a very solid performer for Ireland for a couple of years, never mind that Heineken Cup trial. The funny thing is, people often said I seemed like a classic Lions 'bolter' – a running nine with a bit audacity – but that obviously wasn't true, because I'd now been overlooked for two Lions tours. Oh well – at least Conor wasn't Scottish.

Chapter 12

A Happier Man

The same day the Lions squad was announced, Lanny gave me a call. And after telling me how sorry he was that I hadn't been picked, he moved straight onto the subject of England's summer tour to Argentina. 'It's going to be a different sort of tour,' he said. 'Quite a few of the older lads will be away with the Lions, so the squad will have a younger feel about it. You just tell me what you want to do. If you want to come, I'd love to take you. But I completely understand if you want to recharge your batteries, because you've not had a summer break for a long time.'

He said he'd give me a couple of days to think about it, so I had a chat with my mum and dad and decided that a summer break might be quite nice, as well as beneficial to my career. I was always thinking in terms of cycles, and I thought a bit of time away from rugby might be great for my 2015 World Cup hopes.

When I called Lanny, I explained that my body was a bit sore, I was mentally a bit jaded and a break might be just what the doctor ordered. I assured him I'd tear into pre-season, make a flying start to the Premiership and be in fine fettle for the autumn internationals, if selected. Lanny said he completely understood, wished me the best of luck, and I, along with Jordan Turner-Hall and his best mate, Justin, booked flights to Thailand later that day. We were in Bangkok a couple of days later, seeing things a nice lad from Leeds should never see.

From Bangkok we travelled to Phi Phi, where I bumped into an old schoolmate who was working in a bar, which made drinks even cheaper than they normally are in Thailand. Next stop was Koh Phangan, where Jordy and I booked ourselves in to a seafront apartment and prepared for a Full Moon Party (Justin had flown home by that point, but not before completely losing the plot, which included him getting a new tattoo – the same one that Uges, Jordy and I had got in Las Vegas a few years earlier).

The day of the Full Moon Party, someone handed us a flyer for a pre-party in a nearby hotel, so we bowled down there with a couple of other lads we'd met. And while I was hovering around the buffet, a blonde girl strode in and stopped me in my tracks. I remember it as clear as day, as if it's a scene from a film. When I returned to our table, Jordy asked me what was wrong. 'I've just seen this girl,' I replied. 'I'm gonna have to speak to her.' Jordy said we needed to return to our apartment and get ready for the Full Moon Party, but I wasn't really listening. 'I have to speak to her,' I repeated, as if in a trance. I was well and truly lovestruck, and that had never happened to me before.

I wandered over and started chatting to this girl, whose name was Jodie, and her mate, and I strongly suspect they thought I was a bit of a twat, based on the fact that I was wearing a baseball cap backwards and happened to be shirtless.

I wasn't on Danny Cipriani's level, chat-wise, but I wasn't bad. And neither was Jordy, who was soon chewing the ear off Jodie's mate. And after half an hour, I asked for Jodie's number. 'Oh, I don't have a phone number,' she replied, which is the chatting-up equivalent of getting a custard pie in the face. Who, apart from undiscovered Amazonian tribespeople, didn't have a phone in

2013? The last thing she said to me was, 'If we see each other tonight, it's meant to be. If not, the same.'

Jordy asked me if I was okay on the way back to our apartment – he'd never seen me like that before – and I replied, 'Mate, there's just something about that girl. She's perfect. I think I'm gonna marry her.' Jordy, being a man, responded, 'Whatever, mate. Let's get changed and have a couple of beers …'

There must have been 10,000 people at this Full Moon Party; it was absolutely chaotic. And at some point in the evening, Jordy tapped me on the shoulder and said, 'I've got you a present.' When I turned around, he was standing there with his arm around Jodie. Actually, it was more of a headlock. She was wearing a blue vest, had flowers in her hair and looked even more stunning than she had earlier. Luckily for Jordy, she still had her mate in tow.

Jodie revealed that she was travelling with her brother Luke, who had told her I played rugby. 'He says you're actually pretty good,' she said.

'Do you know any rugby players?' I replied.

'I know nothing about rugby.'

'Brilliant. That's a good start …'

I had a few beers with Luke, assured him that I wasn't a rugby twat, and he gave me his seal of approval. Not that Jodie needed anyone's seal of approval, but it was nice for me to hear.

I spent the rest of the night paddling in the sea, watching the full moon, drinking and dancing on tables, before walking Jodie back to her hotel at about ten o'clock in the morning. Her phone must have miraculously materialised because she gave me her number. The last thing I said to Jordy before hitting the sack was, 'I genuinely think it was love at first sight.'

I invited Jodie to a jungle party a couple of days later and she came to our apartment for a few drinks beforehand. Sitting on the veranda sharing a big bottle of Chang beer, I thought to myself, *Wow, this girl is too good to be true.* We had the best time ever at the party, and she got on great with my mates, which is always a bonus.

Jodie was heading off to Bali, so Jordy and I decided to tag along. That meant we'd miss our flight back to London, but we'd still get back in plenty of time for the start of pre-season training.

As luck would have it, my mate John Spence owned a resort company called Karma Group, so I phoned him while pissed and asked if we could stay in one of his villas in Bali. He said he'd let us stay for free, which I didn't mention to anyone else.

John laid on a lift from the airport, and when we arrived at the resort, there was literally a red carpet laid out for us. The receptionist said to me, 'Ah, Mr Care, good to see you again.' Some waiters appeared with champagne, and everyone apart from Jordy must have thought I owned the place.

Our ten-person crew included a Norwich City diehard called Bill, who we'd met in Thailand and also convinced to get the same tattoo as me and Jordy on his arse: #ELITE (absolutely horrific). There were also two of Jodie's friends, Clare and Laura, and our Quins team-mate Matt Hopper and his wife, Ellie, who were doing a bit of travelling.

The villa we were staying in was more like a Bond villain's secret hideout, set in the mountains and looking out on the ocean. For the next week, we had the time of our lives – cocktails all day, barbecues for breakfast, lunch and dinner – and Jodie and I fell in love, without really knowing it.

Some evenings, we'd all head into Kuta, where all the action takes place. We had a nice little set-up in one of the bars – we'd tip the bouncers and barmen on arrival and they'd look after us – but Bill, who reckoned he was part of Norwich City's firm (I wasn't aware they had one) still managed to get into trouble. Some drunk Aussie pushed him, and Jordy and I told him to leave it, but that wasn't going to happen. I'll never forget what Bill said afterwards: 'Throw the punch first, ask questions later …'

When our time in Bali was up, Jodie still had some travelling to do, including two months in Australia (Norwich Bill was heading there as well and promised to look after her, which I didn't really know what to make of). Meanwhile, I had to get home and sort my life out before pre-season training – Jordy and I were being turfed out of our flat because our tenancy was up, and we hadn't sorted alternative accommodation.

Up until the moment we said goodbye, I didn't know if Jodie and I were destined to be just a holiday romance or not. But just as Jordy and I were about to leave, someone put a sad song on the stereo and Jodie started crying. 'I'm going to miss you,' she said. 'I'm going to miss you, too,' I replied. Then I thought, *Maybe this is going to be something a bit bigger after all. As long as she doesn't get swept off her feet by Brad the surfer from Bondi Beach …*

When Jordy and I got back to the flat, the landlord told us we had to be out by the end of the day, which was nice. Jordy packed up his stuff and drove to Brighton, where he was going to stay with his mum, but that wasn't an option for me, seeing as my mum and dad lived at the other end of the country.

I didn't want to impose on any mates, so I rang one of the concierge guys at Pennyhill Park, the hotel that hosts England's training camps, and asked if I could stay there for a few nights.

EVERYTHING HAPPENS FOR A REASON

To my surprise, he said yes, as well as offering me a friends and family discount. I couldn't sign in with my real name, because I was neither a friend nor a relative of the concierge guy, but it still sounded like a very good deal to me.

When I turned up, the receptionist gave me a big smile and said, 'Good morning, Mr Jones, nice to see you again.' She obviously knew I wasn't Mr Jones because I'd known her for years. For the next three weeks, I lived like Alan Partridge in the Linton Travel Tavern, and I loved every minute of it. If only I'd remembered to bring my big plate for the breakfast buffet.

Just before I checked out of the hotel and moved in with my Quins team-mate Will Skinner, Jodie came home from Australia a month earlier than planned, which I thought was a good sign. We actually spent our first night together in England at Pennyhill Park, which she thought was ridiculous – 'Why on earth are you living in a hotel?' – but quite funny at the same time.

When Jodie's mum, Donna, googled my name, she obviously found out about all my arrests and warned Jodie to be careful. I couldn't really blame her, because a bloke who has misdemeanours and keeps pissing in the street doesn't sound like much of a catch. Luckily, Jodie's dad Paul was a massive rugby fan, while her brother assured their mum that I was a nice bloke really. Weirdly, Jodie had bought her dad, brother and brother-in-law Kev tickets for the 2012 Premiership final. But while that was one of the best days of my life, they were supporting Leicester. Not only that, but they also got horribly sunburnt.

Jodie had done a bit of googling herself, mainly to find out what kind of women I usually went with. I'd only had two serious girlfriends before Jodie, but a couple of flings with women who look like they'd stepped out of a lads' mag had appeared in the tabloids, so Jodie naturally wondered if that was my type. No, I told her, she was my type: naturally beautiful, funny and far smarter than I was (Jodie had done a law degree at the University of Sheffield and was working for Jaguar Land Rover, as a project leader for the chassis engineers, which I always found hilarious for some reason).

After that night at Pennyhill Park, I drove Jodie up to Coventry, where I met Donna and Paul, and her two sisters, Stacey and Sadie. Luke was also home from travelling, which probably helped, and everyone made me feel very welcome. There was a barbecue and beers, and I now understood why Jodie was such a good person, because they were all just so caring.

All in all, my summer break had turned out better than I could possibly have imagined. Not only did I feel refreshed in mind and body, but I'd also discovered the woman of my dreams. Quins made a shaky start to the new season, but I thought I was playing well enough to be recalled to the England team. Then Lanny named his squad for the autumn internationals and my bubble burst: I was omitted.

When I asked Lanny what on earth was going on, he said, 'You didn't want to come to Argentina. And the lads who came played really well, so deserved to stay in the squad.' I couldn't believe what I was hearing. I said to him, 'Stuart, you can't say to someone, "I completely understand if you want to take some time off to freshen up physically and mentally," and then hold it against them when they do exactly that.'

It felt like Lanny was playing games with me, or he'd set a trap, and I was livid. I told him it was complete bollocks, that he'd stitched me up and hung me out to dry. He replied, 'You made the decision not to go, mate.' Had I not met Jodie on my summer break, I'd have been even angrier and may have said something I really regretted.

I hadn't forgotten what Lanny had done for me at Leeds, getting me on the straight and narrow when I could have wandered off down the wrong path, but I was starting to worry that perhaps my face didn't fit in Lanny's regime.

It often felt like guys who questioned things, like Danny Cipriani, Dylan Hartley and Chris Ashton, were risking their place in the team by doing so. I wasn't quite on their level, but usually if I had something to say, I said it. And I was competing for a scrum-half spot with Lee Dickson, who got his head down in training and wouldn't say boo to a goose, never mind to the head coach of the England team.

It says a lot about the capricious nature of professional sport that I was Lanny's number one for the Six Nations a few months later, while Youngsy was third in the pecking order. Suddenly it was him driving home from Pennyhill Park every Tuesday before a game and thinking, *What have I done wrong?*

I assume Lanny was chopping and changing his nines because he was still trying to decide what style to play. But as it was only a year before a World Cup on home soil, the media and fans were starting to worry.

Lanny and his assistant Andy Farrell have gone on to do great things – Lanny with Leinster, Andy with Ireland – but I'm not sure they knew exactly what they wanted England to be back then. Everything seemed to be quite reactive – we'd play well and everyone would think, *Oh, maybe that's what we're meant to be,* but as soon as we played badly, we'd change tack again.

Believe it or not, I've never actually asked a coach why they keep taking players off midway through the second half. It's just something that started happening at some point and now nobody even thinks to question it. I mention it because I was taken off 20 minutes before the end of the Six Nations opener against France, just ahead of three or four other England players. England were playing well and leading at the time, and someone even said to me on the bench, 'Why have they taken you off?' We lost our flow, France got on top and Gaël Fickou went over for the winning try with two minutes to go. The prevailing mood in the changing room after the game was, *Well, that was a bit stupid. We had France on the rack in Paris and let them back into it.*

Beating Scotland 20–0 at Murrayfield was sweet – playing in front of a Scottish crowd with nothing to cheer for is what heaven must be like – but not as sweet as the conversation I had with Jodie the following weekend. I was sitting on the bed in my hotel room when Jodie said the magic words, 'I think I'm pregnant.' It was as if my entire body had been filled with happiness.

We'd only been together for eight months, and while I was still young at 27, Jodie was just 23. Jodie was at a pivotal point in her career – not only was she working for Jaguar Land Rover, but she was also studying for her solicitor exams. Nevertheless, we were both euphoric at the prospect of being parents. I'd always dreamt of my kids watching me play and understanding what I did for a living, and there was no better woman than Jodie to have them with.

I'd been pretty loose for the past ten years, and the news of Jodie's pregnancy had come as a bit of a surprise, so there was some worry and mild panic. But mostly I was incredibly excited about being a dad, and determined to be a good one. I kept thinking, *Bloody hell, a kid's gonna turn up in October – and he's gonna be mine!* And going into the game against Ireland, I felt that everything I did suddenly had more meaning.

I scored one of my favourite ever tries against the Irish at Twickenham. It was an all-Quins affair, with Robbo offloading to Browny and Browny bursting through the middle before slipping the ball inside to me. The icing on the cake was diving through the posts while Brian O'Driscoll and Johnny Sexton gave up the chase. All the emotion came flooding out, and even a few tears. I really believe I was meant to score that try as a little early birthday present to whoever was inside Jodie's tummy.

I was loving life during that Six Nations – playing for England, winning games, a baby on the way – and having scored the winning try against Ireland, I grabbed an early one against Wales a couple of weeks later. Lanny had been going on at me about backing myself and showing what I could do, and I felt trusted by England for the first time. So when the referee gave us a penalty 5 metres out from the Welsh line, I took a quick tap and go and dived over unopposed, when the sensible option would have been to take the three points.

That opening weekend loss to France had put paid to our Grand Slam hopes, and Ireland pipped us to the title, but at least the number nine shirt felt like mine for the first time. Whenever I'd started for England before then, I felt like I was just borrowing the shirt from someone else, usually Youngsy.

○

We beat Bath in the final game of the regular season to pip them to a play-off place, but Saracens were starting to build a formidable squad around that time – they rested their entire first team in their final regular season game against Leicester – and while we managed to stay with them in the first half of our semi-final, they pulled away from us after the break. Exactly how they were able to build such a formidable squad would only become clear five years later.

I travelled to New Zealand that summer with high hopes. I was so looking forward to playing in that great country again, having made my debut there six years earlier, and I really thought we had a chance of beating them. Unfortunately, while the England team did okay, I had a bit of a nightmare.

There are plenty of ways to give your shirt away – playing badly, talking back to the coach, getting arrested – but I'm not sure anyone else has ever attempted a grubber kick, fallen over the ball and knackered their shoulder. This was a couple of days before the first Test in Auckland, and while the rest of the lads thought it was hilarious, I was in agony. I couldn't lift my arm, couldn't lie on it in bed, couldn't sleep. And the worst part of the whole sorry episode was that Youngsy, the man I'd only recently unseated after years of trying, started instead of me.

I was so desperate to play in the second Test that I agreed to have a painkilling injection, which was one of the first times I'd done that in my career. It was like a miracle, and suddenly I understood why I'd seen so many players do it.

Having lost the first Test by five points, we lost the second in Dunedin by one. We were in it the whole game but didn't take our chances, and if you don't take your chances against the All Blacks, they'll find a way to beat you.

I missed the third Test in Hamilton (another defeat, this time by a landslide), before heading home to sort my life out. I was living in a flat in Esher when I found out that Jodie was pregnant, and now I wanted to buy a grown-up house for the three of us.

We decided on a new build in the leafy village of Cobham, which felt like the perfect place for a kid to grow up.

While we were waiting for the purchase to go through, poor Jodie was still up in Coventry, combining work with sitting her solicitor exams while heavily pregnant. They had to provide her with a special desk, because she was now too big to fit behind a normal one, and she felt sick the whole time. She was clearly far stronger than me, I honestly don't know how she did it.

We moved into the house a couple of months before the baby was due, which was a pretty big moment given that we'd never lived together before. Luckily, we got on well. I'm not sure what we would have done had we not. Then, a week before Jodie was due to give birth, I proposed.

I'd asked Jodie's dad, Paul, for permission, which turned out to be more difficult than I'd imagined. I thought I'd do it while playing golf, but Jodie's brother Luke and brother-in-law Kev were also playing, and mine and Paul's balls never landed in the same area. If I hit it right, he'd hit it left. If he found the green, I'd find a bunker. I didn't get a minute with him on my own the entire round. I thought I'd collar him in the pub afterwards, but every time he went to the bar, Luke or Kev went with him. I had to follow him to the toilet in the end. When he emerged from the cubicle, he looked at me suspiciously and asked, 'You alright, mate?' and I mumbled, 'I'd really like your permission to ask Jodie to marry me.' He broke into a smile, gave me a big cuddle and said, 'I always said I'd say no to the next one who asked, just to mess with their head ...'

I wanted to propose in our first house, so I got Snapper's wife, Sally, to take Jodie out for dinner, before my boy Jordy came round to help with the preparations. We hung up lights in the back garden, created a rose petal path through the front door, lit candles, put up nice pics of the two of us (me and Jodie, not me and Jordy) and put some champagne on ice. When Jordy left, I still had half an hour to spare. And while I was sat in the garden, staring at the champagne and a bottle containing a note I'd written for Jodie, I suddenly thought, *What if she says no?* I was pretty sure she'd say yes – after all, we were having a baby together in seven days' time – but I'd never felt so nervous and ended up necking three or four beers.

When Jodie walked through the front door and saw all the romantic paraphernalia, she must have wondered what on earth I was after, or if I'd done something stupid. But I managed to snap her out of her shock and get her into the garden, where I fell to one knee, pulled out the ring and proposed. Luckily for me, she said yes. Unluckily for Jodie, my proposal sent her blood pressure so high that she thought the baby was on its way the following day.

The day before Quins' away game against Leicester, Jodie went into labour, although she didn't know it at the time. We decided to go to hospital anyway, and I could tell from the amount of pain that Jodie was in that the baby was well and truly on its way.

We had planned to have a water birth, but after a couple of hours, the nurse decided to put Jodie on a bed in another room. When I walked in, the nurse (who was brilliant throughout) asked me to go back into the other room and grab the gas and air, as the baby was coming pronto. I did as I was told, yanking something that resembled a mask off the wall, but when I returned to Jodie's room, I received a severe bollocking from a 10cm dilated soon-to-be mother who was in excruciating pain – in my panic, I'd grabbed something completely irrelevant. Mercifully, the nurses were more switched on than me; one of them fetched the correct equipment and we were back to delivering a baby!

It was certainly traumatic for me, so God knows how Jodie felt. She didn't have any pain relief – what a trooper – and was simply incredible throughout. That night, our beautiful baby boy, Blake, was born.

I had no idea how I'd feel when I held Blake for the first time, or even how I was meant to feel. But something just clicked. I was meeting this little human, but he was already the most important thing in my life. It was instant true love. Then I tried to change his nappy and he weed all over me. That's gratitude for you.

Jodie said I should go and play against Leicester, but it really didn't seem that important given what had just taken place. Luckily, Conor always used to say that family comes first, and he told me to look after Jodie and Blake and take the weekend off. That might seem like a no-brainer, but I know plenty of lads who have played on the same day that their baby was born, usually when it was a big game or their side had lots of injuries. And while I didn't get the two weeks' paternity leave that most blokes get, most blokes don't get paid to play sport for a living, so I couldn't really complain.

When the press got wind of Jodie having a baby, there were the inevitable articles about me being a 'changed man'. A lot of that stuff was overplayed. It's not as if I was ever George Best, I just had a rocky few months, which they kept writing about in the papers – but I did make a conscious decision to tidy my life up a bit.

I didn't want Jodie to have to read about me pissing in the street again, and I didn't want to be chucking my money down the drain. I used to love a flutter, and some days a few of us lads would sit in Ladbrokes in Cobham for a few hours after training.

I really enjoyed those afternoons with our Marks & Spencer meal deals followed by drinks and crisps on the house, but now I realised that it was money that could be spent on our baby instead.

I was still sociable and liked a beer, and I'd like to think that my personality hadn't changed at all, but I was just a happier man. It wasn't that I'd been unhappy before, but I didn't have this amazing woman in my life, and I didn't have a baby. In other words, my dreams hadn't come true all at once.

My first game back was eight days later against Castres in the Champions Cup, as the Heineken Cup had been renamed. We won, but it wasn't much of a game. I did, however, score the only try, after a brilliant chip-through from Snapper. Before the game, Conor had asked if I was going to do the so-called Bebeto celebration if I scored – rocking an imaginary baby side to side – and that's exactly what I did, while Jodie and little Blake watched from the sofa.

Chapter 13

A Missed Opportunity

I was back in the starting line-up for the first two autumn internationals against the All Blacks and South Africa, both of which ended in narrow defeat. That meant England had lost five in a row (although four of those games were against New Zealand) and the media were talking about a crisis, which was some turnaround from a few months earlier, when praise was being heaped upon Lanny and the team for finally clicking into place.

That South Africa Test should have been a career highlight, given that it was my 50th cap and I got to lead the boys out. Alas, it turned into a personal disaster. In the first half, I thought I saw a gap down the blind side and threw a looping pass to Kyle Eastmond, only for Jan Serfontein to read it like a book, intercept and canter home unopposed. That's a horrible thing to happen in front of 80,000 people and I just wanted the ground to swallow me up. None of my team-mates said anything to me, but the fact that they couldn't look me in the eye told me everything I needed to know. We only lost by three points, so sitting in the changing room afterwards I thought it was all down to me.

I was presented with my 50th cap at the post-match dinner. Everyone was saying nice things about me and the whole time I was thinking, *I'm the reason we lost*. The newspaper verdicts on my performance were brutal, with the *Sunday Telegraph* calling me 'woeful' and the *Sunday Times* rating me four out of ten.

Lanny must have agreed with them, because he told me on the Monday that I wasn't playing against Samoa the following week.

I couldn't really argue with Lanny's decision, because I hadn't played well. However, I didn't understand why I'd been dropped from the squad completely. If you have a bad game as the starting nine, surely you should then become the reserve nine, especially if you've been performing well for the previous however many games. But I was out of the squad completely, with Youngsy starting and Richard Wigglesworth coming onto the bench.

Then again, Wiggy was a criminally underrated scrum-half who probably should have won more England caps than he did. He was the best box-kicker I've ever seen and always seemed to be in control. Those are two reasons why Saracens won so many trophies with him in the team. I was more of a running threat and would try to hurt teams with my pace, while Youngsy was kind of a hybrid of the two of us, in that he could run, kick and read the game well. The three of us were on a sliding scale, and whenever Wiggy got picked ahead of me, I had to concede that the game plan obviously wasn't suited to me.

I was in the squad for the 2015 Six Nations, but now I was that guy driving home from Pennyhill Park on a Tuesday. And it was a bad time to be out of the picture because England really seemed to have hit on something. They scored 18 tries in the tournament, including seven against France on the final day, and only Ireland got the better of them. They were exciting times for England fans but worrying times for me. Twelve months earlier, the number nine shirt had been mine and I was enjoying playing for England more than ever. Now, I was genuinely concerned that I wouldn't even make the World Cup squad.

It's a cliché, I know, but fatherhood did provide some perspective. Some of my team-mates would finish training and hang around playing pool for hours afterwards, because they didn't want to go home to the family. But I wanted to spend as much time with Blake as possible. I loved bathing him and changing his nappy and all that other stuff that some dads aren't really into. I was head over heels in love with that kid, and just a little smile from Blake would make everything seem okay, whatever was going on with my rugby.

Having said all that, some of the media criticism hurt. I didn't read the newspapers much, but I was aware that Stuart Barnes, who had a column in *The Times*, had never really liked me. He was also a pundit on Sky, so it was impossible to avoid his opinions. Barnes got stuck into me about my box-kicking and said that while my all-round game was perfectly adequate for club rugby, it wasn't good enough for England. I thought that was rubbish, frankly. True, I wasn't as good a box-kicker as Wiggy, and probably couldn't control a game as well as him either, but I felt I could do stuff that he couldn't. I scored and set up more tries than him, I played the game quicker. And while I don't think Lanny read Barnes's columns and thought, *Oh, if Stuart thinks that, I won't pick him*, that sort of commentary can colour a coach's opinion of a player.

Even though England had scored a lot of tries in that Six Nations, I sensed that the mindset had shifted. Whereas 12 months earlier we'd played a high-tempo game, and Lanny had been encouraging me to tap and go whenever I saw fit, now it seemed like physicality and territory were the most important things. If that was Lanny's master plan, I wouldn't have picked me either. But I didn't think we were going to win a World Cup playing that way.

It probably didn't help my cause that Quins were having a rough time of it in the Premiership. Saracens spanked us 39–0 at home in the second game of the season, after which we felt the need to apologise to the fans. There followed heavy defeats by Exeter (twice), Bath, Wasps, Saracens again and even Newcastle in the final game of the season. That meant we finished eighth in the table, 19 points adrift of the play-offs, while Youngsy's Leicester finished third and Wiggy's Saracens finished fourth and went on to win the title.

But if it sounds like Quins were suddenly in the midst of a crisis, that wasn't the case at all. The Premiership is such a competitive league, and the salary cap does its job of making things equal. Unless, of course, some teams decide not to take any notice of it, which can mess up the balance completely.

I was at least picked for England's training camp in Denver in July, along with 44 other players. The pitch was this: you're going to train hard at altitude, while having a bit of fun, and you're going to return to England fitter than any other team. Everyone was on board with that, until we actually got there and realised what their idea of training hard was.

The fitness sessions were ridiculous. They'd explain what we had to do, and we'd all be looking at each other as if to say, 'There's no way we can do that. And why are we doing it anyway?' They'd tell us to run up and down a pitch 40 times and we'd all be blowing out of our arses after one length. By the end of it, some players would be struggling to put one foot in front of the other. And when it came to the actual rugby session, we couldn't string more than three passes together because everyone was in pieces.

Fitness for its own sake has never really been my thing. I was fitter than Youngsy, but not as fit as Wiggy, and as long as I finished all the sessions between them, that was fine with me. I was just keeping my fingers crossed that the coaches knew what they were doing and that we'd all return home feeling superhuman. I certainly wasn't going to say anything, because I felt like I could be chopped at any moment. Even Danny Cipriani stayed schtum.

One day, we went on a whitewater rafting trip that was meant to last for a couple of hours but actually went on for five. To be fair, it was a lot of fun. Somebody nicked the kit man's raft and he spent four hours floating down the river in his lifejacket. And every time we stopped for a few minutes, we'd all start wrestling, even the coaching staff. At one point, Lanny was on a raft on his own, everyone else having fallen overboard, and Haskell swam up behind him. Everyone was watching and thinking, *Oh my God, Hask is gonna attack the head coach*, but after a couple of seconds, when the world seemed to stop, Hask smiled and disappeared beneath the water. In other words, he bottled it.

The day after the rafting, which wasn't exactly a relaxing break, it was back to being flogged and playing terrible rugby as a result. But I still thought we had a great squad, and we'd shown glimpses of how good we could be over the previous year and a half. Plus, the World Cup was on home soil, which had to count for something. I honestly thought we could win the thing. I even started thinking, *If we do win it, we can milk it forever, like the boys who won it in 2003*. I probably shouldn't have had that attitude – I was getting ahead of myself – but I couldn't help it.

Having moved in lock, stock and barrel to Pennyhill Park, Lanny trimmed seven players at the start of August, but not Sam Burgess. Sam had shelved a stellar career with South Sydney Rabbitohs in the National Rugby League with a view to playing for England in a World Cup, but things hadn't really gone to plan. He'd struggled to get to grips with playing centre for Bath and ended up playing flanker. Even so, when I played against him for Quins, they ran one move with him at 12 and he ran straight over the top of Snapper. He was big, he was powerful, he was mean, and he wanted to do some damage.

Whether Sam should have been in the squad or not, he was a great bloke and I loved spending time with him. And I felt quite sorry for him when Lanny decided to put him in charge of the leadership group. Suddenly, this rugby league bloke who had been playing union for one season was explaining our identity to us, telling us all about our heritage and what our values were, and we were sat there thinking, *He's literally just walked into the sport, he's never played for England in rugby union, what does he know about any of this stuff?*

What made it worse was that guys like me and Hask, who had been in and around the squad for the best part of a decade, *weren't* in the leadership group! To his credit, Sam was embarrassed. 'I'm so sorry, lads,' he said, 'they asked me to do it and I didn't think I could say no.' The coaches clearly believed that Sam was going to win us the World Cup, but putting him on a pedestal like that made him uncomfortable and sent out a weird message to the rest of the lads.

Those first few weeks at Pennyhill Park weren't the most relaxing because we knew another eight players still needed to be axed. Everyone was on edge because they constantly felt like they were being judged. We were terrified of making a mistake, on the training ground and off it, whether that meant making the wrong pass, saying the wrong thing, wearing the wrong kit or turning up late for a meeting. One false move and your World Cup dream could be over. We'd hear all these stupid sayings like, 'You should feel comfortable feeling uncomfortable.' But I couldn't help thinking, *Why are there still so many players here? It's just making everyone angsty.*

Our two warm-up games against France clouded the picture even further. Sam played well enough in the first game at Twickenham, which we won, but wasn't even on the bench for the rematch in Paris; Sam's rival for a centre spot, Luther Burrell, played and we lost in dismal fashion.

Luther had been a big part of the squad for a couple of years and was a popular bloke. He'd played under Lanny at Leeds for years (we were in the academy together and he was a really close mate) and was brilliant in the 2014 Six Nations, scoring tries in his first two games and three in the tournament overall. But everyone had done the maths and concluded that there wasn't room in the final squad for him and Sam – it was one or the other. And because they'd made such a song and dance about bringing Sam over from rugby league and put him in charge of the leadership group, everyone could see what was coming.

Meanwhile, I still didn't know if Lanny was going to pick three scrum-halves or not, because that didn't always happen. Then the day before he was due to announce his final squad, Lanny suddenly revealed that we were having an old-school trial match, like the All Blacks had in the amateur days.

Maybe Lanny was giving Luther one last chance to prove that he was a better bet than Sam, because there's no doubt he cared about him, given their history. But to this day, I have no idea why Lanny thought that trial match was a good idea. That's what the warm-up games were meant to be for.

The lads couldn't help taking the piss. Hask and Tom Wood marched down to the training pitch wearing their anthem jackets and headphones, as if it was a proper Test match. People were laughing at me because I'd been picked on the wing, presumably because one of the actual wingers was injured. I didn't find it that funny because it meant I obviously wasn't in the top two scrum-halves, although I ended up having the game of my life. My opposite number, Jack Nowell, actually congratulated me afterwards, and if there had been a man of the match award that day, I'd have been nailed-on for it. Not only did I score two tries, but I also did a no-look chip kick for Alex Goode to score in the corner.

But nobody was really interested in the wing battle between me and Nowellsy; all eyes were on Sam versus Luther in the centres. And when Sam got the ball, ran straight over the top of Luther and scored, there were audible groans. I thought to myself, *Well, that's Luther's World Cup over.* And so it was. Lanny told him that afternoon that he wouldn't be in the final squad, and everyone felt a bit dirty because the affair had been so drawn-out and public.

I've often wondered what would have happened had Luther done to Sam what Sam did to him. Would he have been picked instead? Or was the whole thing a sham?

The full squad was announced the following day – and I was in it. But I didn't really feel elated, I just felt relieved and exhausted. I'd spent the previous two months desperately trying to stay in the room, as had everyone else, and that doesn't make for a great environment. Everyone was out for themselves, and even natural non-conformists morphed into yes men. I think if Lanny had his time again, he'd have cut that squad down to 31 players a lot earlier, which would have made for a more relaxed, collective atmosphere.

You'd have thought the coaches would have let the axed players go straight home, their dreams having just been shattered.

Instead, they insisted on them taking part in one last training session. And it was a completely pointless fitness session, involving fireman carries and pushing sleds around. Even the players who had been picked couldn't be arsed with it, so you can imagine what the likes of Luther, Luke Cowan-Dickie, my old Quins mate Nick Easter and Danny Cipriani, who had all missed the cut, thought of it. At some point during the session, our backs coach Mike Catt had a pop at Cips for not trying hard enough, Cips said something back, and we all thought they were going to come to blows. Looking back, I think we all would have liked to have seen that fight.

○

It was painful having a ringside seat for Luther's long, drawn-out axing, but I never had any problems with Sam being around the place. He was a brilliant bloke and an absolute powerhouse of a rugby player, and if someone had told me to stop playing rugby league in Australia and come home to play in a World Cup for England, I'd have bitten their hand off, whether I thought I was up to it or not.

I think a few of the lads were concerned by the fact that he'd only played a handful of union games, but he was dynamite in training – quick, athletic, good hands, and as big as most of the forwards, even though he was playing as a back.

I was more worried about how drained a lot of the lads looked. Plus, quite a few of the forwards had lost weight because of the madness of Denver, which undermined the entire game plan, which was based on a physical pack beating the opposition forwards up.

By the time the final squad had been picked, we'd all been cooped up like chickens for almost two months. While other teams were based in cities and towns, Pennyhill Park was in the middle of nowhere in Surrey. Presumably, the idea was that we'd have our own space, away from the prying eyes of fans and the media (kind of understandable after what happened in New Zealand in 2011) but instead we felt trapped. We were climbing up the walls because we had nothing to do. If James Haskell hadn't been knocking around the place, the blokes he liked to call the 'bin-juice', who were unlikely to play much part in the tournament, might have lost their minds completely.

It's often said of Hask that you hear him before you see him, and I was hearing about him long before we first met as teenagers in the national academy, when Hask was being talked up as the next Lawrence Dallaglio. At 17 years old, when we was still at school, Hask was already a behemoth, a man. As a person, he seemed like everything I wasn't: a posh, loud rugby bloke who had attended one of the most expensive public schools in the country. He'd always been destined to play rugby for England, while I was a northerner who'd wanted to play football for England. I should have hated him. However, he's been one of my favourite human beings since day one.

No one wore worse clothes than Hask (baggy jeans with terrible trainers wherever he went) and no one told a story better. He'd walk into a room and have everyone laughing and shaking their heads in disbelief within seconds. And he didn't change even after he started winning trophies with Wasps and playing for England.

Some of my early England camps with him were completely bonkers. On Tuesday evenings, we'd all go for dinner at an Italian restaurant called Pazzia, which was about 20 minutes down the road from Pennyhill Park. One night, Dylan Hartley, Chris Ashton, Ben Foden and I were travelling behind Hask's bright red Range Rover. As we were pulling up to some traffic lights, Hask's car started filling up with what looked like green fog. Then he wound his window down, shouted 'Grenade!', and lobbed a smoke bomb onto the road. It rolled under another car and the smoke was going everywhere, to the extent that people were stopping their cars and getting out, to find out what the hell was going on. It was probably the biggest road traffic incident Bagshot has ever seen.

England were sponsored by Land Rover, and one day a load of their employees came to Pennyhill Park and asked us to customise our own cars. We all thought it was going to cost the earth, but they let us have these 5-litre supercharged Range Rover Autobiographies for £400 a month, plus a few quid extra for each added specification. The following week, 25 of these customised Range Rovers pulled up at the front gates of the hotel, which was probably a sign that we'd got a little bit too comfortable as a squad. I'll never forget Hask jumping out of his bright red Range Rover, tossing his keys to the valet and saying, 'Park the car over there, if you don't mind chief, then put the bags in my room ...' Then he fished a tenner out of his wallet, handed it to the valet and marched off, while the rest of us were doubled up laughing.

I, Hask and a few others spent an awful lot of time in the gym during that World Cup, getting more ripped than we'd ever been. The evening's entertainment was normally eating biscuits, watching the football or playing cards. We'd be playing in my room, which I shared with my old Quins buddy Joe Marler, and Jonny May would walk in, look at Joe and say, 'It's on.' That was the signal for Joe and Jonny to strip down and start wrestling on the bed. Joe is obviously miles bigger than Jonny, but Jonny would never give up. Some nights, they'd be at it for half an hour, while the rest of us did our best to ignore them. Jonny is one of the strangest people I've ever met, but also the funniest – he once thought he was possessed by a chicken and would randomly start clucking.

Meanwhile, Lanny seemed to be falling in on himself. He used to be a friendly, happy guy, but it reached the point where I'd walk past him in the corridor and he wouldn't even look at me, never mind say hello. The players knew we were in trouble just by seeing the toll the responsibility was taking on him. He looked like a ghost, as if all the life had been sucked out of him. It was sad to see.

Lanny was so worried about what the media were saying about us, while the players' attitude was, *Who cares what the media say about us? Let's identify what we're all about, practice, then go out and play that way.* But you could tell we hadn't identified what we were all about in our opening game against Fiji, which was pretty close until we scored two late tries. The reason we looked like we didn't know what we were doing is because we didn't. We'd spent too much time on fitness and not enough on skills and a game plan.

I was sitting next to Hask in the stands when we played Wales. We played okay in the first half, and I thought we'd beat them quite handily. But when Gareth Davies scored to give Wales the lead with nine minutes left, Hask turned to me and said, 'God, this is awful.' Then Robbo turned down a late shot at goal which would have levelled the game, asked George Ford to kick to the corner instead and our maul got pushed into touch – and the atmosphere turned toxic. Hask and I and the rest of the bin-juicers had to run to our cars because people were screaming abuse at us. I was thinking, *It wasn't our fault, we didn't play!* And it's not as if the lads who had played didn't try or hadn't put the effort in on the training ground – if anything, they'd been overworked.

The Stuart Lancaster regime was supposed to be about the fine details and leaving no stone unturned, but it had got so many big things wrong. I agreed with all the patriotism stuff in principle – emphasising our culture, what it meant to play for your country and making the English public proud of us again after 2011 – but Lanny spent far too much time on that sort of stuff and not enough time working out how to beat Wales and Australia.

We'd had that period in 2014 when we were playing fast, attacking rugby – which was also winning rugby for the most part – but we'd gone further and further into our shell the closer we got to the World Cup. Frustratingly, we had attack-minded lads having to play within themselves to fit into a conservative system, or not playing at all. It was as if we were playing not to lose, rather than playing to win, which seemed like madness to me.

I think the coaches fell between two stools, style-wise. Saracens had become the dominant team in the Premiership around that time, so maybe the coaches thought that their attritional brand of rugby was the way to go with England. However, we were struggling to impose ourselves up front because the forwards had got too trim (not a problem Sarries ever had) and we looked leggy against Fiji and Wales because of the Denver floggings. Maybe the lads could have run up and down the field 100 times, but they didn't look rugby fit. Meanwhile, New Zealand and Australia were playing some really good stuff, although it was also realistic stuff, involving plenty of kicking.

Poor Robbo was desolate after the Wales game and the lads really had to rally round him, especially his Quins team-mates who knew him best (I thought the criticism he got from the press and fans was over the top, because it wasn't exactly a straight-forward penalty attempt anyway). Sam Burgess got it in the neck as well, although I'm not sure why. He played fine, and as he's pointed out since, we were winning when he got hooked with ten minutes to go.

A more experienced coach would have viewed the predicament we were in as part and parcel of the job – our backs were against the wall, but we'd qualify for the quarter-finals if we beat Australia – but Lanny became even more subdued after the Wales game. I thought he could have mixed things up for Australia, but I was in the stands again. They were going to play things safe, pick the guys least likely to take risks and make mistakes, and I wasn't really that kind of player.

The Aussies blew us away, and they did it playing high-tempo, creative rugby, including some typically intricate training-ground moves. And I just kept thinking, *At least I could have offered something different.* I felt sorry for Sam as well, because he started the game on the bench. That made it look like Lanny held him partially responsible for the Wales defeat, when he'd actually played alright. God knows what Luther was thinking back at home.

The overriding emotion after losing to Australia was embarrassment, and the flak from journalists and fans was brutal. But I stand by the opinion that it wasn't the players' fault. The coaches were responsible for our preparation, fashioning the game plan and picking the team, and they got a lot of it wrong. I genuinely think that the same group of lads could have won the tournament given the talent we had. Instead, we became the first host country in the history of the World Cup not to advance to the knockout stages. What a terrible record to have, what a missed opportunity.

Lanny picked me for our final pool game against Uruguay, and I thought playing at Manchester City's ground would be quite a cool experience. However, despite there being talk from the coaches about displaying 'northern pride', there wasn't much enthusiasm from the players. The final training session was farcical, with every second pass going astray and people dropping balls left, right and centre. But at least Minty had a good game, scoring three tries in his final England appearance. Not bad for a bloke pushing 50.

We knew the RFU would be conducting an inquest after the tournament, and even while it was still going on a couple of lads joked about chucking the coaches under the bus. I didn't agree with leaking to the press – I was angry about not being picked for the first three games, but Lanny was a bloke I had known and respected for years. But the attitude of some of the boys was *Sod him*. A couple of 'anonymous' articles were published in the media – the lads involved know who they are – and I didn't hide my true feelings either. Whenever I was asked about our World Cup exit, I told the truth: poor preparation, wrong game plan, wrong selection.

Lanny resigned a couple of weeks after the World Cup final and I didn't see him again until a chance meeting in Dubai. Jodie and I were having dinner when I noticed Lanny and his wife sitting behind us. I said to Jodie, 'This could be really awkward.' But I eventually plucked up the courage to say hello and I'm glad I did. It's not as if we thrashed things out for hours over five bottles of wine, but I had my say, he had his and I think we patched things up. Saying that, I think Lanny will still be scaring me when I'm in my 70s.

Chapter 14

Eddie

I've come to believe that England's failure in 2015 wasn't really Lanny's fault. Of course he was going to take the job, just as Martin Johnson was going to take the job, so it's the fault of the RFU blazers who offered it to him. Lanny learnt an awful lot from that experience, as did Andy Farrell and the other lads, but coaching the England team shouldn't be a learning opportunity; it should be for people with proven track records at the highest level of the game.

I was delighted when Eddie Jones was appointed as England's head coach because he'd already proved himself to be one of the best operators in world rugby.

He was in charge of Australia when they lost the 2003 World Cup final to England, was part of South Africa's coaching team when they won the 2007 World Cup and masterminded Japan's astonishing upset of the Springboks in 2015. Plus, he was an attack-minded coach who liked to play the game fast, which suited me down to the ground.

Of course, Eddie had been at Saracens when they tried to sign me back in 2006, so I was a little bit worried that he'd hold that against me. But shortly after he was given the England job, I asked his agent if that was good news for me, and he texted back, 'He's a big fan, I think you'll be okay.' I met Eddie after a Quins game in early 2016 and he was really nice, asking loads of questions about me and my life, and he then picked me for the Six Nations.

I'll never forget his maiden team meeting. We were all still desolate after the World Cup, but one of the first things he said to us was, 'I know things didn't go well last year, but there are some brilliant players in this room. And I genuinely think this group can win the World Cup in four years' time.' People had been telling us how bad we were for months, so that was exactly what we needed to hear. At that moment, I thought the sun shone out of his behind.

Eddie was also very honest about what it would take for us to win the World Cup. He said our skills needed to be a lot better. He said we needed to be a lot fitter. He said we needed to be a lot tougher. He said he and his team were going to take us to some very dark places. And if I remember rightly, he finished his speech with, 'If you're ready to do the work, stay in the room. If you're not, fuck off now.' Nobody left.

I liked his brutal bluntness because it meant I knew exactly where I stood and what I needed to do, which was to work harder than I'd ever done. And it soon became clear that Eddie's knowledge was second to none, because he watched so much rugby and studied games in minute detail. But it's not as if he needed to reinvent the wheel with England. As he said, we already had brilliant players, we just needed a style of play that suited us. And once we nailed that style down and started winning, the self-belief would return.

Training was every bit as horrific as Eddie had suggested it would be. He'd have a clock on a big screen, counting down from 60 minutes. I'd look up at it, see that we'd only been going for 20 minutes and think, *I'm already wrecked, there's no way I'm gonna make it to the end.* But I'd carry on running because I knew I'd be out on my ear if I didn't. I swear he had someone messing with that clock because it would get stuck on 20 minutes to go for 10 minutes, or suddenly skip back up from 7 minutes to 15. It was physical, fast, ultra-competitive and incredibly uncomfortable, but Eddie's mantra was, 'The harder you train, the easier the game will feel at the weekend.'

Eddie very quickly worked out who really wanted to be there and who wasn't cut out for that level of ruthlessness. And because he had so many players to choose from, a luxury he'd never had before at international level, he had no qualms about binning people. If someone wasn't up to the task, or was under the weather or injured, it would be a case of, 'Right, step aside, let's get the next bloke in and see what he can do.' It was a very serious, survival-of-the-fittest environment, and not a particularly healthy one long-term, but as long as I was being picked, and we were winning, I was all in.

Robbo having the captaincy taken away was probably the best thing that could have happened to him, because he went to a dark place after the World Cup and his Quins team-mates spent the following season trying to pull him out of his slump. Now he could focus on just being a rugby player again, without having to deal with the media scrutiny and ceremonial duties.

I ended up feeling sorrier for Dylan Hartley, Robbo's successor as England captain. Dyls wasn't the obvious choice because he'd had a few disciplinary issues in his career and was quite abrasive and rough around the edges. But I think Eddie saw a bit of himself in Dyls and used him as an example for the rest of us to follow. That meant pushing him to the absolute limit, physically and mentally.

I recall wandering down for breakfast one morning and finding Dyls wrestling with defence coach Paul Gustard. Dyls had blood all over his face and was drenched in sweat, and they'd been at it since 6am. As far as Eddie was concerned, those early morning wrestling sessions served two purposes: one, to get Dyls fitter; two, to make Dyls's team-mates think, *If this is what the skipper is doing at 6am, maybe I should be doing something similar.* I certainly felt a bit guilty tucking into my scrambled eggs on toast while Dyls and Gussy were grappling in the corner of the room. I don't know how Dyls dealt with being Eddie's example for so long, but he just cracked on and never complained. And most of the rest of the lads fell into line behind him.

We worked hard at Quins, but nothing like under Eddie. Training with Quins involved a lot of condition-based games, but Eddie's sessions were twice as frenetic with full contact thrown in. Every session was like playing a Test, and while I was getting fitter and fitter, I spent a lot of time feeling horrific. Lads would drag themselves off the pitch after a session and head straight to the ice bath or sauna, hoping to recover from whatever knocks they'd taken. But ice baths and saunas don't work miracles and the injuries came thick and fast.

If Eddie was picking you, you liked him, Hask being the perfect example of that. If he wasn't, you didn't, which is where Danny Cipriani comes in. Eddie wasn't one to sugarcoat anything – if he didn't think you were good enough or you weren't pulling your weight, you were out on your ear and that was the end of it – and he couldn't care less what anyone thought about him or his methods, whether that be players, staff, media or fans.

Eddie was constantly playing mind games. For example, he'd ask players if they were tired, to which the correct answer was no. And woe betide anyone who answered yes. If we were having a few beers and someone wasn't drinking, he might say, 'Mate, if you don't want a beer, you may as well leave.'

We called Tuesdays 'Test match Tuesdays' because it would always be a ridiculously hard session. After one of these sessions, Eddie wandered up to Northampton prop Kieran Brookes and asked, 'How did you find it?' Brooksy was a gentle giant, just a nice, softly spoken lad with no side to him, and he replied, 'Yeah, it was tough, but I enjoyed it. I feel good.' Eddie shot back, 'You've obviously not worked fucking hard enough, mate.' After the following week's Tuesday Test match session, Eddie wandered up to Brooksy and asked him the same question. Brooksy thought for a moment, then replied, 'Absolutely exhausted, one of the hardest sessions I've ever done.' To which Eddie responded, 'You're obviously not fucking fit enough, mate.'

He could be excruciatingly cutting. One day, Brooksy showed up with his hair shaved down the sides and waxed on top, and Eddie said to him, 'What the fuck is that on your head?' Brooksy was completely lost for words. Then Eddie pulled out a £20 note, gave it to Brooksy and said, 'Mate, go and change that haircut, otherwise you ain't coming back tomorrow.'

It was all quite weird. For a start, it was just a normal haircut (I can only assume that Eddie preferred his props to be shaven-headed or bald). Second, everyone was laughing, albeit nervously, because we didn't know if he was being serious or not. Remember what it felt like when someone was being bullied at school and you were just glad it wasn't you? That was the vibe.

After the meeting, Brooksy asked everyone what he should do. Some of us thought it might be a test and that Brooksy should give Eddie the 20 quid back, as a sign that he wasn't to be pushed around. But some of us thought he should just borrow someone's clippers and shave it all off. In the end, Brooksy opted for a crew cut, not that it did much for his England prospects:

he only played for Eddie once, and never again after the 2016 Six Nations.

We used to say to each other, 'Just remember, boys, everything's a test,' as if we were characters in a dystopian novel. We'd get given a form to fill out and we'd have to say to any new boys, 'Don't put anything on there that he could use against you.' If the form asked how you felt, you'd say you felt fine, even if your leg was falling off. Because if you didn't, you'd be worried about Eddie calling you into his office and asking if you wanted to go home. Did Eddie rule by fear? Of course he did, everyone was bloody terrified of him. Jonny May probably summed up the situation best: he'd walk in for breakfast, head down, muttering, 'Expect anything today, boys, expect anything ...'

$\bigcirc$

Eddie would tell us what was going to happen in such a matter-of-fact way that we couldn't help believing it. He kept telling us that we'd win the Six Nations, which seemed like a long shot seeing as every other team apart from Italy had got further than us at the World Cup. But we didn't just win the Six Nations, we also won England's first Grand Slam since 2003. It was actually quite spooky how Eddie would seemingly predict the future and we'd go out and do it.

Eddie said all the right things to me before that tournament: 'be a leader,' 'play with your normal high-tempo and run teams ragged' and 'play on top of teams and don't let defences recover.' And when he picked me to start his first game in charge against Scotland at Murrayfield, I was buzzing.

Every coach and every player accepts that you just have to win your first game in a Six Nations; it doesn't matter how you do it. So

Eddie's mindset before our trip to Edinburgh was, 'Let's go up there, get the win, and get out of Scotland as soon as possible.' Smash and grab, in other words. As it turned out, George Kruis scored the first try of Eddie's reign, Jack Nowell added a second after the break and, while we only beat them 15–9, Scotland were never really in it.

I thought I played well and would be starting for the rest of the tournament, but I was relegated to the bench for our second game against Italy. But unlike most of the times I'd been dropped before by England, Eddie made it quite palatable. He said to me, 'You played well, mate, you've just got a different role this week. You're gonna be on the park at the end, running their defence ragged and winning us the game.' I thought, *Well, if you put it like that, no dramas.*

Looking back, it's just more evidence of Eddie's genius: he really just wanted Youngsy on the pitch for longer than me, but he managed to make me feel more valuable than ever. While for other players being dropped was the end of the world – 'Oh my God, I'm on the bench, I'm never gonna play for England again!' – I wasn't bothered. I'd still get to do everything the starting XV did, I'd still get paid the same, I'd still win a cap, but I'd only have to play for 20 or 30 minutes, I'd get to run at tired defences and I'd hopefully be on the pitch when we won.

A small gang of us so-called finishers would even get together and talk about how we could hurt the opposition late on. In truth, it's often difficult to impose yourself on a game as a replacement, not least because you're usually just one of a raft of changes, which can make everything a bit disjointed. But at the time, I bought Eddie's pitch hook, line and sinker.

Eddie gave me the same talk before the wins over Ireland and Wales, both at Twickenham, before suddenly changing tack and picking me to start our final game against France in Paris. 'This is the game for you,' he said to me, and I replied, 'You've used me off the bench for the last three games and it's worked, but now you're changing things up with a Grand Slam on the line. How come?' He just reiterated that I was better suited to start and Youngsy was better suited to finish things off, and all I could do was thank him.

Eddie left most of the pre-match changing room chat to the players, but he would shake everybody's hand and offer a nugget of information just before we went out. And I'll never forget what he said to me that day at the Stade de France: 'Mate, just watch out for their lazy defenders at the breakdown, especially their props on the blind side of the breakdown. I think you could get some pay there.'

Lo and behold, Jonathan Joseph took the ball into contact 11 minutes in, a few of the lads cleared out the ruck and I spotted a gaping hole on the blind side of the ruck where their prop Jefferson Poirot should have been – I ran straight through it, handing Poirot off in the process.

It's not often you get the ball 40 metres out in international rugby and know you're going to score, but their nine was holding the blind side, their full-back was covering the left wing and I dived over unopposed under the posts. It was probably the biggest match I'd ever played in, and my mum, dad and wife were in the crowd, so it was a proper pinch-me moment. And walking back to the halfway line, I thought, *How the hell did Eddie know that was going to happen? He must be some kind of psychic.*

Maybe I'd have scored that try even if Eddie hadn't said anything about lazy props at the breakdown, or maybe Eddie's little nugget had made me score it. I'm thinking the latter. And when Youngsy came on as the finisher just after half-time, he did brilliantly as well, including chipping through for Anthony Watson to score.

A lot of the lads involved in that Six Nations triumph had been through some bad times together, from blown Grand Slams to World Cup fiascos, which made it all the more special. And while there was hardly anyone left in the stadium when we lifted the trophy, that wasn't going to dampen our spirits.

Dyls had done a brilliant job of keeping us in check before then. After every game, he'd say, 'Right lads, no whooping and hollering when we're presented with the trophy.' A few of us lads wanted to have some beers in Rome after beating Italy – who wouldn't? – but Dyls said to us, 'No, no, we'll just go back to the hotel. We're just ticking these games off, that's what Eddie wants. But when we win the big one at the end, we'll go mad.' On the one hand I was thinking, *Yeah, cool, I suppose that makes sense*, but on the other hand I was thinking, *We're missing out on some really good nights here …*

Eddie and Dyls were keeping in mind something I'd forgotten, namely that opportunities to win a Grand Slam don't come along very often. And if you do manage to win one, you might not get the chance to win another. History beckoned, and if we managed to pull it off, we'd remember it for ever. But we'd only pull off the Grand Slam if we retained our focus throughout.

Jamie George and I had been appointed social secretaries, although we hadn't had a lot to do on that front since Eddie took over. But in the lead-up to that France game, I said to our team manager, Charlotte, 'If we win the Grand Slam, can we go big? As in really, really big?'

'Don't worry, Danny,' she replied, 'it's all taken care of.' So after the obligatory changing room madness, we spent some time with our families before heading to a nightclub. Eddie's parting words to us were, 'Celebrate hard, but keep your heads down.'

It was gone midnight by the time we arrived at the nightclub, where someone greeted us off the bus and led us through a side door. I was expecting some dingy little dive, but as we were filing in, the music stopped, a spotlight fell on the doorway and the DJ screamed, 'Ladies and gentlemen, let's give a big welcome to the England rugby team! Grand Slam champions!' They played 'God Save the Queen' as we were taking to the stage, while red rose graphics flashed all over the place. I felt like a movie star – and it was wonderful. But I also remember thinking, *This isn't very heads down, like Eddie had wanted.*

That was one of my best ever nights in rugby. Everyone was just so high on life and all that horrible training Eddie had put us through was briefly forgotten. We'd won the Grand Slam: that was all that mattered.

There are pictures somewhere of Billy Vunipola with a big smile on his face and a tablecloth around his waist, because his trousers had split. Paul Gustard and I ended up in an upstairs room filled with those Swiss balls that women sit on during pregnancy. Gussy was 40, I was almost 30, but we were booting these balls around for about ten minutes, in the dark, like a couple of little kids. We might have spent the whole night in there had a security guy not rumbled us.

Eddie has to take a lot of the credit for that Grand Slam. To take a bunch of lads who were on their knees after what happened at the 2015 World Cup and turn them into a side that suddenly looked like world-beaters in the space of a few months was some feat. I'd liken it to someone taking on a wreck of a boat, getting it shipshape and winning races in it. The RFU had chosen well.

Maybe another coach could have done the same, but the fact that Eddie had been there and done it counted for a lot. When he spoke, we listened and, more importantly, we believed. And Eddie was particularly good at channelling all that collective heartache and all those chip-laden shoulders into something positive. Yes, he said, you can prove a lot of people wrong, but only if you work like dogs. Which is exactly what we did.

All good coaches are lucky coaches, and Eddie had some very strong characters in his ranks. George Ford, a fly-half who never gets enough praise, was brilliant in that tournament, pulling the strings throughout, while my old Quins mate Browny was a rock at full-back. Meanwhile, Saracens lock Maro Itoje had quickly established himself as an integral part of Eddie's team, and while he was different from the rest of the lads in some respects – into art, history and politics – he was every bit as focused on being the best rugby player he could possibly be. Nowadays, Maro will let his hair down at the end of a tournament, maybe with a couple of Malibu and Cokes, but back then it was very much rugby, books and bed.

I first met Maro on England's tour of New Zealand in 2014, when I was asked to present awards at some local games. Maro was down there with England Under-20s (he captained the side that won the Junior World Championship) and he was already a colossus. Most people probably thought that he was the England veteran and I was the under-20s kid. I remember thinking that he had something different about him, a bit of an aura, and when I spoke to a couple of the Sarries lads about him, they confirmed that he was already something special, and might go on to be one of the all-time greats.

Behind Maro in the pack was Billy Vunipola, who was probably at the peak of his powers in the early part of Eddie's reign. I've seen photos of a ten-year-old Billy, sat next to a load of his classmates, and he looks about six years older than them. He grew up to be a serious specimen who made yards for fun, and he was very skilful, which is a deadly combination in a number eight. Billy could be a bit of a nightmare on the beer, as his widely reported recent double-tasering in Mallorca demonstrates (the first shot hit him in the wallet, or so I'm told), but he was a great lad who enjoyed himself on and off the pitch.

I'd known Dan Cole since our England Under-16 days, and while I was never sure what he was up to in the front row – what do they do in there? – apparently he was amazing at it. He was one of the guys in Eddie's ranks who rarely got the plaudits but without whom the team couldn't function properly.

Not many Englishmen can say they scored a try in a Grand Slam-winning game, but me and Coley share that distinction, and how he's managed to last as long as he has playing as a prop is beyond me. He's still being picked for England at the time of writing, 14 years after he won his first cap.

Usually on the other side of the front row was Joe Marler, who is a devastating player as well as a huge personality. Like Coley, he's apparently a tremendous scrummager, and the power and technique of his tackling was second to none. I watched him putting his body through hell for Quins and England, day in, day out, and he never broke.

But perhaps more frightening than that is the number of times I've seen the man's penis, sometimes at very close range. I've roomed with Joe hundreds of times, in hotels all over the world, and his penis has often doubled as an alarm clock. I'll be sound asleep, dreaming about fluffy kittens or some such, only to be rudely awoken by Joe's flaccid member slapping me in the face.

Some of Joe's banter is also dangerously near the knuckle. Joe, our Quins team-mate Mark Lambert (the self-professed 'Chairman of Harlequins' and one of the best club men you could ever wish to have) and I were always really close, and we invented a game that consisted of us saying whatever we wanted about each other's wives. The game had rules: while Joe, Lammy and I could say whatever we wanted, without the need for an apology, if anyone else heard it and laughed, they'd have to apologise; or they could sign up for the game, which would mean agreeing to their wives being talked about in the most horrific terms. Funnily enough, nobody did.

Occasionally, Joe would say nice things about my and Lammy's wives, such as wanting to take them out for a nice dinner followed by a stroll along the river. But his story wouldn't normally end there. In case you were wondering, our wives were aware of the game, although I'm not sure if that makes it more or less acceptable.

But his penis alarm calls and inappropriate comments about my wife aside, I loved, and still love, that man like a brother (although had his member not been flaccid, I might feel differently). There's just so much to admire about the man besides his rugby prowess. He had a few anger issues earlier in his career, but he managed to get on top of that, and you have to salute his bravery for speaking publicly about his mental health, because I know that's helped a lot of people, including himself. Seeing him with his wife, Daisy, and his four amazing kids always cheers me up, as does the fact that his hair is falling out in clumps.

Eddie isn't one to rest on his laurels, and we were back to be flogged on our summer tour of Australia. He allowed us a couple of nights on the piss, but things were so grim in training that we really needed to bring some levity to off-field proceedings. It was on that tour that Jamie and I earned our nicknames of Ant and Dec. I imagine we played a similar role in Eddie's regime to the soldiers who entertained their fellow troops in the Second World War.

When we weren't training, Jamie, Elliot Daly, who got lumbered with all the admin and logistics, and I spent most of our time making daft videos or thinking up game shows. We should have been getting paid extra for it.

Our first show was titled *England's Got No Talent,* and it soon turned weird. Jamie and I had spent hundreds of pounds on prizes out of our own pockets, appointed a judging panel and given about ten of the younger lads two days to come up with an act. At these sorts of events, all kinds of shenanigans take place, from drinking a pint of piss to someone putting a condom up their nose and pulling it out of their mouth. I'd even witnessed one player trying to see how many pencils he could fit up his arse (and making the mistake of inserting them lead-end first). Things got a bit out of hand on this occasion, leading Dyls to close the show early. There were a few boos from the lads, but I think Dyls was worried about CCTV leaks and the subsequent newspaper headlines.

We also did a couple of shows titled *I'm an England Player ... Get Me Out of Here!* Jamie and I dressed up as Steve Irwin, gathered all the lads in a room – without telling them what was coming – and a woman we'd hired from the zoo came in with an arsenal of freaky animals. She had snakes, scorpions, frogs and giant spiders, and people were screaming and squealing like small children. Anyone who'd done anything stupid on tour had to hold one of these creatures, and while Nowellsy ran out of the room when the first snake was revealed, never to return, some of the lads' faces were a picture of joy.

Perhaps the ultimate tourist was Hask. It didn't matter what time of the day it was – early morning, before training, after training, breakfast, lunch, dinner, just before bed – Hask would be holding court. He'd be going on about his latest indiscretion, giving his opinion on some current affair or laying into someone about their hair or something stupid they'd said, and 15 of his team-mates would be hanging on his every word. It's impossible to remember all the funny stuff Hask has said and done because he was on the ball pretty much every day. Someone could mention the weather to Hask and 20 seconds later 15 blokes would be doubled up laughing. We'd be sick of him by the end of the day, but we'd all want him to be there again the following morning. More accurately, we'd *need* him there, because he made everything less serious.

If you asked Eddie to name his five favourite players, I'm certain Hask would be one of them. Not only was Hask fully on board with Eddie's training methods (he's one of the hardest workers I've ever seen), but he was also able to banter with Eddie, which no other player dared to do. Eddie would make some cutting remark, Hask would fire back and Eddie would fall about laughing. On a deeper level, Hask is quite an insecure bloke, by his own admission, and he desperately wants people to like him. So when Eddie showed him a bit of love and made him one of the leaders of the group, which no previous England coach had done, Hask gave him absolutely everything.

Hask and Joe Marler had a curious relationship; they reminded me of two silverback gorillas circling each other in the jungle. They respected each other, and kind of liked each other, but neither could quite work out what the other was about.

I was on the field when Joe squirted water at Hask in a Quins–Wasps game, which was one of the funniest things I've ever seen. First Hask put Joe in a Vulcan death grip, then he grassed Joe up to the referee. Listening to him complain about Joe squirting him with water and pulling his scrum cap down, I couldn't help thinking, *Mate, you couldn't sound more like a private schoolboy if you tried.* What the cameras didn't pick up was me squirting Hask with water as he trudged from the field after being shown a yellow card. In my defence, I had no idea that Joe had already done that, but Hask gave me a long, hard look of pure hatred and I thought he was going to lamp me.

As odd as some of the entertainment was (we honestly would have preferred a bit of tap dancing), we thought we had to come up with something to keep the lads sane. And I think it played a small part in the 3–0 whitewash of the Wallabies, the first time England had beaten Australia in a Test series.

That victory surprised the media and fans, but it wasn't really a surprise to us. Australia had reached the World Cup final the previous autumn, but we thought we had the better players and were fitter and more physical, which is why we were openly talking about whitewashing them beforehand.

The first Test was not only the first time we'd beaten the Wallabies in Brisbane, but a game in which we scored our largest ever points total against them, winning 29–38. The second Test in Melbourne clinched the series: we won 7–23. The third Test in Sydney, which we won 40–44, condemned Australia to their first whitewash in a three-Test series since losing 3–0 to South Africa in 1971. Hask repaid Eddie's love by winning man-of-the-series, his fellow flanker Robbo looked like his old self again, our backs played fast and wide and were a constant threat, we scored a hatful of tries and Owen Farrell couldn't miss from the tee. As for me, I was still happy with my cameos.

Jodie and I got married on our return to England, on 23 July 2016 (I've got the date tattooed on my calf, so I'll never forget). We hired a classic vintage car to bring Jodie to the church, but the bloody thing broke down. I was stood at the front of the church for ages, wondering what the hell was going on. When my brother, who was my best man, told me her car had broken down, I didn't believe him – Jodie is one of those girls who is late for everything. Thankfully, we'd also hired a gospel choir, and I persuaded them to sing a few songs to keep the guests entertained. When Jodie finally arrived, an hour late, I thought I was going to start crying. She looked absolutely stunning. Luckily, Blake, who was a page boy, ran straight towards me and I broke into a massive grin instead.

There were 150 guests and the reception was held in a beautiful old building that was essentially a massive conservatory. It happened to be the hottest day of the year, so the 30 rugby lads, all soaked through with sweat, weren't too happy with me. Still, it was one hell of a do, and seeing my mates from Leeds drinking with Zara Tindall, wife of my old England team-mate Mike and a real-life princess, was surreal. The following day, we jetted off to Dubai for our honeymoon, which was like jumping from a frying pan and into a fire, at least as far as the temperature was concerned. You can't do much sunbathing when it's 45°C.

We followed up the Australia tour with four straight wins in the autumn internationals, over South Africa, Samoa, Argentina and Australia (again), which made us only the second team in the professional era to go unbeaten in a calendar year. And in 2017, we very nearly won the Grand Slam again.

That was the year of one of the strangest games I ever played in, against Italy at Twickenham. I can laugh about it now, but at the time I was quite annoyed.

Eddie had picked me to start for the first time in ages, and before the game he said to me, 'Danny, this is your chance to show what you can do.' I had visions of me carving up the Italian defence and running in a hat-trick in a massive win, but my old Quins coach Conor O'Shea, who had left the Stoop and taken charge of Italy at the end of the previous season, had different ideas.

Conor actually phoned Uges the day before the game, while Uges was sat next to me at the barber's. When Uges told Conor he was with me, Conor said, 'Make sure he knows the rules.' I thought he was just messing around, but it turned out that he was being semi-serious.

It was a lovely spring match day, and I was champing at the bit in the changing room beforehand. But after two or three rucks – or, more correctly, what I assumed were rucks – I genuinely thought I was seeing things. This Italian lad kept standing next to George Ford at fly-half, so I was obviously wondering why the referee wasn't whistling for offside. Then it started to sink in that he couldn't be offside because his team-mates weren't competing at the breakdown.

We'd talked about the possibility of a team doing this against us, but to be honest, I'd never really understood why anyone would. And I certainly didn't expect Conor to come up with something so negative because he had a reputation as one of the game's most attack-minded coaches. Then again, Italy were leading 10–5 at the break, so it must have made perfect sense to them, even though it was one of the worst halves of rugby anyone had witnessed (although there was one moment of comedy when the mic picked up Hask asking referee Romain Poite what a ruck was, and Poite replied, 'I am sorry. I am a referee, not a coach').

When we got back to the changing room, Eddie said, 'Lads, we've talked about this. Start picking and going straight down the middle of them. That way, we can grab defenders and pull them into a ruck whether they like it or not.' We finally got a handle on things in the second half, scoring five tries and winning the game quite comfortably in the end. I took great pleasure in my tap-and-go try, although I still hadn't quite forgiven Conor when he went to shake my hand after the game. I said to him, 'Mate, that was probably my only start in the tournament and you did that to me. Why England, Conor? Why me? I was like the son you never had!' Conor apologised and said they had to try something different after thumping home defeats in their first two games, and then he gave me a big cuddle. We laugh about that game to this day.

Our game against Scotland that year was one of my favourites ever, and not just because we massacred them 61–21 and I scored two tries off the bench.

Scotland wing Tim Visser, who was actually born and raised in the Netherlands and went to school in England, had joined Quins a couple of years earlier. He was a legend of a bloke – very Dutch in his bluntness, walked around everywhere naked, didn't give a damn about rugby convention. The first time I met him was at an England academy camp. He got on the bus, marched straight down the aisle and sat right in the middle of the back seat. Some of us lads had been at the academy for a couple of years, and we had no idea who this weird Dutch kid was and why he was even playing rugby. I thought that maybe he was a bit full of himself, but actually he just didn't care. If someone wanted to get upset about him sitting in the middle of the back seat, sod 'em.

Viss was a great club man – he brought a lot of energy to the changing room and took the piss out of anything that moved, including the coaches. But he suddenly turned a bit Scottish when he started getting picked by Scotland. Before that year's Six Nations game, he did a newspaper interview, in which he said Scotland didn't fear England, didn't fear Twickenham and that they were confident of pulling off one of the greatest wins in their history. One of the Quins boys sent it to me and after I'd finished reading it, I thought, *Brilliant, he couldn't have written a better pre-match team-talk if he'd tried.*

We thought we'd beat Scotland comfortably, but we didn't think we'd beat them by that many. Jonathan Joseph, one of the silkiest players I ever shared a pitch with, sliced through their defence to score after just two minutes and completed his hat-trick shortly after half-time. Everything was working for us and Scotland weren't at the races, and midway through the second half I was itching to get on and grab a slice of the fun.

I'd been out there for about ten minutes when Billy Vunipola peeled off the back of a line-out and put me in for a try. That was a training-ground move, and the ball was meant to go to Ben Te'o, but I nicked the ball off him and crashed over from close range. That's how bad their defending was that day.

I scored my second try in added time, and this time it was Billy's brother, Mako Vunipola, who provided the assist. It was another one of those rare occasions when there were no defenders around me and I could really enjoy it, although some people probably thought my big, loopy dive just made me look like a twat. Wonderfully, a snap of me mid-dive, with Viss in the background, was included in the *Sunday Telegraph*'s pictures of the day. Every time England have played Scotland since, I've posted that picture on social media and tagged Viss in it. I'll probably still be reminding him about it when we're in our 90s.

By the time of our final game against Ireland in Dublin, we'd won 18 games in a row, equalling New Zealand's international record, and 11 consecutive Six Nations games, also a record. No team had won back-to-back Grand Slams in the Six Nations era, and England only did it once, in 1991–92, in the Five Nations era. So we had a lot to play for, and were crazy excited.

Sometimes in sport, as in life, you don't understand what's happening at the time. Only with the benefit of hindsight could I see that Eddie's regime was starting to creak, because it didn't feel like us that day. When we should have been razor sharp, given how much was at stake, all that flogging on the training ground had left us mentally cooked. Physically we were still a match for the Irish, but our minds weren't quite on it. And they have to be on it when you're up against a brilliant side who are hellbent on wrecking all your dreams.

Naturally, we England lads were massively disappointed not to have won back-to-back Grand Slams and extend our record-breaking winning streak, but Dyls pulled us all together before the trophy presentation and said, 'Lads, remember where we were two years ago. Now we're about to lift our second Six Nations trophy in a row. We've lost one game in our last 19. We deserve to enjoy this moment.' He was right. I'd have loved our winning run to go on a bit longer, but I was still proud of what we'd done. So I made sure to smile when Dyls lifted the trophy, and we all had a bloody good night out in Dublin.

Chapter 15

The Grinder

I was gutted when Conor announced he was leaving Quins. Not only had he led us to our first Premiership title in 2012, and the domestic cup the following year, but he'd also created a joyful, stimulating environment to work in.

Conor really was like a second father to me, and lots of other players besides, so there was a lot of sadness around the place, as well as a lot of worry. Who could possibly replace a man like Conor? How different would the place be without him? Would the new regime be anywhere near as much fun?

We only managed to finish seventh in the Premiership in Conor's last season (2015–16), but we did have a chance to send him off with a trophy, having booked a place against Montpellier in the final of the Challenge Cup.

A few days before the game, I received a call from Conor that stopped me in my tracks. Our young prop Seb Adeniran-Olule, a great talent who had played a few games for the first team, had passed away. The news made rugby seem a bit pointless, and there was nothing we could do to make things better for Seb's family. However, we now had an extra responsibility to win the thing.

Montpellier were one hell of a side, including fly-half Demetri Catrakilis, another one of those ridiculously gifted South Africans who never played for the Springboks. Catrakilis, who was joining us the following season, was on fire in Lyon, and while Snapper's goalkicking kept us in touch for most of the game, and Marland Yarde scored a late try, they ran out 26–19 winners.

We actually had a chance to level the scores in added time, but our replacement fly-half Ben Botica decided to kick the ball long and they booted it into touch to end the game. Bots was moving to Montpellier the following season, and the winners of the Challenge Cup automatically qualified for the Champions Cup, so the craic afterwards – once the heartbreak had eased – was that he'd done it on purpose, while Catrakilis's reward for playing out of his skin was appearing in the Challenge Cup for us again. We were obviously only winding Bots up, but Minty, who wasn't one to pull his punches, went straight up to him and said, 'What the hell were you thinking?' Poor Bots looked crushed, and all he could say was, 'Mate, I don't know. I just had a moment …'

I was skipper that season, so I hadn't just wanted to win that final for Conor, Seb and the rest of the lads, I also wanted to win it for my own sake. I'd never had that moment of lifting a trophy on TV, with fireworks going off in the background and glitter falling from the sky, and perhaps I never would.

Being captain, the chief executive, David Ellis, told me to speak to as many players as possible and find out who they wanted as Conor's successor. I thought that was a great idea and I threw myself into the project with vigour, diligence and seriousness (I only wish I'd put that much effort into my schoolwork). And after spending weeks canvassing the opinions of quite a few lads – veterans, academy boys, players halfway between the two – the overwhelming consensus was that the new man needed to have a similar mindset to Conor. That meant first, a great bloke who was committed to the traditional Quins attacking way; second, he needed to have experience of the Premiership or another top

European league; and third, most importantly, he needed to come from outside the club, because while we thought our coaches were great, we didn't think any of them would have been up to the job of director of rugby, and we also thought we needed a new voice to freshen things up a bit.

A couple of the newspapers reported that Quins' senior players had vetoed Stuart Lancaster, but that was a distortion of the truth. The players had no power of veto, so the ultimate decision wasn't ours, it was the board's. But it's fair to say that we didn't think that Lanny was the right fit for the club, for stylistic reasons more than anything else. And the same went for quite a few names that came up.

I was quite proud of all the work I'd put in, and David seemed delighted as well. He told me he'd take our recommendations to the board, that some top names had already applied for the job (one of the rumoured applicants was Scott Robertson, who is now head coach of the All Blacks) and that they'd start conducting interviews soon. I remember one of his lines verbatim: 'We're scouring the world to find the best coach.'

A couple of weeks later, David phoned me and said, 'Danny, just to let you know, we've found our guy.'

'Wow, awesome,' I replied, 'who have you got?'

'We realised the best person for the job was right under our noses,' said David. 'John Kingston.' My heart sank.

'David,' I said, 'what was the point of me speaking to all the players? We all love John Kingston, he's a brilliant coach, which is exactly why he needs to carry on coaching. The players will not respond well if you tell them that you've scoured the world and then given the job to a guy who was already here, and things will not work out with John as director of rugby.' When David told me that JK had interviewed better than everyone else, I said, 'Of course he did, because he's been here for ages, he loves the club, and he's one of the smartest blokes I've ever met.' (JK played in three Varsity matches for Cambridge.)

David thanked me for my feedback, then said they were going to hire JK anyway. I'll never forget the last thing I said to him on that call: 'David, I don't want to speak out of turn here, but in a year or so's time, I think you're going to come back to me and say, "I got this wrong."'

The best coaches coach: they're on the training ground with the players, watching, teaching, motivating, improving their skills and tactical awareness. But being a director of rugby involves running the whole club: the academy, the loan system, player recruitment and contracts, team ethos, team selection – mostly stuff that takes place in offices and meeting rooms.

I suspect most coaches know the difference, but ambition gets the better of them. They think that becoming a director of rugby is the natural career progression. They like the idea of being the main man, of making the big decisions, of earning a few extra quid a month. Then again, there's not huge amounts of money in club coaching, so I don't blame them on that front.

It's not as if I was itching to walk back into David Ellis's office and tell him I told him so, but I could see very early on in JK's tenure as director of rugby that things weren't going to work. We finished sixth in JK's first season in charge and a lot of players weren't happy with the environment and the way we were playing. I think it's fair to say that he'd lost the changing room already.

It didn't help that there were a couple of characters in our squad chipping away at morale, one of them being winger Marland Yarde.

Marland had so much potential – he was strong, seriously quick and a lethal finisher, as he'd proved by scoring eight tries in 13 England appearances – but he could be an unreliable team-mate. He'd be late and sometimes he wouldn't turn up at all. When I was captain, I'd always say to the players, 'Go for a few beers at the weekend, but make sure you're in on time on Monday. You owe that to the rest of the boys.' But Marland would disappear for days.

This happened quite a few times, and it began to undermine JK's authority. But for whatever reason, JK kept defending him. Marland had loads of excuses, including the time he missed a particularly brutal fitness session.

Even when Marland said that a 24-hour sleep caused him to miss a team function, JK was still defending him. I had to say to him, 'Mate, I think you're getting this one wrong. You need to listen to the boys.' In the end, Marland's time ran out and JK had to give him the boot a month or so into the season.

○

I wondered if playing for a struggling Quins side had counted against me when the squad for the 2017 Lions tour to New Zealand was picked.

I wasn't at all surprised when they chose Youngsy, Conor Murray and Welshman Rhys Webb as their three nines, because they were all regular starters for their countries. Then Youngsy dropped out for personal reasons. His sister-in-law Tiff, who was married to Youngsy's brother Tom, had recently found out she had terminal cancer. I was very close with both the Youngs brothers and Tiff. It was devastating news for all involved, and I felt terribly sad for them.

Although I hated the circumstances that had led to this opening on the team, I thought my new role as Eddie's finisher-in-chief might be right up the coaches' alleys. And if anyone was going to be picked ahead of me, surely it would be Gareth Davies, given that Lions head coach Warren Gatland and his assistants Neil Jenkins and Rob Howley were also his coaches with Wales. So when Gatland's scrum coach Graham Rowntree, who was also Quins' forwards coach, told me that Greig Laidlaw was replacing Youngsy, it was tough to take. It was Mike Blair in 2009 all over again, and I felt quite aggrieved.

No, I hadn't been playing that well for Quins, but by my way of thinking, if I had been Scottish, I'd have been playing for Scotland ahead of Greig Laidlaw. This is slightly roundabout logic, I know, but it made perfect sense to me. And while I didn't want to descend into a state of bitterness and cynicism, I couldn't help thinking that Greig had been picked simply to bump up the Scottish contingent, only two Scotsmen having made the original squad. Then again, Greig had been a great player and leader for Scotland for years, and he kicked goals, so maybe they picked him for those reasons. Or maybe Gatland just really didn't like me! I will probably never know.

Being overlooked for the Lions meant an England tour to Argentina, so at least I had an opportunity to impress Eddie, when he wasn't ploughing us into the dirt. There was almost an entire England team away with the Lions, so Eddie called on me, skipper Dyls and a few of the other older lads to grab hold of an otherwise inexperienced team and drive standards.

There were 18 uncapped players on that tour, including Sale back-rows Ben and Tom Curry, who were only 18, and another six lads who were 20 or under. Then there were the more experienced players like myself, Joe Launchbury, Mike Brown and George Ford. I'll never forget the Curry boys, who are the most energetic and physical twins you will ever meet, chop tackling Joe Launchbury the man mountain the day before the first Test match and Joe nearly beating them both up for it. We knew then those two were destined for greatness.

At times it felt like being back at school, but it was a great tour all the same. We won two exciting Test matches, ate some massive steaks, drank a load of very fine red wine and had a big night out to round things off. But the entire time I was there, I stayed across the news, in case one of the Lions nines got injured.

One day, I received a text from an English lad in New Zealand telling me that one of the nines had taken a knock in training. I was all revved up and waiting for the call when I found out that Gatland had already called up four Welsh players, including Gareth Davies, and two Scots as cover.

Unbeknown to me, Gatland had cleared that with all the Home Union coaches before departure, although the English lads were never considered, because we were 6,000 miles away in Argentina. The Scotland and Wales lads were nearby because they'd just finished tours of Australia and the South Pacific respectively and could therefore jump on short-haul flights to New Zealand. That seemed fair enough, until I found out that Gareth Davies had been told before he left for the South Pacific that should any of the nines get injured, he'd be the next man in. That annoyed me, because it suggested decisions were being made for convenience's sake, rather than based on merit.

I think I'd have been a great Lions tourist. I'd have trained like a demon, been a supportive team-mate, hoovered up any cultural experiences on offer and had a lot of fun. I certainly wouldn't have kicked off about being in the midweek team; I'd have played my heart out whatever game I was picked for.

When I speak to lads who were lucky enough to go on a Lions tour, they usually tell me it was the best experience of their careers. So I am sad that I never went on one, although I'm in pretty good company. Some great players never toured with the Lions, including the English quartet of Mike Tindall, Dylan Hartley, Chris Robshaw and Chris Ashton. Not getting picked by the Lions might be the ultimate first-world problem, so I just had to shrug it off, get on with my life and remind myself that everything happens for a reason.

○

Around the time of the Lions squad announcement, my agent called to tell me that Saracens were looking to sign a new scrum-half because South African veteran Neil de Kock was retiring. Their timing was spot-on.

Not only had I grown disillusioned with the situation at Quins, but I was also sick of watching Sarries lift trophy after trophy. Maybe it was better to be one of them, I thought, than grow more and more resentful of their success. Plus, I had a lot of mates in the Sarries team, including Owen Farrell, who I'd forged a decent partnership with for England, and Jamie George, who was fast becoming one of my besties, so I thought I'd slot right in.

I went and met Sarries' director of rugby, Mark McCall, and his right-hand man, Phil Morrow. We had a good chat, and they seemed to think I was a good fit stylistically. When I brought up my old mate Richard Wigglesworth, who had been their first-choice nine for quite a few years and who I really didn't want to upset, they told me he was weighing up an offer from a club in

France. So I left that meeting thinking I might be a Quins player for not much longer.

But after thinking things over for a few days, I concluded that the amount of stick I'd get for leaving Quins and joining Sarries wasn't worth it. And deep down, I didn't want to leave Quins anyway. Yes, we'd had a rough season, but it still felt like home. Luckily, Wiggy told Sarries he didn't want to move to France before they could make me an offer. Given what we know now about the club's finances, it might have been an offer I couldn't have refused.

Nevertheless, in the summer of 2017, I told JK over a pint that I didn't want to be captain anymore. To be fair to JK, it wasn't just because of him. I found it tough coming back from England duty and taking the reins again, and I wasn't being the best player I could be because I was constantly fretting about giving team talks every day and driving standards. I was still happy to be part of the leadership group, but we had former Wallabies skipper James Horwill in our ranks, and Big Kev, as he was nicknamed (something to do with an old Aussie TV advert, in case you were wondering), craved more responsibility. 'You've got your captain right there,' I said to JK, and thankfully he agreed.

Snapper's body had been creaking for a couple of seasons, and while he was still capable of incredible things, he just couldn't stay on the pitch for long enough. I'd say to him, 'Mate, how can we hide you, so that you don't have to make any tackles and risk getting injured?' But he eventually admitted defeat at the end of the 2016–17 season, which was another big blow to the club.

Snapper, who stepped straight into the role of attacking coach, had come up trumps for us in so many clutch moments. Magical players like him only come along once in a blue moon. We thought we had a very good replacement in Demetri Catrakilis, who had killed us in the 2016 Champions Cup final. But poor Demetri got struck in the throat in only his second game, against Gloucester at the Stoop, and almost died on the pitch. He was out of action for about five months, during which time he had to learn how to speak again, and when he returned, he wasn't the same player we'd signed, unsurprisingly.

Demetri's horror injury meant JK had to turn to an 18-year-old kid called Marcus Smith. Marcus was an academy graduate who'd just left Brighton College, and he'd trained with the first team for a couple of days the previous season. I remember JK saying to me, 'This boy is going to be special, let me know what you think.' But it wasn't exactly love at first sight.

Nowadays, most lads straight out of school are ripped to shreds, because they put so much work in at the gym, but Marcus was relatively small and still carrying a bit of baby fat. But he soon put me straight. We were doing an attack drill that involved me passing the ball to him and him having to make the right decision in a four against three. I liked the way he glided with ball in hand, and he picked the right pass three or four times in a row, so I started thinking, *Okay, maybe he does have something.* Then I threw a pass a little too close to his chest and he said to me after finishing the move off, 'Danny, can you put it in front of me so I can run onto it?' My first thought was, *Cheeky little git, who does he think he is?* But I did as I was told anyway, and he ran onto the ball, did a dummy scissors, sliced straight through the defence and scored. *Okay,* I thought, *maybe this kid does know what he's talking about after all …*

Later that same training session, Marcus went up to Joe Marler and started telling him exactly which lines he needed to be running in a certain drill. As Marcus was talking, Joe was looking him up and down as if he was thinking, *Is this kid for real?* But the next time we ran the drill, Joe did what Marcus had suggested, which created a hole that Marcus then floated through. Now there were wide eyes and raised eyebrows all over the field, and everyone was thinking the same thing: this kid knows exactly what's what, he's not afraid to let people know about it and maybe we can learn a few things from him.

When England had a camp down in Brighton, Eddie invited Marcus along to train with us, and he didn't look out of place in that environment either, despite being only 17. If you gave him the ball in a bit of space, he'd do something with it, which is a gift that very few rugby players have. And it's a priceless gift in the modern game, in which space is at a premium.

I got to know him better when he started training with the first team full-time, and I soon realised that he was a really lovely lad. I could tell he'd been raised right even before I met his mum and dad, and when I met them, everything made perfect sense. They clearly loved him, and he clearly loved them. But it was probably because I'd come to like him so much that I felt so sorry for him when Demetri got injured. It's one thing being a prodigiously talented 18-year-old who can wow gnarled veterans on the training field, it's another thing completely trying to run a malfunctioning team at that age.

Marcus's debut was against London Irish at Twickenham, on the first day of the season. A few months earlier, he was carving things up for Brighton College – a very good rugby school, but they don't tend to play against teams containing giant Kiwi, South African and Samoan forwards whose job description includes knocking fly-halves into next week. Neither do they tend to play in front of 56,000 people, which was the attendance that day.

We lost that game, but Marcus did pretty well, all things considered. And a couple of weeks later, he was named man of the match after our narrow victory over Wasps in Coventry. As long as I threw the ball in front of him, just as he'd asked, he'd make stuff happen. Marcus was a great example for youngsters coming through, because he showed that skill was still the deadliest weapon in modern rugby, rather than size and physicality.

But getting a decent tune out of that Quins side was tantamount to turning water into wine. Even a peak Snapper would have struggled. And while Marcus was tremendously gifted, and had Snapper to learn from, he was essentially learning on the job. If the coaches had had a more experienced ten on their books, they would have played him, with Marcus coming in and out for experience.

The board had spent big money on Demetri, former All Blacks centre Francis Saili and Namibia captain and back-row Renaldo Bothma, but they kept getting injured and can only have played about ten games between them that season. Oh for a Nick Easter to steady the ship, but he'd hung his boots up two seasons earlier and was now trying to make a difference as our defence coach.

As a player, Minty was the complete package – crazy strong, smart and a proper leader of men. He was my go-to guy – I knew if I gave him the ball, he'd make yards, and I made so many breaks and scored so many tries from his offloads. So when he told me he was retiring, I felt sad. I thought, *Who's gonna make me look good now?* And I felt almost as sad watching Minty coach. Unfortunately, the timing was all wrong for him, what with all the injuries, players underperforming and JK's struggles as director of rugby.

Because Minty had been such a gifted player, who picked things up quickly and just got on with the job, he couldn't understand why some lads weren't able to do the same. I'd watch him explaining something to someone and get increasingly frustrated that they couldn't understand. In the end, he'd lose his rag and say, 'What is wrong with you? Why do you not know this by now?' It was a seriously steep learning curve for Minty, and while his teaching style did change, he wouldn't be a coach at Quins for much longer.

We produced the odd decent performance (such as when we beat eventual champions Saracens in December), after which everyone would think, *Why can't we do that every week?* But that's not possible when team morale is low, key players are on the treatment table and inexperienced youngsters are plugging the gaps. And mostly we were pretty dreadful. We won only seven of our 22 Premiership games to finish tenth in the table, our worst showing since getting relegated in 2005, and lost five of our six games in the Champions Cup. It was all quite disheartening, and I did start to worry about the direction the club was heading in.

After getting hammered at Sixways, a journalist posed the question: 'How can a team including Mike Brown, Danny Care, Joe Marler, Kyle Sinckler, Chris Robshaw, Jamie Roberts and Marcus Smith concede seven tries against Worcester?' He had a point. Our defence was terrible, we were easy to score against, we were easy to beat. And if that's happening to a team of seasoned internationals, clearly something is wrong with the environment.

JK and the club had parted ways by then, the final straw being a pitiful 35–5 defeat by London Irish at the Stoop. While the lads knew it was the right time for a change, there was only sadness when he told us the news. I certainly took absolutely no pleasure in being proved right about his appointment.

Seeing things fall apart for JK was one of the hardest things I've been through in rugby. He was one of the nicest blokes you could meet, had taught me so much over the years and was always there if I needed someone to speak to, whether it was about rugby or anything else. He just wasn't right for the job they'd given him, although I should make clear that injuries and poor form were also contributing factors. JK knows what I think about his time as director of rugby because we're still very close and I've told him to his face.

The saddest part about the whole situation, at least for me, was that JK couldn't drop back down to being a coach at Quins, which he'd been amazing at for almost 20 years before taking the top job. Club dynamics simply don't allow that to happen. Instead, one of the best coaches I'd ever worked with wandered off into the sunset, although hopefully with a decent-sized cheque in his back pocket.

JK, in case you're reading this, I'd like to finish with a story from happier times. When JK was still head coach, he'd often use a flipchart as a visual aid. Before one big game in 2015, JK was going through these pages while explaining what he wanted from his players – physicality, intensity, enjoyment, that sort of stuff – and when he flipped over to the final page, there was a drawing of a massive cock and balls staring back at him.

As you can imagine, for a bunch of rugby players, some of whom had the mental age of seven, this was just about the funniest thing ever. People were almost falling off their chairs with laughter. But JK, who could normally take a joke, ordered all the coaches out and said, 'Right, I need to know who's done this. We're not going home until whoever did it owns up.' A seething JK then flounced out of the room, probably thinking, *I've got a degree from Cambridge and I'm spending my days with grown men who think a drawing of a cock and balls is the height of comedy.*

The minutes ticked by, but the culprit stayed schtum. And being the captain, I eventually stood up and said, 'Look, lads, whoever did it obviously isn't going to own up, because he's a coward, so someone needs to take the hit for the team.' The lads weren't having that, and when JK came bursting back in, we were still none the wiser. JK then lost the plot completely. 'You're all totally lawless,' he roared, 'you're embarrassing, no wonder the club is in such a state when nobody's taking any responsibility for anything ...' That wiped a few smiles off people's faces – but 'cock-gate' remained unsolved.

In fact, cock-gate ran and ran for months, although most people thought that Nicholas Easter was the man responsible, despite his advancing years. Another prime suspect was Joseph Marler, although he was adamant that he had nothing to do with it either. Some people even suspected me, their skipper, which was nothing short of outrageous.

Cock-gate was only resolved at the end-of-season awards dinner, when the retiring George Robson gave a speech. He said what an absolute pleasure the last ten years had been, thanked everyone at the club, from kit men to coaches, and finished up with, 'The thing I'm most proud of is drawing that cock!' The whole place erupted, including JK, who was wagging his finger at him in mock fury.

Unfortunately for George, it was impossible for him to come out on top in any banter exchange because of what happened when he captained us against Jonny Wilkinson's Toulon in the Challenge Cup in 2012, something I'm sure JK brought up that night.

George, who was filling in for the injured Chris Robshaw, came marching out of the changing room looking mean and moody, slipped on his studs and fell flat on his arse. It was live on Sky, and in the footage you can see me sniggering in the tunnel. I was full-on belly laughing by the time the game started, although thankfully I was on the bench. I laughed even harder when I heard what the commentator said: 'Whoa, George Robson! The first error of the night ...' He must have had a crystal ball, because we were appalling and lost 37–8.

Olly Kohn and Joe Gray had about 50 T-shirts made up of George falling over and the legend: 'Having a bad day? ... Having a Nobson!' We all wore them at the next team meeting. This picture of him falling over was everywhere. When George – or 'Nobson', as we'd started calling him – opened his locker, he saw it; when he opened his bag, he saw it; when he lifted the toilet lid, he saw it; when JK turned a page on his flipchart, he saw it. One day, George finally cracked and started swinging at a team-mate in the physio room, which brought the Nobson era to a close – but it was glorious while it lasted. If a genie said to me, 'Danny, I'm granting you one wish, which is that George stays on his feet and Quins beat Toulon,' I'd reply, 'Stick your wish, I wouldn't change a God damn thing.'

○

England were back to full strength for the 2017 autumn internationals, and you'd have thought that everything was rosy in Camp Eddie judging by the three comfortable wins. But I was feeling increasingly uncomfortable about the culture of fear and loathing in the England set-up – and I almost died the day before the game against Australia. No, really ...

A café in Richmond did the most delicious Mars Bar slices you could imagine – heavenly – but they'd run out of them that day. I've got a severe peanut allergy, so have to be quite care-ful when it comes to cakes and such like. So the waitress having assured me that their chocolate chip cookies didn't contain any nuts, I plumped for one of them. But I knew I was in trouble within seconds of tucking into it. My throat started closing up and the boys were all panicking, thinking their team-mate was going to kick the bucket the day before a Test match. Being an idiot, I didn't have my EpiPen with me, so I had to make myself violently sick in the toilet instead. Meanwhile, Clive Woodward's old T-CUP mantra had kicked in and a couple of the boys bought some antihistamines from a nearby corner-shop, which I got down me immediately post-chunder. They'd also discovered that the categorically 100 per cent nut-free chocolate chip cookie was actually a Reese's Pieces cookie, which is probably the most peanut you can find in a snack.

Jamie George and Elliot Daly hailed a cab and the driver raced back to the hotel as quick as he could. Jamie and Elliot had to virtually drag me to the physio room, where the doctor put me on the bed and clamped an oxygen mask to my face. I had to sit there for two hours until my airways cleared, and even missed the team meeting.

Australia's fly-half Bernard Foley, who was always quite chopsy, gave me some stick for being rubbish when I came on with 20 minutes to go. But the game having been in the balance, I set up two tries for Jonathan Joseph and Jonny May and rounded things off with a try of my own to make the final score 30–6. I believe my old friend Stuart Barnes said he would have named me man of the match had I played for more than 20 minutes, but it was probably the best 20 minutes of my career! God bless that cookie, because I think it was all the oxygen that I'd consumed that made me feel so invincible that game. As for Foley, I couldn't resist giving the silly sausage a little wink after the final whistle.

Near-death experiences aside, it hadn't escaped anybody's notice that players kept disappearing without any explanation. Saracens full-back Alex Goode had been one of the best players in Europe for years and was voted Premiership player of the season in 2016, but after a couple of England appearances under Eddie, he never played for England again. It later came out that Goodey had incurred Eddie's wrath when he had to miss a training day. Goodey had got a dead leg in a Sunday afternoon game. When he couldn't train on the Monday, Eddie declared to Goodey that he was useless to him and sent him straight home, never to be seen again. (While I'm on the subject of Goodey, I'm proud to say that I came up with his nickname 'Jumanji Boy', as he looks exactly like Peter from the original *Jumanji* film, after he cheats at the board game and is turned into a monkey.)

When Manu Tuilagi and Denny Solomona snuck out for a couple of drinks in the middle of a training camp, we found out the following morning that they had both 'left the camp', which was presumably a euphemism for being told to go home and not come back. It made no difference that Manu was arguably the best player in the team at the time.

Eddie had capped 50-odd players by the end of 2017, which shows not only how much depth there is in English rugby, at least compared to other countries, but that Eddie took the same approach to rugby as Russia traditionally takes to war: just keep feeding men into the grinder, as long as we keep winning.

When Wasps hooker Tommy Taylor injured his knee during training before the 2017 tour of Argentina, Eddie said, 'Sorry, mate', and ushered the next bloke on. Tommy was never seen again. Then there's the sorry tale of Wasps flanker Sam Jones, who'd had a couple of great years in the Premiership and looked like being England's long-term seven until he destroyed his ankle while wrestling Maro Itoje at a training camp in Brighton.

Eddie thought that to be more effective in the contact area, we needed to be able to wrestle. Make of that what you will. The backs would make whispered pacts, make it look like they were wrestling hard while actually carrying each other for ten minutes. But forwards aren't made that way. They'd be going at each other like rabid dogs in a pit, which was actually quite scary to watch. Sam was pretty good at it and was getting the better of Maro, until Maro fell on top of him and snapped his ankle pretty much in half.

A couple of the lads picked Sam up and placed him to the side and the wrestling continued. And while Sam was wailing and crying, and the docs were trying to hold his foot in place, Eddie walked up to him and asked, 'Did you strap your ankles, mate?' Sam replied, 'No! I didn't realise it was a full-on wrestling session!' And Eddie said, 'You should have strapped your ankles, mate', before turning back to the wrestling.

That evening, a few of us carried Sam and his bags to a taxi, which ferried him back to London to see a specialist. There was no farewell from Eddie. Sam never played rugby again and was forced to retire in 2018. Sam is now a top sommelier in London. Good for him, although if Eddie hadn't made him wrestle, he might still have been England's number seven.

It was every man for himself in Eddie's training camps. You got your head down, gritted your teeth, said nothing and hoped you stayed in the room. That isn't a healthy environment, because it breeds selfishness, not camaraderie, and it rewards yes-men rather than people who are willing to question things. But whether it's a healthy environment or not, Eddie made it work for a while.

Eddie always had a group of six or seven untouchables – Youngsy, Owen Farrell, George Ford, Dan Cole, Maro Itoje, Billy Vunipola (and his brother Mako for a while) – but the rest of us were expendable, which meant we lived by different rules. We hoped that by toeing the line and saying the right things we'd maybe become an untouchable one day, and then we'd know what it was like to be loved by the master unconditionally. God, Eddie was a clever bastard.

I somehow wormed my way into Eddie's inner circle for a while, but mostly all that yes sir, no sir stuff made me feel a bit sick. Then again, I spent a lot of time wishing I'd said something, so I wasn't being true to myself either.

We were getting paid over 20 grand a game, which was a lot of money for a rugby player. It meant players were desperate not to get dropped for all the wrong reasons, which made for a toxic environment. Some lads had the attitude, *To hell with everyone else, as long as the coach likes me*, which I couldn't get my head around. Other lads would pretend to be fit to play when they weren't. Then again, if saying all the right things and feigning fitness meant earning a few hundred grand a year and maybe paying off your mortgage, what do you expect?

When England were winning games, which they almost always did in the first two years of Eddie's reign, it was easier to excuse his bad behaviour. He'd filled us with an unbelievable self-belief and we had a swagger about us. We felt like we could beat any team on the planet, so why would anyone complain? But when performances started to slip, as they did in the 2018 Six Nations, when we managed only two wins and finished fifth, Eddie's abrasiveness really began to jar.

Analysts would be visibly shaking during presentations because they were so scared of getting something wrong. If a clip didn't appear at the right moment, Eddie would fix them with a menacing stare and say, 'What the fuck are you doing, mate? You're not preparing the fucking team right.' A few players would snigger, then feel bad about doing so. And after we'd all filed out of the room, we'd hear Eddie continuing to berate them. Those analysts worked bloody hard, but some of them ended up as shells of their former selves.

Eddie picked on the odd player, like poor Kieran Brookes, but mostly it was just common or garden piss-taking, the kind of stuff that we were all used to. How he treated his staff – coaches, analysts, medical staff, communications officers – was a different thing completely. We'd hear stories about Eddie texting people in the middle of the night, asking if they'd prepared properly for the morning meeting, the subtext being, *If I'm still working, you should be, too.* He once sent a sports scientist out of the room during a meeting, like a naughty schoolboy. They didn't last much longer. Then there was the time he handed one of his staff a carrier bag and said, 'Here's some steak for you and the missus, sorry about how I spoke to you yesterday.' When the bloke got home and opened the bag, it was actually some sausages. Eddie then sent him a text saying, 'Mate, you're a fucking sausage. You don't deserve steak yet.'

These people were working all hours, so no wonder the turn-over was so high. People would be there one day and gone the next, with no explanation. It was like living in a dictatorship, under a despot who disappeared people. I always thought it was ironic that we went through so many psychologists. I hope they all got the treatment they needed.

When Youngsy got injured early in the Six Nations game against Italy in 2018, I was suddenly England's first-choice nine again. But having scraped past Wales at Twickenham, our 24th win in 25 Tests under Eddie, we then lost three in a row. I became England's most-capped scrum-half in the defeat by Scotland, passing Matt Dawson, but we really weren't great that day.

Training had gone to a whole new level of intensity, which I didn't think was possible. By the time we arrived in Edinburgh, it felt like we'd already played three Tests that week. So when I asked for some extra physicality from the forwards, they couldn't give it to me. We were like a luxury SUV with hardly any fuel in it, so it didn't matter how frantically I pumped the accelerator.

After another mental training session on the Tuesday before the game, a few of the senior players, including the captain, Dyls, plucked up the courage to say something to Eddie about the amount of work we were doing. We suggested we ease off a bit on the Thursday, so that we'd still have a bit in the tank for the game, and he said, 'That's your opinion, is it?' We told him it was, and two days later we all got flogged into oblivion. Sorry about that, lads.

Eddie was unable to see what was right in front of his face because of his obsession with stats. His office was full of screens, and there were graphs and charts plastered all over the walls. His analysts would pin up player metrics in the team room, stuff like how quickly each of us got off the floor after making a tackle. And if you hadn't 'reloaded' quick enough in a session, it would say so in massive red letters. What the printouts didn't show was how knackered the players were, but Eddie didn't seem to think that was important.

I was back on the bench for the final game against Ireland at Twickenham, with Wiggy starting ahead of me. Ireland completely outplayed us that day to win the Grand Slam, and to be fair to Eddie, he was a pretty gracious loser, at least in public. Losing clearly hurt him, but he always gave credit to the opposition and usually took some of the blame. He wasn't one to go mental in the changing room either, although you didn't want to catch his eye. Just the look on his face would tell you you'd disappointed him in some way. For such a small man, he had a very intimidating presence.

Eddie hinted in his post-match interviews that it might be the end of the road for some England players, so when I wasn't picked for that summer's tour of South Africa, I feared the worst. The media reported that I was 'rested', but while Eddie did tell me that I'd had a long year and he wanted to have a look at a couple of other lads (Wasps' Dan Robson and Saracens' Ben Spencer, although Youngsy ended up playing almost every minute of all three Tests), I took it as a dropping, and wondered if I'd be able to fight my way back in.

Snapper and me celebrating Quins' first Premiership title in 2012 – we won it playing rugby the right way.

Back at the Stoop with Mum, Dad and Si. I'd put them through the mill that year, so it was wonderful to make them smile.

Jodie and I dancing on tables in Koh Phangan, where we met in 2013. A random punter sent me this photo a few years later!

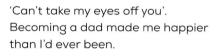

Wife jokes with Marler – whatever Joe has just said, it's probably worse than you can possibly imagine.

'Can't take my eyes off you'. Becoming a dad made me happier than I'd ever been.

Jodie and Blake safely back home 🤍 I now had two great loves in my life.

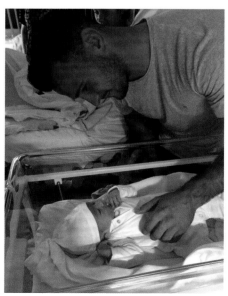

23 July 2016, the day Jodie became Mrs Care – and Blake stole the show.

The Firm – Si (best man), Albear and Crayon on the left, Ugo, Luke (Jodie's brother) and Jordan on the right.

The Old Guard – Joe Gray, Will Collier and Joe Marler after Quins' second Premiership title win in 2021.

With my three beauties 🙂

Back at the Stoop with a happy Mum, Dad and Blake. My parents almost never missed a Quins game.

Will Skinner's famous Transformers costume ... it would look somewhat different by the end of the day.

Just two tough lads about to play a game of rugby. Marler is like another brother to me.

Me and my last England skipper, Jamie George, aka The Bucket Hat Boys – an absolute menace on the golf course.

Preparing for the 2023 World Cup with Marler, Marcus Smith and Owen Farrell – I was so happy to be back in the fold.

Pre-game World Cup coffee with Mum.

Dad bringing the energy to the stadium.

My sister, my brother and my nephew Henry.

Koha with her favourite rugby player and her dad. Blake and Koha are Marcus's biggest fans.

My reason why. I don't know how Jodie managed while I was off playing in the World Cup, but it was so special to have them all on the pitch with me.

My 100th game for England, with Jodie, Blake, Koha, Rocco and Henry –
I'm so glad I got to give them so many happy rugby memories.

Chapter 16

Utter Heartbreak

I wasn't playing particularly well for Quins at the time, despite enjoying working with our new head coach, Paul Gustard. Gussy had been at Saracens for a few years before Eddie appointed him as England defence coach, and I thought he was exactly the kind of bloke we needed at the Stoop. Our leaky defence needed fixing, for sure, but the whole place needed freshening up.

There were some raised eyebrows when it was announced that Gussy was leaving the England set-up a year before the 2019 World Cup, but while he never admitted just how hard it was to work for Eddie, I think it was a big relief to escape that environment. Towards the end of his time with England, Gussy was not the effervescent man he used to be, and while I'm sure he didn't take the decision to jump ship so close to a World Cup lightly, I reckon he just wanted to be able to breathe freely and be his own man again.

The Saracens lads had told me that Gussy would be a bit different, and he was. Meetings were fun, and he was a fan of military analogies (he called high balls 'bombs' that required defusing). But he also ruffled a few feathers. He was very forthright, quite abrupt and not as kindly as Conor or JK had been. And while defence was clearly an issue – we'd had 78 tries scored against us the previous season – Quins had always been more about flair and attack. So when Gussy kept talking about physicality, grind and all the stuff that had been so important to Sarries, a few of the boys didn't like it.

Gussy's attitude was that the traditional Quins way of playing had won us hardly anything, so he was going to try to change our DNA. He didn't explicitly say that he wanted us to play like Saracens, but we knew that's what he meant.

I felt quite conflicted. I was mates with Gussy, he was a lovely guy, and I understood why he thought drastic change was needed. However, loads of the lads were unhappy about it, and they had reason to be. They hadn't joined Quins to play the Saracens way, they'd joined to play the Quins way, which was expressive and fun. We also had Marcus at fly-half, not Owen Farrell. Marcus was a lad who saw the game differently and played what he saw, and suddenly he was being told to put his head where it hurts, make 15 tackles a game and kick, kick, kick. All the backs were told to kick more, which is like taking over from Jürgen Klopp at Liverpool and telling the team to play more long balls.

The biggest problem with Gussy's grand plan was that Sarries played how they did because they had such a massive pack. Because the pack was so dominant, Wiggy was able to put the ball on a dime every single time and Owen could kick for territory over and over without much pressure on him. They had all the right people in all the right places to play that kind of attritional game, but we had a fast, mobile pack and a load of exciting backs who were capable of carving teams up. I was nowhere near the box-kicker that Wiggy was, and no amount of training was going to change that at my age – and we didn't have wingers who were great at chasing and winning the ball back.

Gussy was a brilliant hands-on coach – he'd be able to give you instant feedback on what you'd done right or wrong – but now he was dealing with the bigger picture, which meant spending lots of time worrying about player recruitment and dealing with agents and the media. It was an unsatisfactory situation viewed from every angle.

○

Towards the end of the 2018–19 season, which saw us just miss out on a play-off place, allegations that Saracens had been breaching the salary cap started to emerge, although everyone at Quins had had their suspicions for years.

For a period in the early 2010s, they had former and current Springbok hookers in their squad, plus Jamie George. I'm sure Jamie wasn't on a lot of money back then, but he was learning from two of the greatest hookers ever in John Smit (World Cup winner in 2007) and Schalk Brits (World Cup winner in 2019). Then they had Owen Farrell sharing the ten jersey with Charlie Hodgson, a bloke who had played 38 times for England, for five years; and Wiggy sharing the nine jersey with Neil de Kock, another former Springbok.

Quins used to beat Saracens regularly in my early years at the club. They always had a smattering of decent players, but they never carried any kind of fear factor. Then all of a sudden they got really, really good. Before we played them in the 2014 play-off semi-finals, I looked at their team sheet and thought, *Damn, every single one of their starting XV is an international. How can that be?* Wiggy was on the bench, because Neil de Kock was starting, as was Charlie Hodgson, England A hooker Jamie George, USA winger Chris Wyles and Samoa prop James Johnston (who was one of our own before Saracens made him an offer he couldn't refuse).

We were leading 17–11 at half-time, having played some really good stuff, but when my drop-goal attempt, which was the sweetest I'd ever hit, ricocheted off the post and bounced into the arms of my old Quins team-mate David Strettle, they went the length of the field and scored. Then they changed their entire front row with about 15 minutes left, and two of the replacements were internationals. Meanwhile, we were down to the bare bones. We actually ended up with only 13 men on the field, with me and Tom Guest, who was a number eight, on the wings because Uges and Tommy Williams had gone off injured.

We came off the pitch that day feeling dejected, because there was absolutely nothing we could have done to beat them, but it was only after talking to Conor that I realised what was actually going on. Conor was absolutely convinced they were breaching the salary cap and was furious about it. While they were able to bring on internationals, we had academy lads playing out of position. Plus, all our players looked like they'd crawled out of a coach crash. But Conor couldn't prove anything, so he was hardly going to go public.

I was mates with a load of the Saracens lads, but I grew to hate them as a club. Every time I saw them lift another trophy, I'd think, *How are they being allowed to get away with this? Why is nobody investigating them?* Every time we played against them, we desperately wanted to beat them up, but most of the time we could barely lay a glove on them. They were just too good for us, like they were just too good for every other team in England.

When we got rumbled for Bloodgate, we were punished very severely and rightly so. People lost their jobs, the club's reputation was left in tatters. But the Sarries lads were having a whale of a time. Not only were they winning everything, we would also hear about their lavish celebrations and holidays together, all paid for by the club. There were even rumours about wives being on the payroll and some of their South African players being bought farms back home.

At England get-togethers, we'd give the Sarries lads a bit of stick about the rumours, but they'd just shrug it off – 'We're just players, we don't know what's going on behind the scenes.' But I never wanted any of their names dragged through the mud anyway, because it wasn't their fault.

When it was finally confirmed that Sarries had been breaching salary cap regulations, most players from rival clubs kept their counsel, but I didn't pull any punches on our podcast, the BBC's *Rugby Union Weekly*. Sarries had won four Premiership titles in five years, and I said that it would only be fair if those trophies and medals were taken away from them and given to the teams they beat in the finals, some of whose players have never won anything. And I said what others wouldn't, namely that they'd been outright cheating (I felt that the three Champions Cups they'd won were slightly different, as English clubs were competing against the much higher salary caps of the French and Irish clubs).

Having done it twice, I know that winning the Premiership is the best feeling a player can have in domestic rugby. So how many players were robbed of that feeling by Saracens' rule-breaking? Potentially hundreds – not to mention coaches, backroom staff and tens of thousands of fans. Saracens' cheating also adversely affected England careers. Because they had such a powerful team, and were playing so well week in, week out, obviously England coaches were going to keep picking a load of them.

What's more, having all those internationals – Schalk Brits, John Smit and Jamie George – in the same squad doesn't just make the first team stronger, it makes the academy stronger too, because those young lads have so much experience to learn from.

As it turned out, the powers that be decided to let Saracens keep their titles and trophies, but they were relegated and fined

£5.3 million instead. But what was £5.3 million to Sarries owner Nigel Wray? He was said to be worth about £300 million at the time. And Sarries came straight back up from the Championship and were back winning trophies the following season. To be clear, I never wanted anyone at Saracens to lose their job, but it felt like they'd got off far too lightly.

I have a grudging respect for Nigel Wray because at least he was trying to look after his players with all those property co-investments. If I'd been at Sarries and Nigel Wray had offered to buy half my house or a herd of cows, or whatever, I'd have said yes in a heartbeat. But I found the attitude of some of Saracens' staff quite sickening.

I'll never forget an interview their assistant coach Al Sanderson gave before a game against Gloucester, just after they'd been accused of breaking salary cap regulations: 'To quote Taylor Swift, haters gonna hate, hate, hate, players gonna play, play, play.' The arrogance shocked me. Maybe the coaches didn't know the exact details, but they knew that something dodgy was going on. How did they think they were staying under the salary cap when they were putting out a team of full internationals week after week? So Al Sanderson trying to laugh it off and calling their critics haters blew my mind. And Saracens have still never really said sorry for the whole episode, which is why so many people still hate them.

It turned out that the tour to South Africa was a decent one to miss. We got battered by the Barbarians in the warm-up, with Chris Ashton scoring three tries for them in a sobering 63–45 defeat at Twickenham, before losing the Test series 2–1. And

Eddie clearly didn't trust his second- and third-choice nines for whatever reason because they barely played a part in proceedings.

Ashy's career actually provides a good example of Eddie's capricious nature. After his hat-trick for the Baa-Baas, people were naturally asking the question, 'Why was England's best winger playing for the opposition?' To be fair to Eddie, he couldn't pick Ashy because he was playing for Toulon in France (and getting paid 'silly money', as he'd often remind me). But Eddie asked Ashy to break his contract, so Ashy signed for Sale in the summer of 2018 and he was back in the England squad by the end of the year. Ashy has openly said he found Eddie's training methods frustrating – not the amount of work but the fact that he didn't get the ball in his hands enough – and after a couple more games in the following year's Six Nations, he never played for England again.

Ashy joined Quins in 2020, just before Covid hit, and the abuse that man would give the youngsters was off the scale. Ashy was born and raised in Wigan and spent a couple of seasons with the Warriors in rugby league, and he was always going on about how soft kids were in union nowadays.

Kids are different from 20 years ago, they don't tend to respond well to bluntness, but Ashy wasn't bothered about that. I'd told everyone what a great bloke he was before his arrival, but Ashy gave a couple of youngsters a tongue-lashing in his first training session and never really recovered from there.

Marcus already disliked him because of his behaviour in a game we'd played against Sale the previous season. Ashy kept shouting, 'Marcus! You're killing this team! They were good when you were still at school!' Marcus said to me after the game, 'Is he your mate? He's horrible.' Ashy wasn't horrible really, he just turned into an ultra-competitive animal once he crossed that white line, which is what made him one of the most lethal finishers the game has ever seen (the top try-scorer in Premiership history with 101, plus 20 for England). But because of Covid, no one could get to know him, and he was gone before the end of the season (although he still picked up a Premiership medal to go with the two he won with Saracens and the one he'd later win with Leicester).

Eddie only picked two nines for the 2018 autumn internationals, me and Youngsy. 'I don't want to mess you two around by picking a third scrum-half,' he said. 'You two fight for the shirt.' Obviously, I was chuffed, but I also knew that training was going to be doubly brutal without a third nine to swap in.

I started on the bench when we edged South Africa 12–11, a win that was partly down to some very dodgy officiating – somehow the television match official (TMO) decided that Owen Farrell's late high shot on André Esterhuizen was legal and the Springboks were denied a kickable penalty (when André joined Quins a couple of years later he still hated Owen with a passion and was thirsty for revenge).

The All Blacks beat us by a point the following week, with me on the bench again, and this time a late call went against us. When Sam Underhill seized on Courtney Lawes's charge down and went over in the corner with five minutes to go, we thought we'd won, only for the TMO to rule that Courtney had been ever so slightly offside.

Morale was pretty high going into the Japan game, although not Youngsy's: he got called into Eddie's office and told he wasn't sharp enough. So I was picked to start, Wiggy came onto the bench and Youngsy spent most of the week slogging his guts out in the gym. But while most fans think those games against what used to be called tier-two nations must be a nice break from playing the likes of South Africa and New Zealand, they can actually be quite tricky. The starting XV usually gets chopped and changed, so that it's lots of lads who haven't played together before. So while fans expect us to win those games easily, they often end up being quite disjointed, ugly spectacles.

We looked rusty in training all week, with new combinations not quite clicking, and I went into the game with a bit of a hamstring twinge. And when I dived over for a try after just two minutes, I felt it ping. Still, there was no way I was coming off, because I needed to make the most of a rare start.

Japan were brilliant that day. Not only did they play with their usual pace and attacking verve, but they also ran so low, which made it difficult for us to turn them over. Meanwhile, we were a bit clunky and dropped the ball quite a lot. They ran us ragged and led 15–10 at half-time. All the momentum was with them, while we were almost out on our feet. As we made our way to the tunnel, the crowd were booing, which is never a good sign. But Eddie didn't seem to be unhappy with me for kicking the ball out at the end, and I thought, *Cool, at least I got that decision right.*

I came off for Wiggy with 20 minutes to go and a couple of late tries from debutant Joe Cokanasiga and Dylan Hartley spared our blushes. Joe's try came from a Wiggy box-kick, right on the money, and I thought to myself, *This is not gonna end well for me. After the game, Eddie's gonna say, 'We needed more of that earlier.'* He didn't say that, but he did tell the press that he couldn't believe I'd kicked the ball out to end the first half. Apparently, it showed a negative attitude, although I still had no idea what was about to hit me.

Eddie actually seemed quite positive in the changing room afterwards. He said it wasn't our greatest game but that a win was a win, and then he told us to go home for a couple of nights and get some rest and family time before the Australia game. Then came the bombshell voicemail from Eddie the following evening – 'Danny, Eddie here. Didn't think you were sharp enough at the weekend. Cheers' – followed by our fateful meeting in his office – 'That's a shit attitude, mate. Go back and play for your club and we'll see if you can get back in the room.' My England career had seemingly spontaneously combusted.

The following Saturday, the boys went out and hammered Australia. It was the best England performance for ages. Who knows, maybe Eddie sacrificing me, a bloke who had been a stalwart of his team for three years, stuck a rocket up a few people's arses. But even if it was another stroke of genius by Eddie, I'd still like to think that if I ever attained a position of power, I'd treat human beings very different to the way he did.

○

That period was a black hole for England rugby. So many lads who played in those autumn internationals and the 2019 Six Nations were never seen again: Saracens back Alex Lozowski, Exeter props Alec Hepburn and Ben Moon, Bath back-row Zach Mercer, Worcester centre Ben Te'o, Wasps back-row Brad Shields. Harry Williams, another Exeter prop, crawled out of the hole to play two more games, while Worcester back-row Ted Hill played just one more.

I didn't hear anything from Eddie before the Six Nations squad was announced, and uncapped Wasps scrum-half Dan Robson was picked as Youngsy's understudy. I still hadn't given up hope of making the World Cup, and I kept thinking about one of the last things Eddie had said to me: 'Go back and play for your club and we'll see if you can get back in the room.'

There was a pre-World Cup camp when the season was over, which involved England coaches talking to players who had a chance of going to the tournament, ranging from good chance to cat in hell's chance. It was mainly group meetings about schedules and how fit we'd have to be, but there were also one-on-ones. I hadn't had a proper conversation with Eddie since our meeting in 2018, so I was naturally a bit nervous. But I did think that perhaps he'd reflected and would say, 'Danny, I was out of order, let's shake hands and put it behind us.'

He seemed a bit edgy when I walked in, which I thought might be partly down to embarrassment. He told me I wasn't playing that well, mentioned a couple of things I'd need to improve on if I wanted to be in contention, and said he was looking at four or five nines. He went through the usual suspects – Youngsy, Dan Robson, Ben Spencer – but not Wiggy, which I thought was weird. Then he said, 'And Willi is also in the mix.'

'Who's Willi?' I asked.

'Willi Heinz, mate,' said Eddie. 'Oh,' I said. That was the end of our meeting.

Willi was a Kiwi who had been playing for Gloucester since 2015. I knew he was qualified to play for England, through his gran apparently, because I'd been in a training camp with him in 2017, but he'd never been involved since then. And I walked out of that meeting feeling quite stung. I'd only ever wanted to play for England; that was my dream from the time I started playing the game seriously. I'd given blood, sweat and tears for the England team for over a decade. And now Eddie was considering a lad who had spent the first 26 years of his life in New Zealand, dreaming of playing for the All Blacks.

I went off on holiday with the family and got the call from Eddie while I was lying on a sun lounger: 'Mate, you've not played well enough. I'm going in another direction with my scrum-halves and won't need you for the World Cup.' To which I replied, 'Okay, best of luck. If you need me, just give me a shout.' As soon as I hung up, I thought, *Why didn't I go for him?*

I told Jodie that at least we could have a nice relaxing holiday now, but it's tough pretending to be happy after being told your World Cup dream is over. I'd spent three years thinking that 2019 would finally be the year when I put to bed unhappy memories of 2011 and 2015, so I was utterly heartbroken.

The following day, I phoned one of the lads who'd been selected for the first World Cup camp and asked who the nines were. When he told me that Eddie had picked Youngsy, Saracens' Ben Spencer and Willi Heinz – I was lost for words.

I've got nothing against Willi Heinz as a person. I've met him a few times and I've played against him; he's a nice bloke and a good player. And if I'd grown up in New Zealand, come to play rugby in England and someone had said to me, 'Do you want to play for England in the World Cup?', maybe I'd have said yes too. But did I think I was a better player than Willi? Yes. Did I think I deserved to play for England in a World Cup more than him? Yes.

But it wasn't just me who deserved it more than Willi, it was also Dan Robson, Ben Spencer, Richard Wigglesworth and every other Premiership scrum-half who grew up dreaming of playing for England at a World Cup.

My problem was with the rules rather than with Willi, and I said so in the press. But I didn't labour the point because whenever anyone says anything about that kind of stuff, they get accused of sour grapes, or even of being racist. But a player's heritage or skin colour has nothing to do with it. Billy and Mako Vunipola have lived in the UK since they were small. Manu Tuilagi moved to the UK when he was a kid. The three of them learnt how to play rugby here and came through the English system, just like I did.

The pre-World Cup training camp sounded more mental than ever, and while it was going on I was kind of glad I was out of it. I'd be playing with my little boy while my mates were getting flogged. I'd also sometimes think that I'd been in the room a long time. Far longer than most. Maybe it was the right time to leave. But then the tournament started and I was consumed by envy.

It was a tough couple of months. I'd spent so much time with those lads, so I wanted them to do well, but I didn't want them to win the World Cup. That's a horrible thing to admit to, but it's the truth. I couldn't bring myself to watch any of their pool games, and I secretly hoped that Willi Heinz would come on for a late cameo and sustain a minor injury. Nothing major, obviously, perhaps just a dead leg or a tweaked hamstring. Awful, I know.

I was doing some corporate hospitality work for Guinness on the day of the semi-final against New Zealand, which meant having to watch it with hundreds of other people. The lads were unbelievable that day, producing one of the best ever performances by an England team. And over the course of game, my mindset changed. Because they played such entertaining rugby, I turned into a fan again, cheering along with everyone else. It was impossible not to. I'm not sure I was completely at peace with the situation yet, but I'd stumbled upon a more philosophical outlook. If the boys went and did the business in the final, I could at least say I played a part in the journey.

After the game, I had to do a Q&A on stage with former England fly-half Andy Goode. And his first question to me was, 'Mate, is your phone on?' Andy was referring to the fact that Willi Heinz had indeed sustained an injury.

I had all sorts of crazy thoughts in the taxi home. Eddie couldn't go into a World Cup final with one scrum-half, and surely he was going to call up someone he knew well and trusted. Someone with vast experience. Someone like me.

I kept thinking about Stephen Donald, who wasn't picked for New Zealand's World Cup squad in 2011 but kicked the winning penalty in the final following a spate of injuries. My phone kept pinging because people were tagging me on social media, saying that Eddie should call me up. I found myself staring at my phone and thinking, *Please, please, ring* … I even contemplated texting Eddie and saying, 'Mate, I'm here if you need me.' But when I got home, I turned on Sky Sports and saw the headline: 'Ben Spencer Flying Out to Japan for World Cup Final.'

I couldn't bring myself to watch the final, so we went to a trampoline park as a family instead. While the lads were doing battle with South Africa, I was bouncing up and down with Blake, while Jodie drank coffee on the sidelines. Her excuse for not joining in was that she was expecting our second child at any moment, which was a whopping great silver lining. Then again, while I'd always said I'd be there for the births of my kids no matter what was going on with my rugby, imagine having to choose between that and playing in a World Cup final.

It was my mum who texted to tell me that England had lost, which triggered a range of emotions. I knew exactly how hard the boys had worked to get there, so I felt sorry for them that they'd got so close and not won it. But there was also a tinge of relief. Imagine if Willi Heinz had become an MBE – my mates would have never let me forget it. And four days later, our daughter Koha was born, and not playing in a World Cup final didn't seem important.

Chapter 17

Pure Joy

After Jodie had Blake, she wanted to wait a few years before adding to the brood, in order to fully qualify as a solicitor first. And in early 2019, she found out she was pregnant. She really wanted a girl this time, so we decided to find out the sex, so she'd be able to get her head around things if it wasn't. The plan was for the doctor to tell me first and then I would tell Jodie, and he called me with the news just before an epidural to relieve a pain in my back. To my great joy and surprise, the doc informed me that we were expecting a girl. But just before they put me under, I thought, *I hope I wake up again, otherwise Jodie will remain in the dark ...*

Thankfully, I did wake up, and on my way home from the hospital, I bought pink and blue balloons. Having shown the balloons to Jodie, I got Blake to give her the pink one while she had her eyes closed. When she opened them, she burst into tears of happy shock. Unfortunately, Blake, who hadn't understood the meaning of the pink balloon and desperately wanted a little brother, screamed, 'Nooooo! I wanted it to be a boy!' You'll never see more contrasting emotions at a gender reveal. Luckily, I'd planned ahead and bought him some presents from his unborn sister, and explained that she couldn't wait to meet him. Koha, so-called because Jodie and I met in Koh Phangan, was born on 6 November 2019. We only found out later that Koha means 'gift' in Maori. That was very apt, because she was the best gift imaginable and immediately became the third love of my life.

As odd as Covid was, I actually quite enjoyed the break. Blake was still too young for school anyway, and Koha was only four months old when the first lockdown started, so it was the four of us just hanging out. The weather was great, we had a garden, and we'd all go for walks with the dog over at Quins' training ground in Guildford. I know people struggled during the pandemic and had it really tough, but for a creaking rugby player, it was just what the doctor ordered.

The real weirdness kicked in when we got back to playing rugby, five months after we'd stopped. One of the main reasons anyone plays professional sport is to make a crowd cheer, and suddenly we were playing in empty stadiums. It was particularly disconcerting for rugby players because what's the point in putting your body on the line if nobody's even there to notice. I'd always known how important fans were, but that period underlined it for me.

Quins' squad for that season was almost unrecognisable from the season before. Big characters like Tim Visser and James Horwill had retired, a raft of other players were moved on to other clubs, while 15 new players came in. No wonder our form was so patchy, although a couple of lads really came of age in those vacant, echoey stadiums.

Number eight Alex Dombrandt had joined us from Cardiff Metropolitan University in 2018, having never played in a professional academy. He admitted he'd 'done uni properly', having spent most of his time drinking beer, eating pizza and playing a bit of rugby in between, but he certainly upped his game when he arrived at Quins. I remember watching him during one of his first training sessions and thinking he had excellent hands and ran great lines. He looked like he'd been in a professional environment for years and seemed like a perfect fit for the club (there is lots of serious talent in university rugby, and another Cardiff Met graduate, centre Luke Northmore, joined us the following season).

I said to Gussy one day, 'This kid's got it, he's already class,' but Gussy didn't think Dommers was fit enough and worried about his defence. But Dommers shed 10kg, made his first appearance for England in the summer of 2019 (scoring two tries against the Barbarians) and played like a demon for Quins once he was given a run in the team.

Centre Joe Marchant had been in and around the squad for a couple of years already and was another freakishly good athlete and all-round good egg. I'd love to live in Joe's head for just one day because he's the happiest, most smiley person in the world. A coach would explain a move to him in training and he'd reply, 'Yeah, cool, I've got it.' But I imagine what he was actually thinking about was butterflies and roses and fluffy rabbits. Joe put the fear of God into opposition defences, but he's been to the Harry Potter theme park about ten times and would come out with quotes from the films. He even owns multiple Harry Potter wands.

We finished sixth in the Premiership in that weird Covid-elongated season, miles off the play-off places, and made an early exit from Europe. We did reach the final of the Premiership Cup, but that had always been a youth competition to me. It was only when we reached the semi-finals that Gussy decided to go all in and play our full-strength team. But having mangled Exeter away, Sale did a number on us in the final at their place. And while I made all the right noises about being gutted to miss out on a trophy, I wasn't particularly bothered. There were far more important trophies up for grabs, and we weren't even coming close to winning those.

Before the 2020–21 season, if you'd asked anyone at Quins if we had a hope of winning the title, they'd probably have laughed in your face. We had some great players and backed ourselves to beat anyone on our day, but not many in the squad were over-enamoured of how Gussy wanted us to play.

Our opening game, against defending champions Exeter at home, was an absolute disaster. I thought pre-season had gone okay, but you never really know how sharp you are until you play an actual game. We tried to kick Exeter to death and they just kept running it back and scoring. Their number eight Sam Simmonds ran rings around us, scoring a hat-trick, and we ended up losing 33–3. I thought to myself after the game, *This could be a long old year …*

Gussy already had one foot out of the door by then. It had been a really tough couple of years for him, what with the resistance to his preferred game plan and having to manage a club through the pandemic, and he'd alienated quite a few of the lads on the periphery of the first team. Gussy didn't really speak to them, so they knew they weren't in contention, and they ended up feeling like no more than training-ground fodder. That had never been the case under Dean Richards or Conor O'Shea. They understood that one of the key secrets to success is keeping everybody happy, not just the blokes who are going to play at the weekend.

It didn't help bolster Gussy's popularity that he drove a hard bargain in contract negotiations. I was taking pay cut after pay cut, as were all the veterans, at least as far as I was aware. And when Mike Brown refused a pay cut, choosing instead to see out his existing contract and prove he was still worth more than they were offering, Gussy called him in a few months later and told him he was no longer wanted beyond the end of the season.

It made little sense because he was picking Browny to start every week, and when the lads found out that their meeting had lasted less than five minutes, they were angry on Browny's behalf. He had given everything for Quins for 16 years – you couldn't meet a more professional player, which is why he's still playing for Leicester in his late 30s – so that was an awful way to treat him.

On that subject, rugby players' pay makes no sense at all. You start off on next to nothing as an academy player, start making good money if you're a regular in the first team, and really good money if you play regularly for England. But once you start being viewed as a veteran – in my case when I hit 30 – your club will start chopping your pay season after season, even if you're playing better than you were five years earlier and probably more valuable to the club because you're no longer spending time with England (although the club would no doubt argue that the fact you're no longer playing for England means they're no longer being compensated by the RFU).

In one of my contract negotiations with Gussy, he put two sheets of paper in front of me. On one of the sheets was what I was earning at the time and on the other was their new offer. 'As you can see,' he said, 'it's fair.'

I replied, 'What part of it is fair? It would be fair if you added another 100 grand.' I had a mortgage, and the payments were based on what I had been earning, not what Quins had suddenly decided to pay me. Things got even worse after Covid. Foreign lads were still coming over on big money and it was the English lads who were having to take the cuts to keep the clubs afloat.

Premiership performances did improve, but two weeks after putting 49 points on Northampton at Franklin's Gardens, we got hammered 49–7 by Racing 92, which put paid to our Champions

Cup hopes. The lads knew something needed to change after that one. We were pretty disillusioned by the game plan, which was all defence and box-kicking and oh so joyless. Marcus was being told what to do and when to do it, which didn't suit him or the team. It was like asking a great artist to paint by numbers.

Proof that nothing was going to change Gussy's philosophy came in the form of England rugby league legend Sean Long, who was brought in to help Snapper with our attack. Being a big rugby league fan growing up, I was so excited to work with Longy. He was slight for a rugby league player but had great control, sublime skills and plenty of swagger, and I thought we could learn plenty from him.

Sure enough, Longy was keen as mustard and full of ideas, a real breath of fresh air. He was open about the fact that he didn't know all the ins and outs of rugby union, but he seemed quite bewildered that we weren't keeping the ball in hands more and kept kicking it away. He was also shocked by the skill levels of some of the lads. For example, he couldn't get his head around the fact that some of them couldn't pass off their 'wrong' hands.

But while Longy came up with a lot of interesting ideas, most of them got shot down. The lads wanted more of him, especially Marcus, who was probably the only bloke at the club as skilful as him, but Longy left at the end of 2020. Just after his departure, he said in an interview, 'I'd put my ideas forward and be told, "No one does that." I'd say, "Why can't we be the first team to do it?" I became so frustrated.' Imagine how the players felt.

Ironically, Gussy had turned into a mini-Eddie, which happens to a lot of coaches who work with him. By his own admission, Gussy was too intense. He'd send messages to the players and staff WhatsApp groups at 4 or 5am – stuff like, 'Let's make today a winning day.' Imagine being one of the lads he wasn't picking and getting woken up by that. He'd get frustrated that some of his staff weren't as driven as him. He'd have his nose in every bit of the business, presumably because he didn't trust people to do their jobs properly.

I even said to him a few times, 'Gussy, you need to chill out, it's too much for you to be worrying about everything. Give the players some responsibility and let the coaches do their thing.' The following day, Gussy would be on the training ground, interrupting drills and generally getting under the coaches' feet. Maybe more experienced coaches would have got him in a room and told him to stay in his lane, but that was never going to happen.

Gussy once said to me, 'I want to be the best coach in the world,' and I replied, 'We don't need you to be the best coach in the world, just be the best coach for us.' And that was the real sadness of the situation. Gussy was working all hours under the sun trying to get things right at Quins when he might as well have been bashing his head against a brick wall. Quins played exciting rugby – it was in our DNA – so even if Gussy *had* been the best coach in the world, he was never going to be the right coach for us.

Gussy was finally let go at the end of January 2021. I felt terrible about it, just as I did when JK went. We were close, as were our wives, and I felt I'd let him down by not playing well enough. Worse, the coaches thought Gussy had been ousted by some of the senior players, which made for an awkward atmosphere.

With Gussy out of the picture, Billy Millard, who had been the general manager, became director of rugby. One of Billy's first tasks was patching up the strained relationship between the players and the coaches. To that end, he created a senior player group and stuck us in a room with the coaches, so that we could thrash things out and hopefully find some common ground.

The coaches said their bit about the players not performing to their potential and we said our bit about the coaches needing to focus on the parts of the game they'd been hired to focus on, which hadn't been happening enough when Gussy was in charge. When Billy asked the players what we wanted to happen, the first thing on our list was scrapping the captain's run the day before a game. If any aspiring coaches are reading this, the captain's run is a rugby tradition that is a complete waste of time. It normally involves lads travelling into training to jog through the moves that they'll be running the next day. None of the lads want to be there and it's mainly a box-ticking exercise for the coaches. If you don't know your detail by Thursday at the latest, you shouldn't be playing at the weekend anyway. We also thought that another day away from the club, recovering and spending time with friends and family, would give us more energy to take on the opposition at the weekend.

We also said that we had to go back to playing the Harlequins way; that we didn't want to be spending all our time in training kicking and chasing and trying to perfect defensive formations; and that training needed to be fun again, which meant playing lots of games. As for our fitness, that would come naturally because those games would be so free and fast. To be fair to them, the coaches' reaction was, 'Why not? Let's go for it and see what happens.'

Almost overnight, the club became a happy place again. Even the lads who hadn't played a minute all season had smiles on their faces. Actually, they probably had the biggest smiles of all. Andy Sanger, a former bomb disposal specialist in the army and now our player development guy, would bring in coffee and cakes every Tuesday, and we'd all sit round gossiping and laughing. A fish and chip van would turn up after training sessions and – whisper it quietly – we sometimes even had a few beers.

Rugby players are simple creatures. Create a nice environment for them and they will work hard for you. Make the work fun and it won't feel like work at all. Suddenly, we were a bunch of mates chucking a ball around a park. And Harlequins, a club that needs to do things differently, felt like the best place to be playing rugby in the whole world.

We were seventh in the table when Gussy left, having won two of our first seven games. And having been partly responsible for a good man losing his job, demanded changes and been given those changes, the players now had a responsibility to perform on the weekend. Which is exactly what we did. It's amazing what can happen when you empower a group of players.

Against Wasps at their place, we threw the ball around with abandon, scored six tries and won 49–17. We followed that up with comfortable wins over Bath, Leicester and Sale, before Dean Richards's Newcastle pipped us up at Kingston Park (I couldn't begrudge him that). The big wins kept coming after that – 37–19 against Northampton, 59–24 against Gloucester, 50–26 against Worcester – but perhaps the two games that best demonstrated how far we'd come were the one-point defeat at Exeter and two-point defeat at Bristol. Both those sides were already nailed-on for the play-offs, so we knew that if we grabbed that fourth spot, we had a chance of beating them.

It was the perfect scenario for me personally. Not only was I no longer being asked to box-kick all the time, but I also didn't have that nagging feeling that every mistake might cost me a place in the England team. That chapter of my life was over, and now I could go back to being the 17-year-old me, except with thinner hair and creakier knees. If I tried something and it didn't come off, so be it, and we had a squad full of players with the same mindset.

Marcus wasn't ready to run the team in his first couple of seasons, but there's no better way to learn than on the job. And by the 2020–21 season, Marcus had developed into the full package. He was certainly the perfect half-back partner for me. We saw the game the same way: we both wanted to attack at every opportunity and beat teams with speed and skill rather than by repeatedly bludgeoning them over the head.

Marcus and I have a competition every year to see who can provide the most assists, and while I'm not sure who won that season, some of his play was magical. But he wasn't just a flair player, like some outsiders seemed to think he was, he could also control games. On top of that, his goalkicking was impeccable, the reason being that he worked harder than anyone else at it. And all that success and praise hadn't gone to his head. He remained humble, eager to learn, and far more sensible than I was at his age. You weren't going to read a headline about Marcus getting arrested for being drunk and disorderly.

Towards the back end of the regular season, it started to feel a lot like 2012 again. Our skipper Stephan Lewies, another one of those brilliant South Africans who'd found his way to our door, was great at rallying the players. He started talking quite early on about us winning the title – none of that 'let's take it one game at a time' stuff from Stephan – and everyone was on board with it. And the closer we got to the play-offs, the more we dared to dream. Screw it, we thought, let's prove that you can win this league by playing expressive, attacking rugby, by being true to yourselves, rather than how Saracens and Exeter have won it in the recent past. How cool would that be?

It shouldn't be forgotten that it was Gussy who brought Stephan to the club, along with his best mate André Esterhuizen and two other key South Africans in full-back Tyrone Green and prop Wilco Louw, all of whom played a big part in our successes that season. However, while Gussy had probably brought them in for their South African grit and physicality, they came to love being part of a club that did things very differently from what they were used to.

André never got injured, never missed a game and was the best player on the pitch every single week. The only downside for him was that Owen Farrell was playing that season in the Championship for Saracens, which meant he couldn't get his revenge. And he managed to be great despite living off braai for dinner every night, rum and Coke and vapes. We'd be in a serious team meeting, a coach would be talking and I'd suddenly get a whiff of fruit. When I turned around, I'd see André blowing out great plumes of vape smoke. I'm not sure he could have got away with that at any other club, but no one ever said anything to him at Quins because he was doing the business on the pitch.

Tyrone Green was another great character. Not long after he came over from Johannesburg with his wife, who he'd been with since he was 13 or 14, they found out they were pregnant. And a few weeks before the due date, he said to me, 'Danny, I'm thinking about getting a dog.' I was a lot older than Tyrone, which he reminded me of every single day, so I tried to pass on a little bit of my wisdom every now and again. And on this occasion, I said, 'Mate, can I just stop you there. Getting a dog now is not a good decision.'

'But I really want to get a dog,' he said.

'But you're just about to have a baby,' I said. 'You don't seem to understand how drastically your life is going to change.' Tyrone looked slightly sad, then said, 'Alright, yeah, you're probably right …' A week later, I heard that Tyrone had gone out and bought a husky.

When the rest of the lads found out about Tyrone's husky, they tore into him. He was living in a small house with a tiny garden and this poor dog, which was supposed to be walked for a couple of hours a day, had nowhere to roam. And a week after that, Tyrone's wife gave birth, bang on schedule.

The next time I saw him, he looked absolutely terrible. 'Oh my God,' he said to me, 'I've had an absolute shocker. The baby's keeping me up all night and the husky keeps howling and eating all the furniture. I don't know what to do.' Two or three months went by, I walked into the gym one morning, and André said to me, 'DC, ask Tyrone how his dog's getting on. And while you're on the subject, ask him how many dogs he's got.' It turned out that Tyrone hadn't just bought one husky, he'd bought two, but was too embarrassed to tell anyone. The biggest irony of the whole situation is that Tyrone was, and is, famously laid-back. And before the baby and huskies turned up, he and his wife liked nothing more than lying in bed all day watching anime cartoons.

I'm happy to relate that Tyrone, his family and his dogs did eventually move to a bigger house. I'm slightly less happy to relate that he leaves his doors open at night, even in winter, so that the dogs can wander in and out. When I suggested that might be a bit risky – I'm basically the Yoda of Harlequins nowadays – Tyrone said, 'If anyone tries to burgle us, our two huskies will rip their heads off.'

When a play-off place was virtually assured, Stephan pulled me aside before a team meeting and asked me to say a few words about what winning the Premiership back in 2012 meant to me and the club. He wanted the boys who weren't there that day, which was most of them, to be able to visualise it. Because when you're able to visualise something you want, and know how it will make you feel, you're more likely to make it happen, or so the theory goes.

I described what it was like to walk out with your best mates at Twickenham – the lads you spend more time with than your own family – what it was like to thrill a crowd as big as that by playing rugby as it was meant to be played; the feeling of euphoria at the final whistle; the ecstasy of lifting the trophy; the hugs and kisses with my loved ones; the heady celebrations that went long into the night. I told them that it was one of the best days of my life, not just in rugby, and what made it even better was that we'd done it fairly.

$$\bigcirc$$

That Quins side was like Kevin Keegan's Newcastle United – you score three, we'll score four. We never thought we were out of a game because our attack was on a different level to everyone else's.

The best example of our Keeganesque philosophy was the game against Wasps towards the end of the season. Wasps nine Dan Robson had the game of his life that day, partly because of where I was asked to defend. I like to be right behind the ruck, so that I can man-mark my opposite number, but Jerry Flannery wanted me out wide, which meant I could only watch as Dan ran the show in the first half, setting up two tries and scoring one. If they'd named him man of the match there and then I don't think anyone would have complained, although we still led by two, mainly because Marcus was having a ridiculous game himself.

Jerry let me try to man-mark Dan from behind the ruck in the second half, but when Browny accidentally trod on Tommy Taylor's head and got sent off, we looked doomed. However, Dommers and I both grabbed tries to keep the game alive, before Marcus took over. First, he kicked a penalty from out wide; then he sparked and finished a blind-side move that levelled the scores bang on 80 minutes; then he popped over the extras for a 48–46 win. The only downside – and it was a big one – was Browny's subsequent six-week ban, meaning he'd never play for Quins again.

As any true fan of rugby will know, the backs can only do their thing if the forwards win them the ball, and we had a pack to rival anyone's. Joe Marler was in full beast mode that season, and he had either Wilco Louw or Will Collier, both amazing scrummagers, on the other side of the front row. In between was Welshman Scott Baldwin, who once got bitten by a lion he tried to pet in South Africa – he's a legend of a bloke and one hell of a hooker. Elsewhere in the pack were unsung English guys like Matt Symons, Jack Kenningham and James Chisholm, our inspirational skipper Stephan Lewies, and Alex Dombrandt, who provided a bit of dash. And on the bench for Scott was my old mate Joe Gray, who had returned from a spell at Saracens. Without the quick front-foot ball those boys provided, and the number of penalties they won at scrum-time, we backs wouldn't have been able to attack like we did.

We secured a play-off spot with a 44–33 win over Bath – another thriller – meaning we'd play table-toppers in the semi-finals.

The last time we'd played Bristol, a few months earlier, we walked off the pitch thinking we knew how to beat them, even though they pipped us 35–33 that day (Kyle Sinckler scored a last-minute try that quite clearly should have been disallowed). It was a strangely similar feeling to nine years earlier, when we lost to Leicester towards the end of the season before beating them in the final.

Browny's ban was a shame, although it allowed Tyrone Green to come in and show what he could do in the 15 shirt. But a definite spanner in the works was the fact that Joe Marler's wife was expecting a baby the weekend of the semis. The rest of the lads kept telling him we couldn't do without him, but Joe told the bosses straight that he wouldn't be able to play. No disrespect to Santiago García Botta, who was Joe's very able understudy, but I think even Santi would say that we needed Marler to play. Not just for his dominant scrummaging and tackling, but also because he drove standards and got team-mates up for it.

If Joe was struggling with his mental health, he'd say before training or a meeting, 'I can't contribute much today,' which everyone was fine with. But when he was on it, which was most of the time, nobody was as inspirational as him. I'd never seen Joe as hellbent on winning the league as he was that year. He was also refreshingly honest and forthright, and it didn't matter how many points we were losing by, Joe never stopped believing we could win.

Luckily, Joe also sits just below the CEO in the club's hierarchy, and Laurie Dalrymple decided to charter a helicopter to ferry him to and from the match. So while the rest of the team stayed in a hotel the night before, Joe got choppered in on the Saturday morning, safe in the knowledge that if his wife went into labour, he'd be choppered straight to the hospital after the game.

Joe landed on the playing fields of a nearby school, to a rapturous reception. He was wearing yet another bespoke Adidas tracksuit – he must have spent about five grand on tracksuits that season – and if he wasn't waving like the Queen, he should have been. And this was a man who claimed he didn't like the limelight. I'd never seen anything so playboy in my life.

Having been so confident of victory, Bristol came out like orcs, with their overseas superstars – Siale and Charles Piutau, Fiji centre Semi Radradra and former All Blacks flanker Steve Luatua – running riot. Max Malins bagged a couple of early tries and we were 28–0 down after as many minutes, not knowing what the hell had hit us. I'll never forget standing under the posts after yet another try, struggling to catch my breath. When Joe Marler and I looked at each other, we couldn't help smiling. Never mind all the pre-match hope, it didn't look like we were coming back this time.

Almost nothing went right for us in the first half, but moments after Dommers had knocked-on a few metres from their line, Marcus put up a speculative bomb, Malins dropped it and Dommers went over in the corner. We still trailed by 21 points at the break, but at least it was something.

Walking towards the tunnel, I noticed that some of their boys were laughing and joking, as if to say, 'Jesus, these boys are rubbish.' They were right, we were, or at least we had been for those 40 minutes. Stephan Lewies asked the coaches if he could have a few minutes with just the players in the changing room at half-time, and as soon as they closed the door behind them, we all burst out laughing.

Stephan and a few of the senior players spoke, and because we still thought we could win, we said so, forcefully. We thought we were fitter than them and would finish the game stronger, when some of their superstars were already off the pitch. And we thought that without their superstars, Bristol were a pretty average team. When the coaches came back in, Stephan said to them, 'Sweet, we've fixed what we needed to fix.' We'd talked a bit about defensive spacing, slowing down their ball, being more physical, but it's not as if we'd come up with some genius plan. We were just going to attack them, like we always did. If we got the first score, it was game on.

Ten minutes after the restart, we were back in the game, courtesy of tries from Tyrone Green and James Chisholm. I started giving them a bit of stick at that point: 'You can't bottle this, boys, surely!' And when Dommers put Louis Lynagh in for another try, we were suddenly only four points behind, and I could see the panic in the Bristol lads' faces. They weren't chirping away like they had been in the first half, and they certainly weren't laughing. And every mistake one of their players made would be followed by bitching.

A penalty put Bristol seven points ahead with 15 minutes to go, but by that time Charles Piutau and Luatua were off the pitch and Radradra wasn't looking anything like as threatening, just as we'd hoped. We also knew that Bristol couldn't manage a game like Exeter or Saracens could and that their director of rugby, Pat Lam, would just be telling them to carry on throwing the ball around, which didn't make as much sense with their big dogs missing.

Then with three minutes left on the clock, we did a training-ground move off the back of a scrum: Marcus put Tyrone away down the left, Tyrone offloaded to Joe Marchant and Joe touched down in the corner. It wasn't a straightforward conversion, but Marcus slotted it to take the game to extra time.

All the momentum was with us and there was no way we were going to lose the game from there, especially given the away support we had. It was only a small crowd because of Covid restrictions, but 500 Quins fans had made the trip and I'd never heard them as loud. Leading the chants with his top off was our flanker Will Evans, who had been brilliant for us earlier in the season before breaking his leg. Will is a big Norwich City fan, so is used to all that kind of madness, and he and some of the boys were even doing the Poznań celebration at one point, jumping up and down with their backs to the pitch while whirling their shirts around their heads.

Callum Sheedy hit the post with a long-range penalty attempt a few minutes into extra time, but it was Tyrone who broke the deadlock, putting us ahead for the first time in the match with his second try, six minutes into first-half added time. Tyrone was unbelievable that day – he really came of age. But, brilliant try that it was, the forwards had done the spadework. And who was still out there scrummaging like a demon? That's right, Joe Marler. That he was able to last so long that day boggled the mind.

I was replaced by Martín Landajo with seven minutes left, and Malins completed his hat-trick a couple of minutes later. Thankfully, Sheedy's drop-goal conversion hit the post, which meant we still led by two, before Marcus put Joe Marchant over in the corner. We couldn't celebrate straight away because the referee, Wayne Barnes, had to look at a potential high shot from Luke Northmore on Siale Piutau. But when Barnes rightly ruled that Luke hadn't made contact with Piutau's head, we could finally cut loose.

I had wondered if I'd ever get back to Twickenham with Quins, and we'd looked dead and buried just over an hour earlier, so I'm not ashamed to say I had a tear in my eye. And talk about a fine margin. Had Max Malins caught that high kick from Marcus just before half-time, they'd have gone on to win the game, no doubt about it. As it was, Dommers's try gave us a sniff, and that's all we needed to complete the 'Miracle of Bristanbul'! As for Bristol, I think we stole a part of their soul that day.

After a few songs and a bit of dancing with the fans, who included Jodie and the kids, the lads retired to the changing room. And once he'd got us to quieten down, Stephan said, 'Shall we do it again at Twickenham next week?' (And in case you were wondering, Joe Marler's chopper arrived home in time for the birth.)

Some in the media made out that the lunatics were running the asylum after Gussy's departure, which sounded dramatic but wasn't actually true.

The coaches had been close to Gussy, so their irritation when he left was hardly surprising. Adam Jones and Jerry Flannery were probably also worried about their own futures, because Gussy had hired them. But despite the strangeness of the situation, and the coaches' obvious unease to begin with, I thought they came into their own once Gussy wasn't around.

Because Adam, Jerry and Snapper had only recently retired, they understood what the players needed and were open to conversations. Snapper and Charlie Mulchrone were in their element working on attack with Marcus, while Jerry managed to find a way of tightening up our defence while not making us less expansive with ball in hand.

Jerry had played the game at the highest level for many years and coached at Munster, but Gussy hired him as a line-out guru and he'd never coached defence before. Jerry would say to a player, Joe Marler for example, 'What you thinking, Joe?' And

Joe would reply, 'Mate, how am I meant to know?' But Jerry worked bloody hard to get to grips with defensive principles and intricacies, and he ended up learning so much that South Africa hired him as their defence coach a couple of years later.

Meanwhile, our forwards loved working with Adam Jones, not only because he knew everything there was to know about scrummaging and all that other weird stuff they get up to, but also because he was a great guy to have around the place (he actually still refers to himself as a 'Welsh icon', which amuses me no end). And above them all was Billy Millard, who didn't get involved in the coaching side of things but would organise and co-ordinate the whole set-up, give speeches and show the odd motivational video. He and the legend that is Andy Sanger must take a massive amount of credit for creating that winning environment.

The coaches picked the team by committee, with Nick and Charlie deciding on the backs and Jerry and Adam deciding on the forwards. It's not what they expected to be doing when they signed up, but it worked. Whether a set-up like that could ever work long-term is doubtful because the players also had a lot more say than usual. It's inevitable that at some point a power struggle would break out: among the coaches, among the players, or between the two groups. But as long as we were winning, that wasn't an issue.

Standing in the way of a second Premiership title were Exeter, who were playing in their sixth consecutive final, which was a remarkable achievement.

When I first started playing for Quins, Exeter had never been in the top division, and they were a bit of easy touch for their first few years in the Premiership. But they eventually got the blend of talented local lads and overseas stars right and became a really formidable outfit. Had the authorities punished Saracens as they could have, Exeter could have had four or five Premiership trophies in their cabinet, instead of only one.

Exeter, who beat Sale in the play-off semis, had class all over the pitch. Sam Simmonds was the Premiership's top scorer that season with 21, despite being a number eight (I finished second with 12). Sam was short for a number eight, only six foot, and had the pace of a winger. As such, he scored lots of tries off the back of line-outs but also some absolute worldies from open play.

Their front row had all played for England, they had Scotland stalwart Jonny Gray in the second row, and their backline was very respectable as well, with Sam Simmonds's brother Joe at fly-half, Jack Nowell at full-back, Henry Slade and Ollie Devoto, both England internationals, in the centres, Wales's Alex Cuthbert on the wing and Scotland's Stuart Hogg on the bench.

Exeter weren't as sexy as some teams, but they were more than the sum of their parts and knew how to win big games. We knew we'd have to be bang on form, although we weren't going to change a thing. We'd be smart when we needed to be smart, but if we had an opportunity to run, we were running hard.

Jodie, the kids and I had just moved into a new house, which was being renovated, and it was an absolute tip. There were piles of our belongings all over the floor, wires hanging out of walls, boxes everywhere and we didn't have any curtains up, not even in our bedroom. But when I opened my eyes and saw a blazing sun on the morning of the final, I smiled and thought, *This has to be our day.* Nobody plays better in the sun than Harlequins, and the weather was glorious when we won the title in 2012.

Blake wandered in as I was packing my gear, then we brushed our teeth together in the mirror. By then, Blake had become a

Quins super-fan (Marcus was, and is, his favourite player, ahead of me and Dommers in joint-second), and he wasn't afraid to offer his views on the game, despite only being six.

'Are you excited about the game, Blake?' I asked.

'I can't wait,' said Blake.

'Do you think we're gonna win?'

'Honestly, Dad, no. Exeter have played really well this year so it's going to be a tough day. But if you do win the trophy, Dad, could you bring it home?'

I looked at him and said, 'Mate, I will do everything I possibly can to make that happen.'

I loved that Blake knew what his dad did for a living – not many players have that privilege – but that little chat did put a bit of extra pressure on me.

Because of Covid, they only allowed 10,000 fans into Twickenham that day, which wasn't ideal but was better than nothing. We'd only been allowed to play in front of hundreds for weeks, so Twickenham felt like it was full. As nine years earlier, loads of our fans turned up three hours before kick-off and lined the way from the Stoop (best fans in the game, no doubt about it), and after the Twickenham debutants had had a look around, Stephan gathered us together and said, 'Go and have some fun, lads. Let's bring the trophy home and have the biggest party imaginable.' That was a message everyone could buy into.

Unlike the Bristol game, this one was nip and tuck from start to finish. It was two tries apiece at the break, before André Esterhuizen's try early in the second half sparked an Exeter onslaught. Tries from Sam Simmonds and Devoto gave them the lead and a Joe Simmonds penalty increased their lead to five points with 15 minutes remaining. And just when we needed a bit of magic,

Marcus started waving his wand about. First, he goose-stepped through a tackle and put Louis Lynagh in for a try, then he drew a couple of defenders and found Tyrone in space, before Tyrone passed to Louis for his second try of the day. What a moment for a very nice lad in front of his mum and dad, Michael, who won the World Cup with Australia at the same ground in 1991.

I didn't think Exeter were coming back from that, although I did have a few doubts when Stuart Hogg went over with a couple of minutes left on the clock. But when they turned the ball over right on their 22, I knew we were home and hosed. I remember looking at the clock and thinking, *Ten seconds and we've done it. And I'm not passing the ball to anyone, I'm booting it out myself.* And when I did, it triggered wild celebrations on the pitch and in the stands.

That was my favourite ever moment on a rugby pitch, even better than anything I did with England. I still get goosebumps thinking about it. I'll never forget the scenes on the final whistle, including sharing a big hug with Ben Tapuai, one of the best blokes you could meet. Every day, in his charming Aussie way, Ben would say, 'Best job in the world, boys.' On this day, it really was!

You could make a film about that season. Not many people would watch it apart from the players' families and Quins fans, but it would have a compelling narrative, especially if you jazzed it up a bit: a disillusioned, underperforming bunch of lads take over the running of the team after a terrible start to the season, start playing like the Harlem Globetrotters and win the title. Although of course, the real story isn't quite as romantic as that.

Gussy played a big part in our success that season – for starters, we wouldn't have done it without the signings he made – while the four coaches who remained at the club after his departure, plus Billy, did one hell of a job in highly unusual circumstances. Plus, there was still plenty of Conor and John Kingston in that team, not to mention so many of the players who had come and gone over the previous nine years.

I was very lucky to win the Premiership as a young, free and single young man, but it was even better winning it as a responsible adult (if you can call a man who laughs at a drawing of a cock and balls responsible). Sharing success with loved ones might be the best thing about being a professional sportsperson, and I'd never seen a smile like the one Blake gave me on the pitch after the game. He'd lost his first tooth celebrating, so I gave him the biggest cuddle once I'd stopped laughing at the big gap in his face.

I'd brought ski goggles to protect my eyes against champagne spray (bold move to pack a pair of ski goggles for a final, I know, but I'd seen LeBron James do it) and they came in very handy in the changing room, because the stuff was flying everywhere. Then we all piled into the Cabbage Patch, probably the greatest pub on earth.

We'd told the landlord, Stu, that we'd keep the numbers down to 50 or 60, but there must have been 200 people in there that night. There was dancing on tables, there was karaoke all through the night, it was just hours and hours of happiness. One of my biggest motivations for success that year was desperately wanting the young boys to experience what I had nine years earlier, and I spent a lot of time watching Marcus, Dommers, Joe Marchant, Louis Lynagh and the like and basking in their pure, unadulterated joy. And unlike the first time I did it, I was very aware that I might never have that feeling again.

Playing professional sport can, frankly, be a bit of a nightmare. We'd had to go through a lot to reach that moment, but that made the triumph so much sweeter, which is why I wouldn't change a thing. And not only could we say that we were the best team in the league, but we had also shown that exciting, attacking rugby, the kind of stuff that gets fans off their feet and squealing in delight, could be winning rugby. And we did it fair and square.

After Saracens' ill-gotten and not particularly inspiring domination, the bleakness of Covid and various clubs' financial struggles, Quins provided a welcome dash of fun and romance. And we'd gone from being the most hated club in the country after Bloodgate to everyone's second team. People would come up to me in the street and say, 'I'm a Bath/Leicester etc. fan, but I love what you Harlequins boys do.' People told me their kids wanted to take up the game because they saw our semi and final.

The day after the night before, we went out in Brighton in full fancy dress. On the Monday, it was an all-day affair in the Ship in Wandsworth – us lads, a load of Quins fans and a trophy full of champagne. Jodie heard me coming down our street at about midnight. When she looked through the bedroom window, she expected to see half the team, but it was just me singing songs with the trophy in my arms.

Before hitting the hay, I snuck into Blake's room, like Santa Claus on Christmas Eve, except far more drunk, and placed the trophy at the end of his bed. And the following morning, he appeared in our room with the trophy, which was almost as big as him, and said, 'I can't believe you brought it home.'

'You said you wanted it,' I replied, 'so Daddy helped win it for you.' And he broke into one of those beautiful gap-toothed smiles again. Playing sport can be a serious business, but it's mainly about making people happy.

Chapter 18

Back in the Room

Some people expected me to retire after that final, but it actually reinvigorated me. Why would I want to give up experiences like that if I was still able?

I hadn't given up hope of playing for England again, even though Eddie was still the man in charge, and I hadn't spoken to him about rugby for years (we'd met at a couple of games and corporate events but only engaged in small talk). But being out of the picture had freed me up to play the way I wanted to play, which ironically meant I was performing as well as any scrum-half in the country. At least that's what some journalists and pundits were saying.

I even thought I might be in with a shout of a Lions call-up, especially after Youngsy ruled himself out of contention. For the fourth time in my career, I received the famous Lions letter, informing me that I was being considered, and there was a bit of chatter in the papers about me going to South Africa (although I only knew that because people kept sending me articles on social media).

Warren Gatland, the Lions head coach for a third time, had been in the stands when Quins narrowly lost to Bristol in March, and I walked off the pitch after the final whistle happy with how I'd performed in front of him. Then I heard that Sam Warburton, who had been Gatland's captain on the last two Lions tours and was now a pundit, had tipped me to go. Sam was obviously close to Gatland, so I couldn't help wondering if he had some inside information.

I watched the squad announcement at home with Jodie. They did it in alphabetical order, backs first, so when they went straight from Bundee Aki to Elliot Daly, I slammed my laptop shut. The nines turned out to be Conor Murray, Gareth Davies and Scotland's Ali Price – trumped by a Scot again!

No disrespect to Ali Price – he'd had a couple of good seasons and ended up starting two of the three Tests ahead of the tour captain, Murray – but Gregor Townsend was one of Gatland's assistants, and he'd been working with Ali for the previous seven years with first Glasgow and then Scotland. Plus, the rest of Gatland's team were Welsh, so I do wonder what might have happened if there had been an English voice in the room.

From what I've heard, it was one of the loosest Lions tours ever, shenanigans-wise, despite the Covid restrictions. As for the actual rugby, it was like watching paint dry, so maybe I was best out of it.

I had a chance to write my autobiography around that time, and it wouldn't have been very complimentary about Eddie. Not that I've given him an easy ride in this book, but had it been published back then, I might never have played for England again, which is why I decided against it. Besides, things weren't looking great for Eddie.

England had a pretty poor Six Nations in 2022 and Eddie was getting quite a bit of flak from the media and fans. Reaching the World Cup final in 2019 was a distant memory, England weren't playing great rugby, and more and more stories about Eddie's oppressive methods were leaking. Then on 30 April, a month or so after England's defeat by France in Paris, Eddie sent me a text saying, 'Well done on 250 not out. Eddie' (he was referring to my 250th Premiership game for Quins). I replied saying, 'Thanks mate, hope you're keeping well, can we catch up over 🍷 at some point? I'd give anything for another crack, would love to help with another whitewash' (the lads were touring Australia again that summer). 'Yes, will do mate,' Eddie texted back, 'let me find a time.' The following morning, he asked me to meet him at the Twickenham Marriott a couple of days later. I was meant to be playing golf, but I quickly cancelled that. If Eddie suggests a date, you say yes.

We had coffee instead of wine because it was 9am, and Eddie was nicer than I'd ever seen him. He spent the first ten minutes talking about Jodie and the kids, and I was thinking, *Is this some kind of a trap?* Then he suddenly said, 'Firstly, Danny, I want to tell you that I don't have a problem with you. Loads of people have asked me why I haven't been picking you, and they assume we've had a falling out, but the reason I didn't pick you was because you weren't playing well enough.' I told him it felt a bit more personal than that, but I was also very aware that one careless phrase might be the end of me – Eddie could go from affable uncle to malevolent dictator in a nanosecond. 'Look,' Eddie said, 'I think you've been playing really well this season and I'm ready to have another look at you.' That was all I wanted to hear. I left that meeting elated. Then I didn't hear from him for the rest of the season.

Quins had continued where we'd left off the previous year. New Zealander Tabai Matson had been brought in as director of rugby, the rest of the coaches had stayed the same, and we'd played some great rugby on the way to finishing third in the table, which had been our aim. That meant a play-off semi-final against Saracens on that god-awful 4G pitch of theirs, which is terrible on the joints and leaves players with brutal cuts (promotes a better brand of rugby, apparently, never mind player welfare).

We'd had quite a few injuries towards the end of the season and our squad was very stretched, but we were desperate to beat Sarries. Because of their cheating they'd been down in the Championship when we won the Premiership title, so we wanted to prove we could win it with them involved.

Their players had obviously heard what some of our players, including me, had said about them, which made for quite a fractious atmosphere that day. We made a great start, with Dommers going over early and Marcus dancing around a few players before putting me in for a try after 20 minutes, but Sarries came on strong in the second half. Ben Earl was at his electric best in the back row, which was irritating, because he was extremely annoying to play against. Every time Sarries won a turnover or a scrum penalty, he'd be whooping, fist pumping, jumping up and down and slapping people on the back. It made us angry, especially when they started winning.

As much as I despised Saracens, they were a very good team, and had a knack of edging tight matches. Still, we could have won that game. We kept dropping the ball and butchered some exits, which gifted them a couple of soft tries. We also couldn't make the most of the fact their players kept getting sin-binned (three in the second half, and a couple could have been reds). Our winger Cadan Murley did go over to reduce the deficit to ten points, but when Tommy Lawday was held up over the line when he reached out to score, when he could have placed it back for another phase of attack, the momentum swung back their way and Ben Earl finished us off with his third try.

I was devastated at the final whistle, and gutted when I walked into the changing room. I noticed a couple of staff members and a few of the lads were already dressed for the end-of-season social, laughing and getting stuck into the beers. It felt like we'd just been happy to be there rather than desperate to win, which didn't sit well with me and a few of the other more experienced players. That drive that had propelled us to such heights the previous season had evaporated without me noticing.

That evening, I texted Eddie to ask if we could have a chat – I wanted to know if I was in with a chance of touring Australia or if I could go on holiday with the family – and he called me back after the second semi. He told me he was finalising selection and that he'd let me know if I was needed for the game against the Barbarians the following weekend. I had to tell Eddie that the Barbarians had asked me to play for them and expected me to fly to the south of France for a training camp (week-long piss-up) the following morning. Eddie said he'd call me then, which didn't help me at all.

I texted Eddie again on the way to the airport, to tell him that the Barbarians were flying out at 11.30am. 'Sorry to ask again,' I wrote, 'but I just need to know if I should get on the plane or not. Can you let me know?'

He texted back 15 minutes later to say that he was still final-ising his squad. The taxi was just pulling into the rank when he texted again: 'Mate, you're in for the Barbarians game.'

'Amazing,' I wrote back, 'I'll turn the taxi around 😂.'

'Good,' replied Eddie. He wasn't really an emoji kind of guy.

I'm sure Eddie could have told me the night before and saved me the mental torture, but I was nonetheless extremely grateful. It just so happened that Blake was playing in a football tournament near Heathrow, so I paid him a surprise visit. Jodie was pleased to see me – she was pregnant with our third child so probably hadn't been over the moon about the prospect of me going off for a week-long piss-up. Then again, if I played well against the Baa-Baas, I might be spending a month in Australia instead.

Steve Berrick, the guy who organises the Baa-Baas tours, was very understanding, but couldn't resist telling me that they were going to give England a mullering – which is exactly what they did. It was a mainly French Barbarians outfit and they were unbelievable that day, winning 52–21 despite playing with 14 men for 43 minutes (Australian lock Will Skelton was the first player in Baa-Baas history to get sent off). That was former England lock George Kruis's final game, and whenever I'd text him to find out how training was going, he'd told me they'd hardly done any and were on the piss every day. After backheeling a conversion through the posts, he gave me a cheeky wink.

England were flying to Australia the following day, so Eddie spent that evening tapping players on the shoulder and telling them if they were going or not. Players were walking back to the team dinner and saying, 'Nah, going home ...' When Eddie pulled me aside, he kicked off with, 'You'd better go home to see your wife and kids,' which didn't sound good, before adding, 'because you're coming to Australia.'

Somehow, I'd managed to get back in the room. And while some wives might have been annoyed about their husband pissing off for a month in the middle of a pregnancy, Jodie just said, 'Go and do your thing.'

Courtney Lawes was captain for that tour, and he must be the most chilled leader England have ever had, off the field at least. We'd be on the bus to a game against South Africa and Courtney would be watching cartoons on his phone. I'd walk into his room at Pennyhill Park and he'd be laid out on his bed with icy aircon blowing right in his face. He'd have three different laptops on the go – one for gaming, one for Netflix, one for any other business he needed to take care of – and be surrounded by food. Because he was naturally so lean, he was the only person in the squad allowed to eat everything on the menu, but he'd also get Nando's or Wagamama delivered. His team-mates would come to his room to scavenge for scraps. Courtney never changed and never conformed, much like Joe Marler.

While his fellow forwards were banging their heads against the walls before a game, Courtney would be as cool as a cucumber. He only spoke when he absolutely had to, even when he was captain, but that only gave his words more weight. And he was happy to let other senior players lead their different areas. But once he stepped over the whitewash, he became one of the most physical players I ever played with, an absolute animal who just loved melting people. To play as long as he did as a second row, make that many tackles, and suffer that many injuries, it's a wonder he's still standing. What's more, he wasn't afraid to stand up for the lads. If Courtney thought we'd done enough training, he'd say, 'Right, the boys are ready,' and Eddie would go along with it. It helped that Eddie seemed to have worked out by then that we didn't need flogging at the end of a long, hard season.

I was picked to start the first Test in Perth (Youngsy missed the tour for personal reasons), and although we lost, I thought I looked pretty sharp. When Jack van Poortvliet replaced me and scored a try with one of his first touches, I was genuinely buzzing for him. Some young lads nowadays don't ask the old boys questions, presumably because they think they've cracked it already, but Jack was very eager to learn and we'd become quite close already.

When Eddie told me that Jack was starting the second Test in Brisbane and that I'd go back to my traditional finishing role,

I had no complaints. Jack had a blinder, as if he was born to play in that kind of arena; I played the last 15 minutes, and we levelled the series. I assumed I'd be on the bench again the following week at the Sydney Cricket Ground, but Eddie pulled me aside on the Monday and told me he needed my experience from the first whistle. I couldn't understand his rationale – Jack had just had a great game, the team had played well and we'd won to level the series – but I wasn't going to argue.

I trained well all week and felt good going into the game, but we arrived at the ground late, had a rushed warm-up and started slowly. They scored a try halfway through the first half, I had a box-kick charged down for the first time in ages, but it wasn't a train wreck by any means. However, when I glanced over at the bench on 35 minutes, I saw Jack stripped off ready to come on. I had instant flashbacks to England's last tour of Australia, when Luther Burrell was hooked after just 28 minutes of the first Test and Teimana Harrison was hooked after just 31 minutes of the third Test. On both occasions, I was sat on the bench when they came off. They were in a state of shock, and I knew there was nothing I could say to make them feel okay, so I just put my arm around them and said sorry.

Jack gave me an embarrassed look, and I gave him an embarrassed look back. I thought it had ended four years earlier, Eddie had brought me back in against all odds, after four long years, and now he was doing this to me. Why?

Aussies in the crowd were laughing at me as I took my place on the bench. Most of my team-mates were making a tremendous effort not to look me in the eye, and the ones who were able to said sorry. And if people are feeling sorry for you as a rugby player, you know things have gone badly wrong. When someone stuck a camera in my face, I wanted the ground to swallow me up.

Freddie Steward scored just before half-time to give us a one-point lead, so the lads were in good spirits in the changing room. All except for me. Our attack coach, Martin Gleeson, gave me a big cuddle and said, 'One of you was going and it just happened to be you,' which I thought was a bit weird. Then one of Eddie's long-suffering analysts showed me a piece of paper listing all the players and how they needed to play. And in a gold box was written '30-minute substitution' and three names: Mako Vunipola, Jamie George and Danny Care.

It later transpired that Eddie had been speaking to some Aussie rules coaching guru, who had told him that if your team is slightly off it in the early stages of a game, you'll get a more positive reaction from the players if you hook someone before half-time rather than during or just after the break. And, apparently, I'd made more mistakes than Mako or Jamie.

Credit where it's due, Eddie's plan worked. The lads were even better in the second half, ending up 21–17 winners, and maybe they were thinking, *Damn, I don't want what happened to Danny to happen to me.* And I'm kind of glad it did happen to me instead of one of the younger lads, like Marcus Smith or our winger Tommy Freeman, who was only 21 and playing his second Test. It hurt, and it was very embarrassing, but I was experienced enough to take it on the chin without it having any long-term psychological consequences.

Eddie wasn't paid to keep everyone happy, he was paid to make the team win, so I couldn't help but have a grudging respect for his tactics that day. We won the game, we won the series, job done. But I was still angry. I'd waited four years for a recall and it felt like another power play on Eddie's part. *Screw you*, I imagined him thinking, *I'm gonna take you off, we're gonna play better, we're gonna win, and people will see I was right all along.*

We all went out that night in Sydney, but I wasn't really in a celebrating mood. I'd been stuck on 84 England caps for so long and now I had the sinking feeling that I'd be finishing my career on 87. And while we'd won another series against Australia, I didn't really feel like I'd been part of it. Courtney put his arm around me and said, 'Mate, forget about it, it doesn't matter.' But I couldn't forget about it. I didn't think I was coming back from that.

I asked Eddie about it before flying home and he said he had to change something because we needed fresh impetus, and it just happened to be me. Snapper offered an alternative version of events when I spoke to him a week later. 'I reckon the only reason he recalled you was to do that to you,' he said. Maybe Snapper was right, but it's not really what I wanted to hear.

Our third child, Rocco, was born on 8 October 2022, the day before Blake's birthday (both Jodie and my birthdays are in January, and all three of our kids were born about nine months later!). Like most youngest children, including my little sister, poor Rocco gets dragged along for the ride, whether it's Blake's football or Koha's ballet, but he doesn't seem to mind. He's the most happy-go-lucky, chilled-out lad and loves being outside and chucking himself off and into everything. He, Blake and Koha are the most perfect little trio.

I didn't hear from Eddie before the 2022 autumn internationals, and I honestly wasn't that bothered. I'd have loved to have played a few more games with Marcus as my half-back partner, for sure, but the environment hadn't changed in the four years I'd been away. Players were still walking on eggshells and staff still looked terrified of making a mistake. Having been immersed in such a fun environment at Quins, it was really quite jarring. Besides, '87 was the year of my birth, so finishing up on 87 England caps felt quite poetic.

Having said that, certain players seemed able to get away with murder. Luke Cowan-Dickie, who's as loose as the loosest goose you'll ever come across, didn't stop drinking the whole night before we left Australia and turned up to the team meeting wearing sunglasses and carrying four vodka Red Bulls. I expected Eddie to chuck him out, but instead he said, 'Love that you feel comfortable enough to do that, mate. Every team needs someone like you …'

I couldn't get my head around it. I love Dickie, he's a great bloke with a heart of gold, but even I was thinking he'd gone too far. It felt almost staged, as if Eddie was using Dickie as a pawn in another of his mind games: 'Everyone look at this guy! Who said you couldn't have fun in my England set-up?'

Then we moved on to the team debrief, which involved the team psychologist. She was trying to get us to talk about what needed to be done to improve England rugby, but none of the lads were engaging. Dickie had an obvious excuse, but it felt like the rest of them feared saying something that Eddie might use against them. I felt a bit daft to be honest: this was the room I'd been dreaming of getting back into for the last four years – and it was toxic.

After a run of just five wins in 12 Tests, including defeats by Argentina and South Africa in his final autumn international series, Eddie was sacked in December 2022. It was quite ballsy of the RFU to get rid of him less than a year before the 2023 World

Cup, but I also thought he'd overstayed his welcome by two or three years because his methods were unsustainable.

Having said that, I owe Eddie a lot. When others had tried to reshape me to fit into a team, he was the first England coach who told me, 'Be yourself and you'll be fine.' And I like to think he recalled me to the team having decided he'd been a bit harsh on me, despite what happened later in Australia. There has to be a heart in there somewhere. I didn't always agree with Eddie's methods, but he was a genius coach and desperate for England to do well.

Nobody was ever comfortable working under Eddie – not even Luke Cowan-Dickie – but I'm sure some of the untouchables who were still knocking around the squad were looking over their shoulders for the first time in years. And you had to feel sorry for someone like Zach Mercer, who fell into that black hole along with me and a load of other players around 2018–19, before moving to Montpellier in 2021 and winning a Top 14 title and player of the season award. Eddie told Zach he'd be part of his plans again if he returned to England, but he'd only been playing for Gloucester for a couple of months when Eddie got binned. He's still waiting for an England recall.

On the other hand, I think the majority of players thought it was time for someone else to have a go, and none of them would have been surprised when Steve Borthwick got the job. Borthers had done his time as an England player and captain and coached under Eddie for Japan and England, before leading Leicester to their first Premiership title in nine years in 2022. He knew English rugby inside out and I thought he was the perfect man for the job.

Borthers was quite chopsy as a player, always chirping away at opposition players and getting in the referee's ear, as befits the skipper of a Saracens team I'd already begun to hate (I said to

Borthers when he was appointed assistant coach under Eddie, 'Mate, I'm going to have to apologise for all the things I've said to you on the pitch.' He just replied, 'Danny, we've all said things we didn't mean, and I'm sure I said some horrible things to you as well'). But when he was my captain for England, I really liked him.

Borthers was phenomenally hardworking and always talking about how much it meant to represent your country, although he's since talked openly about living in constant fear of losing his place in the team, which is why he didn't enjoy the experience as much as he should have done. I'm not sure he enjoyed being a coach under Eddie, either, which is why he was so determined to create an environment in which players and staff felt like they were having the time of their lives, rather than wanting to be anywhere else but there.

The RFU also needed a bloke who could get a decent tune out of the England team in time for the World Cup, which was only nine months away, and Borthers had shown with Leicester that he could turn things around quickly (he transformed them from relegation candidates to Premiership champions in 18 months). Not that I was part of Borthers's rebuilding plans initially, and I must admit that I was disappointed not to get a call from him before the 2023 Six Nations. Then again, some of the best matches are those you don't play in, because coaches can see what they're missing.

Quins finished sixth in the Premiership in the 2022–23 season, but we hadn't missed out on the play-offs by much and I'd played pretty well for a bloke in his mid-30s. My partnership with Marcus was certainly still fizzing. But despite thinking that England had lacked a bit of leadership during the Six Nations – we only won two games, lost to Scotland and got pummelled by

France at Twickenham – I still hadn't heard from Borthers weeks after my season was over. Then, one day, I was sat on the toilet when a breathless Blake knocked on the door and said, 'Dad, Steve Borthwick's calling you!'

Every now and again, Blake would ask me, 'Do you think you'll ever play for England again?', and I'd reply, 'Obviously I'd love to, but we'll have to wait and see if Steve wants to pick me.' So he was mad excited that Borthers was now on the phone. And as soon as I'd finished my business, I phoned Borthers back.

The first thing that struck me was how friendly Borthers sounded. He was so softly spoken, and I had to squeeze the phone against my face to hear everything he was saying. And after the usual pleasantries, he suddenly said, 'Look mate, I know this is a big ask, and something you'll have to discuss with the family, but would you be up for coming on the next England camp with a view to making the squad for the World Cup?' He went on to explain that England were missing some scrum-half experience and guidance in the Six Nations, and when he'd finished his pitch, I replied, 'Steve, the answer is yes.'

Me preparing for and potentially playing in a World Cup would mean Jodie holding the fort for months. We were still renovating our house and the crappy little rental we were living in had mice running around the place and nails hanging out of the floor, and Rocco was only a toddler. But she said to me, 'Danny, you've been dying for this to happen. Do it.' As for Blake, while he'd found me disappearing off to Australia the previous summer quite tough – I'd been around for the previous four years – he'd aged about 25 years in the 12 months since. 'Dad,' he said to me, sounding like a wise old man, 'it's a great opportunity, so you've got to take it.'

The three nines in the Six Nations were Jack van Poortvliet, Northampton's Alex Mitchell and Youngsy, who only played about 20 minutes. And while Jack and Alex didn't play badly, I think Borthers was concerned about taking two inexperienced nines to a World Cup. But I wasn't getting ahead of myself. I'd only been invited to a training camp, and I'd still have to show that my creaking old legs were up to it and I could fit into Borthers's system.

Borthers told me to be myself, off the field as well as on it. It's not that he wanted me to be some kind of team jester, but he thought the environment needed loosening up after the Eddie years. He even suggested Jamie and I revive our roles as social secretaries, to get the players smiling. Why would he suggest Ant and Dec get back together if he wasn't planning on taking me to France? There didn't seem to be any mind games with Borthers – he was as honest as they came – so I thought that was a pretty good sign.

That was probably the hardest England camp I'd ever been in, partly because of my advancing years, partly because Borthers had the same very high standards as Eddie when it came to training. But a key difference between Borthers and Eddie was that once training was over, players could switch off from rugby and relax. We'd have a meeting every day just before dinner and nothing afterwards, which meant we could do whatever we wanted.

Under Eddie's regime, the schedule would be packed with events, some of which were impromptu. You could be sat in your room at eight o'clock in the evening and suddenly you'd get a call telling you to be downstairs for a meeting in half an hour, and that meeting might go on until almost ten. Players would be worried about having an early night, however exhausted they were, in case they missed something. It was a bit like that

Channel 4 programme *SAS: Who Dares Wins*, in that anything could happen at any moment, just as Jonny May always used to say. God help any players who were on the anxious side.

My old mate and rival Richard Wigglesworth was one of Borthers's coaches, and having kept his secrets very close to his chest for years, he was suddenly teaching me everything I needed to know about box-kicking. I said to him, 'Mate, could you not have told me all this stuff five or six years ago?' I also loved working with Kevin Sinfield, who was a Leeds rugby league legend and a bit of a hero of mine growing up. It was a great environment, and I felt like I trained really well. I certainly didn't feel shown up by the youngsters.

We only had one warm-up game before the final squad announcement, against Wales in Cardiff, and I didn't really want to play in it. I'd got injured in a warm-up against Wales in 2011, and I'd seen quite a few team-mates play themselves out of contention in warm-up games in the intervening years. But Borthers had to pick someone to play scrum-half, and that someone was me.

Alex Mitchell had already been sent home, leaving just me, Youngsy and Jack van Poortvliet, and I still didn't know if Borthers planned to take two or three scrum-halves to France. So when we lost that game in Cardiff, I was half expecting a tap on the shoulder. I hadn't played badly, but it had been a pretty average performance overall. But when I mentioned my doubts to Wiggy, he said, 'Mate, there are only three nines here and he's taking three. Surely you know that?' I felt a bit pathetic. I was a 36-year-old man living in constant fear of getting canned, although it also showed how much it meant to me.

The following Monday, Borthers asked me to go for a walk with him. And despite what Wiggy had told me, I was crapping myself. I actually thought, *By the time this walk is over, I will no longer be an England player.*

We spent the first ten minutes talking about family, and then he suddenly stopped and said, 'I just wanted to clear something up. I'm obviously taking you to the World Cup.' I felt like hugging him, until I remembered that Borthers was England's head coach and not really a hugging kind of guy, so I shook his hand instead. 'Amazing,' I said, 'thanks so much.' He looked at me as if I was mad and said, 'How did you not know I was taking you?'

I wish Borthers had just told me he was taking me after sending Alex Mitchell home, but my doubt was more a legacy of previous regimes than any miscommunication on Borthers's part. I always suspected I had more to give, but my self-belief had taken a bit of a battering over the previous four years. Borthers had told me a few times that he wanted me to feel comfortable, but I kept thinking of poor Luther Burrell in 2015 and all those players that Eddie had given hope to before discarding.

After we'd returned to the hotel, I got straight on the phone to Jodie. 'We've done it,' I told her, 'I'm on the plane.'

Chapter 19

Actually Pretty Good

The media were having a full-on meltdown after the rest of our World Cup warm-ups. We were pretty ordinary in beating Wales at Twickenham and well-beaten by Ireland in Dublin, before being ambushed by Fiji. That was the first time they'd ever beaten us, and we'd now lost five of our last six games. There was talk about us being one of the worst England teams ever, of us not making it out of the pool stage, but there was no sense of panic in the England camp.

Borthers had spent just a week with the England lads before the Six Nations, which is a tough tournament to compete in at the best of times. He could have gone two ways: let's just chuck the ball about and see what happens (what you might call the Quins solution); or let's try to shore up our defence, sharpen up our kick-chase game and become a really difficult team to beat. He chose the second option, which was actually quite brave of him, because he must have known that fans and the media would complain about the spectacle.

Borthers didn't worry about what the media thought about him or his team. He certainly didn't go into press conferences planning to say something funny or confounding, like Eddie often did (although Borthers has tweaked his approach slightly, having realised that if you throw the media a few crumbs, they're less likely to savage you). But I remember watching that Six Nations and thinking, *It's not great rugby, but they do look hard to beat –*

apart from the France game, obviously, but even then I could see what they'd got wrong.

When I got into Borthers's England set-up, I was amazed by his attention to detail. He had a load of computer boffins working for him, and they'd run simulations, almost like *Football Manager*. They'd punch in two teams' stats over the previous however many months, play them against each other, and the simulator would come up with a probable winner.

But Borthers combined all that number crunching with a personal touch. He'd say, 'I'll only ever ask you to do something for a reason,' then show us some stats. And the stat that really stopped me in my tracks was that every 50-50 kick a team wins back in Test match rugby increases their chances of winning by five per cent. That didn't sound right to me, but when I gave it some thought, it actually made perfect sense. Contested kicks are one of the few ways a team can create a bit of unstructured chaos, because when the kick goes up, defences are spread and there are gaps all over the field. As such, if the ball does come back on your side, there's likely to be a chance to attack when the defence isn't set and ready.

I'd spent my entire rugby career moaning about people box-kicking, and being told by England coaches to improve my 'consistency of kick', and I finally understood – at the age of 36 – why they did it. And I was lucky enough to have one of the best box-kickers ever in Wiggy to teach me all about it (having said that, I still maintain that box-kicking should only be one part of a team's arsenal, not the be-all and end-all).

Borthers didn't have time to be romantic even if he'd wanted to be. It was about identifying parts of the game we could get good at quickly – a solid set-piece, exiting well, being hard to score against – and I never doubted his methods even after we lost to Fiji. I understood why the media and fans were worried – I would have been as an outsider looking in – but Borthers kept saying, 'I promise you, boys, things are about to click, I'm seeing it in training.' I believed him, and that Fiji game did us a favour, because it meant we travelled to the World Cup knowing we still had a lot more work to do.

Le Touquet was the perfect base for us. It's only 40 minutes from Calais, the weather is similar to England's – it was pissing down when we arrived – and it was quite low-key without there being nothing to do. We could go out for a coffee or a couple of beers without being hassled, there were lots of golf courses and padel courts, or you could just go for a nice walk on the beach.

It felt like the whole of Le Touquet came out to watch our first training session, and we gave them a pretty good show. Things suddenly clicked, just as Borthers said they would. It was like watching a blurry photo suddenly come into focus. We were creating quick ruck ball, we were fizzing the ball around, we were running hard. Marcus was carving things up, Owen Farrell and George Ford looked sharp, Ben Earl and Bath centre Ollie Lawrence were hitting great lines. I remember thinking, *Damn, we're actually a pretty good team.* Everyone knew the game plan, everyone was on board with it, and I think we were all quietly confident that we were going to prove a lot of people wrong.

Before Ben Earl came into the England fold, I'd say to Jamie George, 'What's he like? He seems like a total bellend on the pitch.' Jamie would reply, 'Danny, you would absolutely love him if he was on your team.' Jamie was right, I fell in love with him almost straight away. I even came to enjoy all that celebrating he did every time a team-mate turned the ball over. Well, kind of.

Ben is very well-educated and very posh, not dissimilar to Haskell, but I loved spending time with him, especially on the golf course. He's got a handicap of three, because he's been playing it all his life, but he's the easiest person ever to wind up. Jamie George and I have formed a formidable partnership throughout the years, on and off the field, but we did our best work on the golf course. Jamie used his contacts at Nike to get us kitted out with seven matching outfits for the World Cup, including a bucket hat to complete each look. That's how the 'Bucket Hat Boys' were born. The Bucket Hat Boys dovetailed exquisitely; we backed ourselves against any opponent and intimidated our opposition with unrivalled swagger (facing us must have felt like going up against Tiger Woods in his absolute prime). However, Ben wasn't a huge fan. We could mentally destroy him with a single comment about his swing or grip, and he always went mad when he lost a hole and we'd play 'Another One Bites the Dust' on my phone. He once told me he wanted to wrap his driver round my head. But he's like that because he's so incredibly competitive.

Ben took a hammering from Eddie when he first came into the England team. Eddie had developed a dislike of public schoolboys; he thought they were too soft and that there were too many in English rugby, and Ben was as public schoolboy as they came. I found out that during a Six Nations tournament, Eddie told Ben that he wasn't performing well enough because he'd been raised wrong. I thought that was an outrageous thing to say to a young player, but Ben took it on the chin, kept working on his game and seized the opportunity when it came. I'll be shocked if Ben doesn't captain the side one day because he's the perfect Test match animal. He can play in the forwards, he can play in the backs, he can do almost anything.

Borthers leant on a few experienced players, saying stuff like, 'It's your last World Cup, boys, this is your only chance to win one. So whatever you can do to help this team, do it.' I was fully on board with that. Borthers had believed in me and given me another chance at 36, so I'd have done almost anything for him.

We'd have to do without Owen Farrell for our opener against Argentina because he'd been banned following a high shot against Wales in Cardiff (we were down to 12 men at one stage in that game and they had to bring extra chairs into the sin-bin – there's a great photo of Faz, Ellis Genge and Freddie Steward sat side by side looking glum), but there was relief in the England camp that Faz would at least be back for our third game against Chile.

Faz was the ultimate leader; I'd never met a bloke who was more passionate about playing for England or more determined to win. He drove standards among others by demanding the most of himself, and while that ruffled a few feathers and some people couldn't handle it, I always loved that about him. It made me a better player and improved the whole team.

I think even Faz would admit that he was too much of a rugby obsessive in his early days, but he's mellowed over recent years (having kids will do that to you). Then again, maybe he had to be completely consumed by rugby to get to where he did. Faz wasn't the quickest, or the strongest, or the most athletic, but he did work the hardest and have more mental resilience than anyone else I ever played with. Plus, he was far more skilful than people gave him credit for. I suspect Faz will be one of those players who only gets the respect he deserves once he's disappeared into the sunset. The Premiership and England will certainly miss him now he's decided to try his luck in France with Racing 92.

As to why some people never took to Faz, maybe it was the fact he preferred not to reveal too much of himself to the media; maybe it was his association with a dominant Saracens side that didn't play the most thrilling rugby, and was later found to have cheated (he had nothing to do with that, but he was the bloke kicking all the goals and lifting all the trophies, which made him guilty by association in some people's eyes); maybe it's just that people don't understand rugby and therefore how good he was. Whatever the reasons, a lot of nonsense was written and said about Faz, although he didn't care what anyone thought about him. All he cared about was helping the team win, whether he was wearing the red of Saracens or the white of England.

Those who know Faz well will vouch for what a lovely bloke he is. He adores his family, loves a joke and can sing like an angel, which will surprise a few people. I can hold a tune, but the first time I heard that silky voice of Faz's, I felt like punching him. He's one of those lads who's annoyingly good at everything – football, golf, table tennis, although I can beat him at pool – so to find out he sang miles better than me as well was like a dagger to the heart.

There was no moping about from Faz before the Argentina game; he was as influential as ever – still speaking in meetings, still busting a gut. He was like an extra coach on the training ground, always helping others, as well as being the best player. There was no better preparation for the lads than going up against Faz all week – Argentina fly-half Santiago Carreras was decent, but he wasn't a patch on Faz – and once we were all done for the day, Faz would do extra fitness sessions to make up for the fact he wasn't playing at the weekend.

We were confident of beating Argentina – and then Tom Curry got sent off after three minutes (Was it high? Yes. Was it in any way malicious? Of course not). Step forward George Ford, who was playing fly-half instead of Faz and gave one of the greatest individual performances in World Cup history.

Borthers would often tell us to 'find our advantage', and he'd talk a lot about drop goals in the build-up, even though they'd kind of gone out of fashion, for reasons that are a mystery to me. Our fly-halves would practice them every day, as would I (Borthers would have me hitting them from the base of rucks), and George slotted three of them against the Pumas, as well as six penalties. (I was winding George up about the fact I had more international drop goals than him that week, which is probably why he went out and smashed my tally!) We outclassed Argentina and made them look average, which they weren't. And beating any team with 14 men does great things for team spirit.

I found myself in the stands for our second game against Japan, Youngsy having taken my place on the bench, while Alex Mitchell was starting again, having not been in Borthers's original squad. Mitch was called up after Jack van Poortvliet got injured in camp, and it was a running joke that he'd had the best World Cup ever, missing out on four weeks of horrendous training and those awful warm-up games and being parachuted in for the good stuff.

Youngsy and I were a bit put out at first, but Mitch was so chilled about it – 'You want me to start? Yeah, sweet, I can do that' – that it was impossible to be jealous of him. Besides, he repaid Borthers's faith in spades against Argentina. He'd worked so hard on his kicking game, played at a high tempo and was exactly what we needed. Still, I was gutted not to be involved, especially as Jodie and our good friends Paul and Gill Fleming were over for the weekend.

The evening before the game, I'd met Jodie, Gill and 'FlemDog', as Paul likes to be known, for a bit of dinner. I'd requested somewhere low-key, because I didn't want to get spotted drinking a glass of wine by any fans or journalists, but within five minutes of turning up at this restaurant in Cannes, the music had been cranked up, burlesque dancers had taken to the stage, and people were up dancing on tables. If Carlsberg did restaurants, they'd look a lot like this one, and I couldn't help getting a little bit caught up in all the fun. Even so, every time another bottle of wine appeared on the table, I'd think, *Anything could happen in tomorrow's warm-up. What if one of our nines gets injured?*

Thankfully, the game against Japan kicked off at 9pm, so I had the whole day to recover, and Mitch and Youngsy made it through the warm-up unscathed. Even better, we won fairly emphatically, scoring four tries to none.

I played 50 minutes of our 71–0 victory over Chile, before starting on the bench against Samoa. Samoa had lost two of their first three games and had almost no hope of qualifying for the knockout stages, but you wouldn't have known it. We started pretty well, Manu Tuilagi making plenty of yards against the country of his birth and Ollie Chessum going over for an early try, but they had us on the ropes after that. Winger Nigel Ah Wong scored two quick tries, before Duncan Paia'aua pounced on a box-kick from Mitch and dived over for what appeared to be Samoa's third. Had that try stood, we would have been 11 points down at the break. As it was, the ref ruled it out for a slight knock-on.

We chopped and changed personnel after the break but still couldn't find a way through. And things got very shabby when Faz was timed-out by the shot clock when lining up a straightforward penalty attempt. But with seven minutes left, Samoa went to sleep at the scrum and I scampered over unopposed for my first World Cup try, which made it 16–17. When Faz knocked over the extras for the win, it was 'phews' all round in camp England.

Our reward for finishing top of the pool was a quarter-final against Fiji, who had already beaten Australia and given Wales a scare, although also lost to Portugal. We took that Portugal result with a pinch of salt and prepared for the side that had pulled our pants down at Twickenham two months earlier.

Fiji had always been incredible athletes – big, powerful and skilful – but they'd added some nastiness to their game, which made them even harder to beat. Tries from Manu Tuilagi and Joe Marchant gave us an 11-point cushion at half-time, but things went tits up after I came on with 20 minutes to go. Their two quick tries had nothing to do with me (one of them came from a ridiculous offload from Bristol's Semi Radradra) but suddenly it was 24–24 and I was thinking, *We're about to lose to Fiji and people are gonna blame me …*

We held an emergency meeting under the posts, the findings of which were: be more physical in defence, stay out of rucks, fill the field, keep hold of the ball and get it down their end. We spent the next five minutes battering away at their line, and maybe could have scored if we'd spun it wide, but maybe wasn't good enough. So after quite a few phases, I turned around and shouted to Faz, 'Three! Drop goal!' There was no defender within 10 metres of him when he received the ball, and he popped it over with ease.

Everyone always goes on about how lovely Fijians are, but I want to dispel that myth right now. I was about to put the ball into a scrum when their replacement scrum-half stamped on my foot. A few opposition nines had leant on my feet before – that was just a classic bad scrum-half thing to do – and I'd always told them to stop being a twat. But this time, when I'd recovered from the shock and the pain, I said to the ref and linesman, who were both standing a few feet away, 'Lads, I'm not being funny, but he's just full-on stamped on my foot right in front of you.' They claimed they hadn't seen it – and then he did it again.

Only after the game did I remember that Kuruvoli had ruffled my hair after scoring against us at Twickenham, so he had form on the bellend front. My left foot hurts to this day.

Ben Earl very nearly scored one of the tries of the tournament with a few minutes left, before Faz knocked over a penalty to give us a six-point lead. And when Courtney Lawes won a turn-over five minutes into added time, that was the end of it. When I shook Kuruvoli's hand, I couldn't resist saying to him, 'Have a safe flight home.' I was quite happy with that remark.

Everyone was going on about Faz's amazing game management after the game, and I was thinking, *That drop goal was my idea!* But I didn't really care who got the credit. We were through to the semi-finals, when every other European team had fallen by the wayside, and my crazy dream was still alive.

Not many people gave us a chance of beating reigning champions South Africa, but Borthers and his team did, and that was all that really mattered.

Borthers's boffins had fed every stat imaginable into their super-computer, played the game a million times and predicted a South Africa win by two points. So Borthers kept saying to us, 'Lads, that's one penalty or one drop goal. Come up with one of those and we'll be into a World Cup final.'

The game plan was essentially what we'd been doing all tournament. We weren't going to kick long to their back three, especially not to the frighteningly quick and elusive Cheslin Kolbe on the left wing; we were going to keep box-kicking and keep trying to win the ball back. If we only won three all game, that would increase our chances of beating the Springboks by 15 per cent.

While Kolbe and his opposite wing Kurt-Lee Arendse could be deadly in space, they were both unusually small. So we were confident that Jonny May and Elliot Daly, two of the best kick-chasers in the world, would give them hell. And whenever they won the ball back, we had the players to move it quickly and exploit the space. For any of this to happen, our forwards would need to match them physically. And we knew that would be the case as long as Joe Marler and Dan Cole, those two front-row warhorses, were on the field.

You can usually tell quite early in a game whether you've got your planning right, and I knew we'd got it bang on for that one. We subjected South Africa to a barrage from the opening minute, and they struggled to cope. Mitch kept putting the ball on a dime, Elliot and Jonny kept outleaping and outmuscling Kolbe and Arendse, and the only way South Africa could prevent us from scoring tries was by giving away penalties, which Faz kept kicking.

When Faz knocked over his third penalty to make it 9–3, I couldn't help thinking, *Bloody hell, we're actually gonna win this ...*

We led 12–6 at the break, and while we certainly didn't feel comfortable – you never do against the Springboks – we were calm in the changing room. We knew they hadn't worked out how to combat our game plan, and they'd gone to the well a couple of times already in the tournament, having narrowly lost to Ireland in the pool stage and pipped France in the quarter-finals.

Those two games had the intensity of World Cup finals and must have taken a big physical and mental toll. Then again, maybe they made them more battle-hardened than us. And always at the back of our minds was their so-called Bomb Squad, their formidable front-row replacements who usually made an appearance with about 30 minutes to go.

One of my first acts as a replacement was passing the ball to Faz for a long-range drop-goal attempt. What a kick that was: an absolute monster to make it 15–6 with 27 minutes remaining. Shortly afterwards, the third member of the Bomb Squad came on and the Springboks scrum really started turning the screw. First, they drove us off our ball on their own line, which earned them a penalty. Then with 12 minutes to go, they kicked to the corner after a collapsed scrum and their giant lock RG Snyman, another sub, barged over for a try. And having felt in control for most of the game, we suddenly felt hunted.

Those kinds of games often hinge on seemingly insignificant moments, in this case Freddie Steward's decision to kick an up-and-under on halfway instead of kicking long with five minutes to play. We knocked the ball on, which gave them a scrum. They won a penalty, for what I still don't really know, and Handré Pollard, possibly the best clutch goalkicker in the world, had a chance to win the game with three minutes remaining. I don't really believe in God, but I asked him to make Pollard miss. If He does exist, He wasn't listening. It was a beautiful strike, straight through the middle.

We still had a couple of minutes to win it, and I'm certain there were a few infringements at the breakdown which should have given Faz a chance from the tee, but it wasn't to be. We'd lost a game we probably should have won, despite nobody giving us a cat in hell's chance of winning it in the first place. That's gonna mess with your mind a bit.

We were incredibly proud of what we'd achieved. We'd stood toe-to-toe with the best team in the world and were beating them for 77 minutes. But as any boxer will know, if you get knocked out in the final round, it doesn't really matter if you were winning before that. As such, our pride was mixed with dejection. I'd dreamt of that moment since I was a 16-year-old kid watching England win the World Cup in 2003. And I knew I'd never get the chance to do it again.

It could have been worse, because I very nearly punched Willie le Roux at the final whistle. Le Roux was screaming and hollering from a couple of yards away, and when he did it right in Faz's face, I thought, *Shall I swing at him?* I'm glad I resisted – it might have made me feel better for a couple of seconds but would have been disastrous long-term – although I did tell him to mind his own business and celebrate with his own team-mates instead of rubbing our noses in it.

My three best mates from school – Albear, Wiff and Crayon – had been there for me every step of the way in my career, and lost an awful lot of money betting on me with their hearts rather than their heads. And I felt terrible for them on this occasion because they'd shelled out a fortune to come and watch me and had already made plans for the final. As for my family, they were all in floods of tears. I felt a bit guilty that I hadn't won the game for Jodie and the kids, because they'd been carrying on without me for the last two months. So thank God for Blake and his ice-breaking pearls of wisdom. Apparently, he got up and said, 'Listen, guys, they've done so well to get this far. Let's just be proud of the fact that they've got us to a semi-final. And we've all had an amazing time.' Everyone was doubled up laughing. I took Blake and my nephew Henry with me on a lap of honour, and the sight of the two of them high-fiving the likes of Siya Kolisi and Faf de Klerk will stay with me forever.

I thought we would have caused the All Blacks similar problems if we'd made the final. But we didn't, so instead of going into pointless hypotheticals, I'll tell you about the most pointless fixture in rugby instead: the dreaded 'bronze' final, against Argentina.

I say pointless, but finishing third is obviously better than finishing fourth, and there were actually a few emotions attached to it. Youngsy announced beforehand that it was going to be his last game for England, and while Courtney Lawes wanted the semi-final to be his international swansong, he was also bowing out after the tournament.

After a day on the piss with my old England team-mates James Haskell and Mike Tindall, among many others, I got back down to it. And while we were going through our walkthroughs on the Monday before the game, Borthers came over to me and said, 'Danny, not that I'm ageist or anything, but a couple of the older boys are playing their last game on Friday, so I just wanted to find out what you had planned.' I told him I'd thought about retiring, because I was very aware that I was the oldest person in the squad, but that I wasn't going to call it quits just yet. I thanked him for bringing me back into the fold, told him I'd loved every second of it, reminded him that I was on 95 caps, and said I'd love to reach 100. 'But if you want to go in a different direction,' I added, 'I completely understand.'

Steve replied, 'I'm glad you said that. I'd love to see you get a hundred caps because I think you deserve it.'

'Amazing,' I said. 'I'll just crack on then. But I really could do with you picking me five more times.'

Borthers laughed, before adding, 'Well, you're gonna get one of those caps on Friday because you're starting on the bench.'

We sneaked past Argentina 26–23 before heading back to the hotel for many drinks, although I had to be at the airport at five in the morning because Jodie's sister, Sadie, was getting married in Cyprus. I just hope Youngsy and Courtney enjoyed themselves. They'd played 232 times for their country between them, so they deserved a rest. But England was going to miss them.

Chapter 20

That'll Do Me

We spent the build-up to the 2024 Six Nations trying to add some attacking verve to our game plan, but it didn't quite click in our first few games. We were nearly rumbled by Italy in our opener in Rome, before sneaking past Wales at Twickenham. Scotland then beat us for the fourth time in a row, and while I was glad to be homing in on 100 caps, we weren't showing what we were really capable of.

I felt a bit sorry for our new skipper, Jamie George, because he kept telling the media that things were about to click. I started the Scotland game because Mitch was injured, and while it's never nice to lose to them (they'll be talking about that result for a thousand years), and our attack still wasn't functioning properly, there were signs that we would hit our straps soon.

Our new defence coach, Felix Jones, had just helped South Africa win the World Cup, so he obviously knew his stuff, and his philosophy was aggressive line speed, which we spent all our time training against. (I played against Felix for England U20s, and he loves to remind me that his Irish team beat us quite convincingly that day in Athlone. Meanwhile, I like to remind him that he has the skinniest, palest legs, which is why, since his retirement from playing, you will never see him in a pair of shorts again.) However, the Scottish defence was quite passive in comparison, so we had more time and space than we were used to. It might sound daft, and we should have adjusted better, but it messed with our timings. Either attacking players were nowhere near where they should have been or the whole line was too flat. So after that game, we realised we had to tailor our training more to the opposition. And while everyone was saying how terrible we were, and that we'd gone backwards since the World Cup, we knew that things sometimes had to get worse before they got better.

The week leading up to my hundredth cap against Ireland at Twickenham was very special. On the Monday, Borthers told the boys he wasn't going to announce the team until Thursday, except for me. 'Danny's gonna win his hundredth cap,' said Borthers, 'either from the start or from the bench. Probably from the bench.' Everyone laughed. 'Whatever happens,' continued Borthers, 'we're gonna beat Ireland and make it a special week for him and his family.'

Jamie George and Joe Marler, bless them, had gathered video messages from loads of different sportspeople, including David Beckham, Liverpool manager Jürgen Klopp, Liverpool players Jordan Henderson and Curtis Jones, and England cricket captain Ben Stokes. They hadn't messed about. Stokes recorded his in a toilet, just before a coin toss in India. No less wonderful were the messages from friends and family, including Mum, Dad, Jodie and the kids. The boys finished the video montage, which I'm not ashamed to say moved me to tears, by saying, 'Let's get the win for him.'

Jodie and Koha snuck into my hotel room while I was training and filled it with a load of balloons and '100' signs, plus a cake. The kids also made me a big 'Congratulations' banner. It made me appreciate who I'd been doing it for all those years, and who had allowed me to do it. It was a special week, although maybe not the best way to toughen up for a team as ferocious as Ireland.

Before the game, my old man texted me to say I'd played at Twickenham more than 90 times, which might be more than anyone else in history. I first played there for my school and followed up with appearances for various England age-group teams. I also played some sevens there, and obviously quite a few games for Quins. I must have covered every blade of grass on that pitch, and to win my hundredth cap for England there felt really quite magical.

Ireland had for years been every non-Irish person's second favourite team, but people seemed to have grown a bit sick of them by then (probably because they were so good), and I kept getting messages from neutral fans on social media saying they wanted us to beat them. As someone who'd spent 16 years feeling hated by anyone who wasn't English (as well as a lot of people who *were* English), that was a pleasant novelty.

Jamie asked if I wanted to lead the team out, which I wasn't sure about, seeing as I was starting on the bench. But he insisted, and even suggested I do it with my kids. While I was standing at the head of the team in the tunnel, which I'd never done before, Ireland skipper Peter O'Mahony leant over and said, 'Congratulations, Danny. Enjoy it, mate.' Then I walked out to a packed Twickenham with my three prized possessions – Blake, Koha and Rocco, all wearing England shirts with 'Care 100' on the back – and tried desperately not to cry.

All that ceremony would have felt a bit hollow had we lost, but the boys were awesome from the first whistle. We'd been making a conscious effort to move the ball a bit more through-out the tournament, without much success, but we finally got it going against Ireland.

We attacked with ambition, pace and accuracy, and had scored three tries to one by the time I was introduced with 14 minutes to go. James Lowe did his best to ruin my Twickenham farewell, scoring to give Ireland the lead with seven minutes remaining, but Marcus won the game for England with a drop goal in added time. I was slightly irritated that I didn't kick that goal myself – we had the advantage anyway, and some of my mates had a bet on me being the last scorer – but we'd beaten tournament favourites Ireland and prevented them from winning a Grand Slam.

Having been booed off the pitch after losing to Fiji just months earlier, which was a horrible experience, we were now being cheered to the rafters. I felt so proud that the England fans were behind us again.

Afterwards, I told Borthers, Jamie and a couple of other lads that the France game would be my last for England. I'd had one hell of a run, but now it was time to spend more time at home with the family and let someone else have a go. I'd been away for a long time over the previous nine months, what with the World Cup and the Six Nations, and it wouldn't have been fair on Jodie or the kids to carry on. Besides, being allowed a few more whirls around the dancefloor meant I no longer needed one last fix. And that performance against Ireland was the surest sign yet that the team was on the right track.

I can't remember what I'd had for dinner the evening before the France game, but I woke up the following morning with a terrible stomachache. I soldiered through the team run but still felt rough at the evening meeting, at which Manu Tuilagi and I announced that it was going to be our final game for England (Manu had signed for Bayonne).

After a couple of hours shivering in bed, with regular breaks for evacuations from both ends, I texted the team doctor, Katy, who told me to stay in my room. She then texted back to say they were calling up Bristol scrum-half Harry Randall. Harry's partner had just had twins, so now I felt terrible about that as well.

Luckily, it was a night game in Lyon, so I spent most of the day in my room eating as much food as I could keep down and drinking gallons of electrolytes. And at about five o'clock, I started feeling okay. I apologised to Harry when I saw him, but he was actually quite happy because he hadn't had a wink of sleep for two weeks and he couldn't wait to spend a quiet night in a hotel.

I still felt a bit washed out sitting on the bench but was sure the adrenalin would get me through a ten-minute cameo. Then Mitch dislocated his wrist in the first tackle of the game. I thought, *Oh my God, there's absolutely no way I can last 79 minutes against one of the best teams in the world.* But fair play to Mitch, he strapped it up and carried on. And the boys played brilliantly, even better than they had the previous week against Ireland.

Having trailed 16–3 at the break, we blitzed them with three tries in five minutes at the start of the second half, the first two from the irrepressible Ollie Lawrence. The third, from Marcus, was everything the team wanted to be in a nutshell, Ben Earl punching straight through the middle and Marcus flying up outside him to finish things off. It was physical, it was fast, it was skilful, it got fans on their feet. Most of all, it was young players playing with freedom. I thought, *That's it. Borthers has nailed it. This team is in very good hands.*

I didn't get the fairytale ending – France came back to win 33–31 courtesy of a controversial last-minute penalty – but it was a perfect final game in other ways. For me, rugby had always been about entertaining people, and suddenly England were one of the most entertaining teams in town.

I took a great deal of satisfaction from playing a part, however small, in turning England's fortunes around. The seemingly constant criticism from the media and fans had annoyed me over the years, no doubt about that – it often felt like they wanted us to fail – but even I was one of those people watching England in the 2022 Six Nations and wondering what the hell they were doing. So bowing out knowing that everyone was behind the team was extremely gratifying. As was the fact that I was leaving on my own terms, without the bitterness and regret I'd felt when Eddie had discarded me six years earlier.

When I look back on my England career, my fondest memories are of that final year playing under Borthers. I'd spent the previous four years like a kid looking through the window of a sweetshop, and when Borthers finally let me back in, it was everything I'd dreamt of and more. Borthers showed me love and made me feel like I was wanted. For the first time in my England career, I felt like an important part of the team, rather than expendable.

Even under Borthers, I still had imposter syndrome. I felt like I was blagging it and never stopped wondering if I was good enough or not. In my head, I was just a little lad from Leeds who probably should have been playing football instead. But I'm kind of glad that was the case because it shows what's possible if you never give up and keep chasing the unlikeliest of dreams.

I know some people thought I should have given up the ghost a few years earlier, but everyone was very nice when I announced my England retirement after the game, even on social media. And I was chuffed that people remembered me as a bloke who played with a bit of devil and a smile on his face and showed that you can have fun on a rugby pitch and still compete.

Borthers used to say to the senior players, 'Given the amount of talent in this group, we haven't won enough big games or trophies.' We finished third in my final Six Nations, and I certainly should have won more during my England career. A couple more Six Nations titles would have been lovely, as would another Grand Slam. And, of course, a World Cup. But I'm content with what I achieved overall. Yes, I spent quite a lot of time on the bench, mostly watching Youngsy do his thing, but I don't care how many minutes I played. I got to play for England 101 times, and if you'd told me that when I was 14, I'd have replied, *Wow, I am going to have one hell of a football career ...*

I strongly believe that England are set fair for the foreseeable future. The recent resignations, in quick succession, of Felix Jones, strength and conditioning coach Aled Walters and fitness coach Tom Tombleson are a slight concern (I don't know the reasons why, but I do know that Borthers is a demanding boss), but I still think they've got the right man in charge. I also think they've got the right captain in Jamie George – a guy you'd go to war for – and a brilliant young squad with a few old stagers still showing the way.

One of the biggest challenges for an England head coach is to create the right environment, and Borthers has got it spot-on. The players and staff can be themselves and are happy, and I'm envious of young lads like Marcus, Ben Earl and Manny Feyi-Waboso, because they're going to be in that environment for a long, long time.

If England want to take their game to the next level and win Grand Slams and World Cups, Marcus has to be nailed-on at ten. To beat the top teams, you have to mix smarts with attacking rugby, and Marcus can do things other fly-halves can't. But he's not just a box of tricks, all goose-steps and dummies – he can also control games. People were questioning his goalkicking after the recent 2–0 series defeat in New Zealand, but kickers can have bad days, as he did in the first Test, and he proved the doubters wrong in the second. I also refer people to the Premiership final in 2021, when Marcus slotted every single kick under intense pressure, quite a few of them from out wide. My guess is that George Ford will be there beside him for a few years yet, helping him every step of the way.

Ben Earl was probably our best player at the 2023 World Cup and is fast turning into a superstar of the game. He'll be an England stalwart for many years, fitness permitting, and I can see him taking over as captain when Jamie George decides to call it a day for England. And he'd be a great one.

Joe Marler reckons young Quins prop Fin Baxter is the real deal, and Joe knows quite a lot about propping. Fin made his debut against the All Blacks in Dunedin in 2024 – Joe having got injured after 18 minutes – started the following week in Auckland and did magnificently on both occasions. He looks about 12, but I can see him having a massive role in that team for years.

Quins flanker Chandler Cunningham-South is a great replacement for Courtney Lawes – powerful, aggressive and a player who wants to hurt people, which is something you can't teach – while Exeter wing Manny Feyi-Waboso is a very smart lad with electric pace and great try-scoring ability. Thank God he chose England over Wales. Manu Tuilagi's various injuries meant England struggled to nail their midfield combination for years, but they've got a gem of a 12 in Bath's Ollie Lawrence, who is a lot more than just a crash-ball merchant. And Northampton's full-back George Furbank looks set to wear the 15 shirt for years and has added a new dimension to England's attack.

Those two narrow defeats against the All Blacks in New Zealand suggest that Borthers's young side will be in very good shape for the 2027 World Cup. What are the odds of Marcus doing a Jonny in the final? I wouldn't be at all surprised.

○

The simple reason I carried on playing for Quins after retiring from England was because I could. My knee wasn't as it should be, and I had a couple of bulging discs in my back, but the medics thought I still had a few games in me. And as long as I felt I could help the team, and wasn't letting the lads down repeatedly, I'd keep patching myself up and putting myself out there.

I'd love to win one more trophy with the club, and we gave it a bloody good go in the Champions Cup in 2023–24. Quins had underachieved in the Champions Cup during my time at the club, never getting further than the quarter-finals, although the French clubs had been playing by different rules: their higher salary cap allowed for bigger squads and more top internationals (like the Irish teams, whose players are centrally contracted and therefore play nowhere near as much rugby as in England).

We have had some success in France, but mainly because we view those games as a fun trip away, given that we're highly unlikely to be standing there with the trophy at the end of the season. Attack with pace from the get-go, keep the ball moving and throw in some trick plays, and you're likely to cause French teams problems. But if you try to feel your way into a game, you'll get eaten up, because their league is more physical and set-piece dominated.

We had a great comeback win over Racing 92 in the pool stage in December 2023 – at their place, by the way – before a completely bonkers game against Bordeaux in the quarter-finals. Bordeaux had thrashed Saracens twice in the pool stage, and had home advantage, but we threw the kitchen sink at them and won a 12-try thriller 42–41. I say 'we', but I was actually resting up in Turkey with the family. I was alternating between watching the kids go down a water slide and watching the lads run riot on my phone. And I couldn't help thinking, *Of all the games to miss, I had to choose this one* … When I got home, people kept telling me it was one of the greatest games they'd ever seen.

Next up was Toulouse, who battered us at the Stoop in the pool stage and put 60 points on Exeter in their quarter-final. We weren't expected to lay a glove on them, but we actually stood toe to toe with them for most of the game, only to run out of gas down the stretch. They ended up winning 38–26, and despite thinking we'd kept Antoine Dupont unusually quiet, he still scored two tries, which is yet more proof of what an incredible player he is.

I first played against Dupont when he was a teenager at Castres, back in 2015. In the tunnel before the game, Chris Robshaw said to the lads, 'I was watching their scrum-half in the warm-up and he looked like he was crapping himself. Let's make his life hell.' Halfway through the first half, this kid made a dart from a scrum, beat Robbo, stepped Nick Easter, handed off Nick Evans and scored under the sticks. 'Bloody hell, lads,' said Robbo, 'watch out for their nine, he's handy …' We were all pissing ourselves laughing.

Dupont felt like a rock when I tried to tackle him, but he was also incredibly agile and elusive. We went on to win that game comfortably, and afterwards he wanted to swap shirts with me (I've still got it at home), but I suspected even then that he'd surpass anything I've achieved in the game.

Since joining Toulouse, Dupont has taken scrum-half play to a whole new level. He can do all the things the other great nines I played against could do – Australia's Will Genia, South Africa's Fourie du Preez, New Zealand's Aaron Smith – but that much better. He somehow manages to be the fastest, the strongest, the most athletic, the best at making breaks, the best offloader, the best kicker, the best passer and the most consistent. Maintaining such high standards year after year in an attritional game like rugby is incredibly difficult, but Dupont has been the best player in the world for four or five years now, and the really scary thing is that he seems to be getting better and better. He even led France to a gold medal in sevens at the Paris Olympics. What a year, what a player.

Fighting on two fronts – being bombarded by French power-houses one week, scrapping for a Premiership play-off place the next – caused us to run out of ammunition towards the back end of the season, and we just missed out on a play-off place again. But while it might sound hopelessly romantic, Quins have a higher purpose than just winning matches. We want to entertain, put smiles on people's faces and inspire kids to play the game. We want to do things differently, which is why it is and always will be the perfect club for me.

$\bigcirc$

After I retired from England duty, Koha would sometimes ask me as I was walking out the front door, 'Is this just Harlequins training? You'll pick me up from school?' I'd tell her yes and she'd look so happy and relieved. In moments like that, I knew I'd made the right decision.

I still craved a bit of adventure, however, and finally got the chance to play for the Barbarians against Fiji in June 2024, something that had always been on my bucket list. Fellow Yorkshireman and former England international John Spencer told all the boys how special the Baa-Baas were at the start of the week, and he was dead right. I was born to play for that team and the whole experience was everything I'd hoped it would be and more. I knew it would probably be the only time I'd get to wear that famous black-and-white shirt, and I bought into the whole process – the drinking, the training – from start to finish. It felt like I was falling in love with rugby all over again.

Great players flew in from all over the world – New Zealand's Sam Whitelock, Chay Fihaki, Fergus Burke and Leicester Fainga'anuku, France's Gael Fickou, Cameron Woki and Virimi Vakatawa, Australia's Scott Sio – and within hours of meeting, I was sipping beers and becoming lifelong friends with lads I'd played against many times. There were also plenty of old England team-mates in the side – Kyle Sinckler, Jonathan Joseph, Kieran Brookes and Ben Youngs, the last of whom I roomed with for the first time in 15 years of playing together – and we played some amazing rugby to beat a quality Fiji side 45–32 at Twickenham (although I somehow managed to pick up a yellow card!).

I also thought about playing a season or two abroad. The lads kept telling me to move to France, and a couple of years in the south of the country sounded marvellous on paper – sun, sea and sand, mad passionate fans, a complimentary house and car, the chance for the kids to learn French. And, as Chris Ashton always said, silly money.

I had Zoom meetings with Perpignan and Bayonne, and both clubs sounded very keen to sign me. But then I wouldn't hear from them for weeks. It felt like the early days of a romance in which I didn't know where I stood, although it was just nice to feel wanted at the age of 37. Meanwhile, Quins kept asking me what my plans were. They were doing their salary cap calculations for the following season and needed to know if they should get a new scrum-half.

Quins had offered me another one-year deal, but not for any more money, so France made a lot of sense financially – we could rent out our house in Cobham and save a load of cash for a rainy day. On the other hand, what if Jodie and the kids didn't like living in France? Would it blow up my chances of working for Quins in some capacity in the future? (I'd always told them I'd finish my career there and help find a replacement.) Would disappearing for one or two years kybosh my chances of working in the UK media? After all, ex-players are often quickly forgotten, however many times they played for England.

In the end, both clubs took too long to come up with a formal offer and I didn't want to mess Quins around. Besides, Quins ended up offering me a slightly improved contract, which included a clause saying I'd have every Monday off. The lads couldn't believe that – 'You're kidding me? You don't work Mondays?!' That was mainly to help manage the load on my knee, but also so I could commit to recording my podcast with the BBC every week – you're welcome, listeners!

I'm still a Harlequins player at the time of writing, although whether I'll make it to the end of another season remains to be seen. I'll be 38 by then, and that much creakier. I hope having Mondays off will help, and I've just gone out and bought myself a sauna and an ice bath, but the pain in my knee and shoulder isn't getting any easier and there are times when I'd rather be anywhere else than on a training ground. Rugby is no sport for old men.

Me and a few of the older boys sometimes discuss the pros and cons of being a rugby player, and the toll it takes on the body is chief among the cons. I'll see a team-mate laid out unconscious or barely able to walk after a game and think, *How is this meant to be fun? Will it have been worth it if I'm in pain every day when I'm 50?* The old boys' conclusion is always that it will have been, although I should add that I've been far luckier than most.

While I have cherished memories of scoring tries for England in front of 80,000 at Twickenham and lifting trophies for Quins, many players toil day after day, year after year for not much glory. And for every England regular or overseas superstar, there are dozens of players earning no more than 30 grand a season. That's not a lot of money when you consider the risks and the shortness of a rugby career.

I've not had many concussions over the years, touch wood, because scrum-halves tend to steer clear of big collisions. I wouldn't have played the game if it had meant running into brick walls in training over and over again. One of the many ridiculous things I've seen forwards do in training is the one-minute drill, which involves three forwards running as hard as they can into three other forwards for 60 seconds. No gaps, just head down and get banged, and they have to be as committed as possible to get a quick ball for the team. I'd be the bloke passing them the ball, and I said to Wiggy one day, 'How is that someone's job?' Sometimes I'm embarrassed to call myself a rugby player because their job is nothing like mine. And that was just a training session.

Thankfully, the mindset has shifted over the past decade or so. The days of players getting concussed in training and playing on a weekend, however big the game, are mostly gone. I'm amazed at how much contact training some clubs still do – Eddie seemed to think that players crawling off the pitch at the end of a session was a good thing, but it actually just meant they were knackered for the weekend. Quins' training is a lot less attritional than it used to be, which has extended my career. Smarter training means players go on for longer, and the longer players go on for, the smarter they tend to get.

I feel for those players who took too many whacks to the head, who kept having smelling salts wafted under their noses and getting chucked back into the fray. So many lads from the generation before me are struggling with brain injuries in retirement, and I'm grateful that I came along when player welfare started being taken more seriously. But those in charge of the game should never forget that rugby's main selling point is its gladiatorial nature. Rugby as we know and love it is never going to be completely safe, so they need to be careful not to water the physicality down too much. No one is paying to watch a game of tag, and they should write that on a wall at World Rugby's HQ.

Rugby has plenty of problems, no doubt about that, its rickety financial state chief among them. Some grand old clubs have gone under in the past few years – Wasps, London Irish, Worcester – and the sport as a whole still hasn't worked out how to be profitable. But I've always been a glass-half-full kind of bloke. The product, both in the Premiership and internationally, is as good as it's ever been – especially if you've got a Quins season ticket – and if the powers that be can get their acts together on the marketing front, it will fly.

◯

I need rugby to fly from a selfish point of view because I still want to make a living from it when I retire from playing. I'd love to stay connected and potentially work at Quins, or maybe I'll get an ambassadorial role or a spot on the board. I'm also about to launch a YouTube channel – definitely not another podcast! – which I'm excited about. It's not going to make me millions but it's another way of staying involved with rugby and hopefully branching out into a few other sports. I'm told that all the kids watch YouTube nowadays – it's the future.

But the best thing about not playing anymore will be spending time with the family, because Jodie and our kids are my proudest achievements – they're far more important than anything I did on a rugby field.

When I met Jodie, I honestly didn't know that a woman as fabulous as her existed, and I sometimes wonder how my life would have panned out if I hadn't plucked up the courage to talk to her that day in Thailand, looking like a bit of a twat with a baseball cap on backwards and no shirt on. That has to go down as the best decision I ever made: even better than the one that led to my try against France in 2016.

Professional sportspeople need to be selfish to be success-ful, as well as surrounded by people who are fully on board with the lifestyle their sport demands. If someone isn't on board, they either won't stay in your life for very long or they'll end up sabo-taging your career. I certainly wouldn't have been able to do everything I've done without Jodie. She's made sacrifices in her own work and has always been there for the kids, whatever part of the world I was chucking a ball about in (not forgetting looking after a sickly French Bulldog who hates other mutts). Jodie ended up being a wife, a mum and a best friend rolled into one, and not many blokes are lucky enough to find someone like that.

I can't thank Jodie enough for everything she's done for me, and I hope my rugby career has provided her and the kids with at least a few good memories. It's those memories I was able to share with the family, towards the back end of my playing days, that are most special to me. And even if Jodie and the kids are only half as proud of my achievements as I am of theirs, that's enough for me.

As for Mum and Dad, I think they're sadder at the prospect of me retiring than I am. I keep saying to Mum, 'You'll be able to do whatever you want on a Saturday.' As it is, they schlep from Northamptonshire, where they now live, to watch me play almost every weekend, before schlepping home again. It doesn't matter how many times I tell them to just watch it on TV, they keep coming, and they won't stop until I've played my final game.

They've been doing that since I joined Quins 18 years ago, and they were doing it for many years before that. Sometimes, I'd be playing in the arse end of nowhere in Yorkshire and one or the other of them would be the only parent there. Other kids would tease me about my parents' presence on the touchline week after week, but that didn't bother me. Them being there was comforting and made me play better, because I wanted to make them proud. Even now, if I play badly, such as when we got battered 52–7 by Saracens at Tottenham Hotspur Stadium, I feel the need to apologise afterwards. It might sound silly, but I feel like I've let them down after everything they've done for me.

Those four years I was out of the picture, they were always saying to me, 'I still think you've got a chance.' And I'm so glad I was recalled and gave them some memories they never thought they'd have. When I phoned to tell them I was going to the World Cup in France, Mum cried her eyes out. When I played my hundredth game for England, she cried her eyes out again. After I played my final game, she told me how glad she was that I never gave up. I may or may not have said to her, 'Mum, everything happens for a reason.'

Whether I was playing mini rugby at West Park or playing for England at Twickenham, I never stopped being one of their babies. And I know they feel the same about my brother, Simon, whose own rugby career was ended by a dislocated shoulder before he went to university to study medicine, failed his first year twice and ended up working as a banker in the City; and my little sister, Samantha, who would get dragged along to watch me play every weekend, was also very sporty and now works in events in London. You can't choose your parents, but if we could, we'd have chosen ours in a heartbeat.

Whatever Blake, Koha and Rocco choose to do in life, I want to be the same kind of parent to them as my mum and dad were to me. Whether it's standing on the touchline in the cold, wind and rain, ferrying them halfway across the country to dance or play music, or whatever it is they end up doing, I'll be there. And maybe they'll end up making it their living like I did.

I still sometimes think to myself, *How is rugby my job?* Then again, which is the stranger way to make a living: sitting behind a computer screen in an office bored out of your mind or throwing a ball about with your mates?

At the time of writing, I've just started my 20th pre-season as a professional rugby player (at least I would have done if my knee wasn't playing up). Not many people get to do a job they love for so long, and not many people get to work at a place like Harlequins that lets them be themselves (you get a lot of empty promises in sport, but Dean Richards wasn't lying when he said he wanted Quins to feel like home to me – it has done for 18 years). I've been extremely lucky on both fronts, not to mention my 101 caps for England.

My old man is a bit of a rugby geek, and he reckons I'm the longest-serving England player ever, from first cap to last: fifteen years, nine months and two days. He also reckons I'm one of the only people to have played for England Under-16s, -18s, -19s, -20s, -21s, Saxons, Sevens and the big team. But while I'm grateful for Dad's research, that sort of stuff doesn't matter much in the grand scheme of things.

Statistics do not make a person – they certainly don't tend to crop up in funeral eulogies – and I don't really care if people think I was any good at rugby or not. But I do hope that rugby fans remember me as someone who made the game look fun and never gave up. I also hope that anyone I've known over the years thinks of me as someone they'd like to have a beer with. What more can a man want than to be known as a decent bloke? Yep, that'll do me.

Acknowledgements

This book is for everyone that ever believed in me, none more so than Al and Shez. Mum and Dad, I owe it all to you. Thank you for being the best parents we could wish for and for never giving up on me.

Si and Sam and all the rest of the Care clan, thank you for all your love and support on this wild ride.

Albear, Crayon and Wiff. Apologies again for all the money you lost betting on me. However, how good were a few of those wins?! Beers on me if this goes well!

Pete Latham, Prince Henry's Grammar School. Thank you for constantly twisting my arm and tempting me towards this beautiful game. 'Henry's till we die'!!

To Harlequins, my first thank you is to our owners, Charles and Duncan. Thank you for your unwavering support and belief.

Dean Richards, Conor O'Shea, John Kingston. Parts of you will forever be in the Quins DNA. Thank you for everything you did for me, on and off the pitch. Danny Wilson, Laurie Dalrymple and Billy Millard – our amazing club is in great hands with these three leading the way.

Martin Johnson, Stuart Lancaster, Eddie Jones – we've had our ups and downs but I really appreciate your impact on my rugby career. Lanny, I'm genuinely really happy you're getting to show what a great coach you are.

Eddie, I still hope we can share a glass of wine together at some point.

ACKNOWLEDGEMENTS

This game is nothing without the fans and we've got some special ones. Thank you for all the love over the years!

Thank you to every coach who picked me, dropped me, picked me again, dropped me again, loved me or hated me. Hopefully I've shown that you should never give up.

To all the boys that I've had the pleasure of sharing a changing room and a pitch with over the years, thank you for the unbelievable memories, the ridiculous childish behaviour and the constant piss-taking. I still can't believe this can be called a job!

To Charlotte Hardman, Jasmin Kaur, Lucy Brown, Shelise Robertson, Jess Anderson and the amazing team at Ebury, thank you for making this such an enjoyable experience and bringing it all to life!

David Luxton, my literary agent, and my commercial agent, Ryan Shahin, for all their hard work in making this all happen and of course to the best ghostwriter/semi-pro golfer I've come across, Ben Dirs, for bringing the magic to the pages!

Lastly, to Jodie, Blake, Koha and Rocco. As I said at the start you are my biggest achievement and my best friends. I can't wait to make and share a million more memories with you. Thank you for letting me chase my dreams, I'll do anything I can to help you chase yours. I love you with all my heart.

DC x

Image Credits

Image Section 1
QBE (Image 16)
KICKPHOTO (Image 18)
Sportsbeat Images Ltd (Image 20)
Gallo Images/Stringer/Getty Images (Image 21)

Image Section 2
Rebecca Goddard (Image 7, 8)
David Rogers/Getty Images (Image 9)
Warren Little/Staff/Getty Images (Image 10)
Fred Ellis/England Rugby (Image 19)
Joel Stocker/England Rugby (Image 20)